Scaling Social Impact

Social Entrepreneurship

Series Editors:

Paul N. Bloom, Adjunct Professor of Social Entrepreneurship and Marketing, Duke University's Fuqua School of Business, Faculty Director of CASE

Matt Nash, Managing Director of CASE

Social entrepreneurship is a growing field of practice and scholarship. Spurred by the financial support and encouragement of organizations like the Skoll Foundation, Ashoka, the Schwab Foundation, Echoing Green, and the Acumen Fund, many individuals and organizations have labeled themselves as "social entrepreneurs" and are drawing upon the best thinking in both the business and philanthropic worlds to develop innovative approaches to addressing critical social needs in health, poverty, the environment, and other domains. With this growth in the number of practitioners has come a concomitant growth in the number of students, consultants, teachers, and researchers who want to learn more about social entrepreneurship. A deep hunger for knowledge about this field has emerged, and the Center for the Advancement of Social Entrepreneurship (CASE) at Duke University's Fuqua School of Business has led the way in seeking to serve that hunger. The *Social Entrepreneurship Series* represents a new and exciting knowledge dissemination initiative. The series will contain monographs and compendia of papers offering the latest thinking about how to become more effective at social entrepreneurship.

Scaling Social Impact: New Thinking
Edited by Paul N. Bloom and Edward Skloot

Scaling Social Impact

New Thinking

Edited by

Paul N. Bloom and Edward Skloot

palgrave
macmillan

SCALING SOCIAL IMPACT

First published in 2010 by
PALGRAVE MACMILLAN®
in the United States—a division of St. Martin's Press LLC,
175 Fifth Avenue, New York, NY 10010.

Where this book is distributed in the UK, Europe and the rest of the world,
this is by Palgrave Macmillan, a division of Macmillan Publishers Limited,
registered in England, company number 785998, of Houndmills,
Basingstoke, Hampshire RG21 6XS.

Palgrave Macmillan is the global academic imprint of the above companies
and has companies and representatives throughout the world.

Palgrave® and Macmillan® are registered trademarks in the United States,
the United Kingdom, Europe and other countries.

ISBN: 978–0–230–10437–2

Library of Congress Cataloging-in-Publication Data

Scaling social impact : new thinking / Paul N. Bloom, Edward Skloot,
editors.
    p. cm.
    Includes bibliographical references and index.
    ISBN 978–0–230–10437–2
    1. Social change. 2. Social entrepreneurship. 3. Social marketing.
4. Nonprofit organizations. I. Bloom, Paul N. II. Skloot, Edward.

HM831.S353 2010
303.48—dc22   2010003250

A catalogue record of the book is available from the British Library.

Design by Newgen Imaging Systems (P) Ltd., Chennai, India.

First edition: October 2010

D 10 9 8 7 6 5 4 3

Printed in the United States of America.

Contents

Illustrations

Figures

Tables

Foreword: From Scaling Organizations to Scaling Impact

Jeffrey L. Bradach (The Bridgespan Group)

When I started doing research on the challenges of "going to scale" fifteen years ago, the topic could fairly be described as under the radar, both in the university and out in the field. My focus was growth through replication, and when I presented papers and case studies to nonprofit audiences, the ideas were often dismissed as too corporate. As one audience member said to me at one such presentation: "We are not McDonalds. You cannot use a cookie cutter to replicate the work we do."

At almost exactly the same time, however, a cadre of social entrepreneurs was developing new models for organizations that would grow to significant size through replication in new locations. Nonprofits that are now nationally recognized names, such as Teach for America and Habitat for Humanity, and some that are better known in other parts of the globe, such as Bangladesh-based BRAC, have grown from small entities to major organizations active in many parts of the country and/or the world. While they have indeed found that scaling is anything but "cookie cutter," one of the most notable aspects of the past few decades is the emergence of a wave of relatively large, rapidly growing nonprofit organizations.

Today, there may be no idea with greater currency in the social sector than "scaling what works." In its first year, the Obama administration has announced several multimillion or billion dollar initiatives that focus on identifying programs that work (typically using rigorous evaluation standards) and investing in their capacity to expand to new locations and reach more beneficiaries. As the president put it, "Instead of wasting taxpayer money on programs that are obsolete or ineffective, government should be seeking out creative, results-oriented programs...and helping them replicate their efforts across America" (Obama, 2009).

What has happened over the past twenty or so years that makes it possible for the Obama administration—and many philanthropists—to bet on strategies that center on identifying, investing in and scaling what works as a central lever for addressing intractable social problems? And what are the new questions that are already emerging among leaders in the field who are grappling with how to scale impact?

What has Propelled the Focus on Going to Scale?

Generally speaking, it is difficult to trace the causes of social change; but in this case it is clear that a few significant dynamics came together to make "going to scale" a focus for many in the nonprofit sector.

First, powerful ideas emanated from the for-profit sector that propelled new thinking and behavior in the nonprofit one. The rise of venture capital offered an analogy for how the nonprofit sector might operate—an analogy that Chris Letts, William Ryan, and Allan Grossman developed in their pathbreaking 1997 *Harvard Business Review* article, "Virtuous Capital: What Foundations Can Learn from Venture Capitalists." This pivotal article articulated a model of social change centered on investing in promising organizations, strengthening their organizational capacity, and helping them to scale.

Individual philanthropists such as Don and Doris Fisher took this idea to heart and invested millions in helping entrepreneurial organizations such as KIPP and Teach for America to scale their work dramatically. Others used new wealth to create "venture philanthropy" funds committed to scaling promising, high-performing nonprofits. New Profit, New Schools Venture Fund, Venture Philanthropy Partners, Klaus and Hilde Schwab Foundation for Social Entrepreneurship, and Omidyar Network are among the many institutions now applying some version of this new philanthropic model. Simultaneously, a few well-established philanthropies such as Edna McConnell Clark shifted their grant-making to a new paradigm centered on big, multiyear investments aimed in many instances at helping high-impact organizations to scale.[1]

The celebration of entrepreneurs proved similarly contagious, with the concept of finding and supporting nonprofit entrepreneurs becoming an explicit strategy for social change enjoying unprecedented levels of support. Bill Drayton, the founder of Ashoka, was a pioneer in pursuing this approach; since 1981, Ashoka has provided more than two thousand social entrepreneurs—Ashoka Fellows—with living stipends, professional support, and access to a global network of peers in more than sixty countries. There are now a number of philanthropic institutions including the Skoll Foundation, Draper Richards Foundation, and Echoing Green that select and support social entrepreneurs with an eye to helping them take their ideas to scale.

The continued importance of this trend is evident in the extraordinary growth of university-based programs in "social enterprise" and "social entrepreneurship." These classes are enormously popular—even with students who don't plan to enter the nonprofit world vocationally, but do intend to remain involved as donors and volunteers. An important moment in the evolution of the field was the launch of the Harvard Business School social enterprise initiative in 1994, which sparked the creation of similar programs in the United States and around the world. Today, over 150 full-time global MBA programs participate in the Aspen Institute's biennial *Beyond Grey Pinstripes* survey, which ranks schools according to the "integration of issues concerning social and environmental stewardship" into their curricula. The survey shows that in the United States alone, MBA schools increased course offerings relating to social benefit and social sector management by 79 percent between 2005 and 2007.[2]

A second force propelling the focus on scale has been the unprecedented influx of money from new philanthropists. The technology-driven economy of the 1990s—culminating in the dot-com boom—was the platform for the creation and accumulation of massive wealth, as were the financial markets—right up until 2009. Some of this wealth has already flowed into philanthropy: 75 percent of all existing private foundations have been founded since 1980, for example (Foundation Center, 2008). But with more than twenty-one trillion dollars projected to flow into philanthropy as part of the baby-boomer intergenerational wealth transfer in the next fifty years (Schervish et al., 2006), we may have only begun to see the impact of these resources on philanthropic strategies designed to build stronger organizations capable of sustaining major growth.

Third, there has been a tremendous shift in the sector toward focusing on "results." The move by many government agencies to contract with nonprofit and private-sector providers of services has been an important underlying force propelling this shift. In many spheres where nonprofits operate, government is the largest funder of their work, and its heightened emphasis on results—often through the use of performance-based contracts—has contributed to the trend of identifying and investing in what works. This pressure, along with rising interest from philanthropy and the general public, has put a spotlight on the issue of results; and it has led to efforts by many organizations to assess their performance in more concrete, objective ways, despite the inherent—and legitimate—challenges and complexities that presents. While it is still early days, we *may* be beginning to see the emergence of a virtuous cycle in which funders and nonprofits not only invest more in measurement, but also devise strategies that can more reliably produce results, thereby creating more momentum for replicating what we know works and investing in the ingredients (such as organizational infrastructure) that undergird the ability to sustain and improve results.

Thanks to all these dynamics, both leaders in the field and academics have a much better understanding of what it takes to build and scale strong nonprofit organizations. For example, we have a much deeper knowledge of the funding models that support growth (Foster et al., 2009; Miller, 2005; Overholser, 2010). Similarly, the work on capacity building has sharpened our understanding of some of the key organizational dimensions that need to be in place if nonprofits are to scale effectively (Enright, 2006; Hubbard, 2006; Kramer, 2008; Wolfred, 2008). While big, open questions remain to be answered—the absence of a capital market that supports the growth of nonprofits from one stage to the next, the lack of practical tools for assessing outputs and outcomes, and the systematic underinvestment in "overhead" being three very notable issues—we have made significant progress in learning what it takes to produce and scale results at the organizational level—even if it remains enormously difficult to do that.

From Scaling Organizations to Scaling Impact

At the same time, it has become increasingly clear that *scaling organizations is not the only way to scale impact, nor is it enough.* This is not news to most people, but the emphasis on organization-building in the last two decades has oftentimes conflated the two.[3] What are some of the ways that leaders are amplifying social impact beyond scaling organizations?

- *Technology: "Bricks to Clicks."* Kaboom!, which helps communities organize projects to build new playgrounds for children, has shifted from hands-on management of projects—Kaboom! staff on the ground—to using a web-based platform to help communities organize their projects. In its first ten years, Kaboom! built nearly 750 playgrounds; since its shift to the new model, it has built approximately 4,000 in three years. Similar experiments with bricks-to-clicks models are underway in mentoring, advocacy and other fields.
- *Intermediaries: Knowledge-sharing and technical assistance.* Intermediaries play a critical role in many fields by increasing the performance of constituent organizations and/or serving needs that extend beyond the capacity or interest of any one provider. For example, Microfinance Information Exchange (MIX) provides data that enable microfinance lenders to compare their performance and practices, learn, and improve. Mentor plays a similar role in the mentoring field, as does Local Initiatives Support Corporation (LISC) in community development.
- *Talent-centered models.* A growing number of organizations are pursuing strategies for broader impact that center on developing leaders who will pollinate a field. Education is a prime example. In some cases, New Leaders for New Schools and Recruiting Teachers for example, the production of talent is the strategy; in others, such as Teach for America, it is a by-product of working in the organization, with alumni leaving and becoming influential players in education-related issues and institutions.
- *Catalyzing changes in markets or social systems.* Some nonprofits (and their funders) are stimulating change by expanding the realm of what's possible. In microfinance, nonprofit institutions pointed the way to for-profit companies investing substantial capital in serving previously unrecognized market segments. Some of these for-profit players are creating significant, self-sustaining markets that reach at least some of the segments of the population that were originally targeted by the nonprofits. Charter schools have triggered changes in school districts across the country—far out of proportion to the number of children they serve directly. In many cases, these changes hinge on demonstrating that change is possible and employing intentional communication strategies that inspire and/or force others to adjust.
- *Blending direct service and advocacy.* City Year's vision is "that one day the most commonly asked question of a young person will be, 'Where are you

going to do your service year?'" It has pursued that mission for twenty years by growing to twenty sites and engaging fifteen hundred young people each year. But an explicit part of City Year's strategy has always been to advocate for federal policies and funding for public service work. The organization was instrumental in the creation of the Corporation for National Service (CNS) in 1993 and, most recently, was a critical player in the passage of the Kennedy Serve-America Act. In 2010, seventy-five thousand people will be involved in service through the CNS-funded programs for which City Year has been a model and an active advocate.

- *Networks.* Many of today's most prominent nonprofit networks first took shape and gained momentum early in the twentieth century. Service providers such as Big Brothers Big Sisters of America, Boys and Girls Clubs of America, Goodwill, and the American Red Cross spread across the country—paralleling the growth of Sears and other pioneering for-profit businesses. These large nonprofit networks ultimately became a critical source of programming and services, especially for young people and the poor.[4] Later in the century, another type of network, centered on local implementation of a common idea and model, emerged. The hospice movement and Alcoholics Anonymous, which both became major forces in society without a central organization driving their growth, are two fine examples (Dees, 2004). Today, virtual networks are proliferating with people brought together around a common interest via the Internet. Through websites and social networking technology, enormous numbers of people are able to donate money, volunteer, advocate, and organize.

- *Social marketing campaigns: Changing attitudes and behaviors.* Through the creative use of marketing techniques, some organizations are pursuing direct and widespread changes in "what's acceptable." The "designated driver" campaign, conceived and designed by the Harvard Alcohol Project at the School of Public Health, built on the platform created by Mothers Against Drunk Driving to change—and stiffen—public attitudes toward "driving under the influence." Social marketing strategies targeting behavior and culture change are currently being pursued in a variety of arenas beyond public health, including the environment and education.

While not exhaustive, this set of illustrations highlights some important ways to scale impact. It also provokes two last thoughts: First, even though these approaches are all about scaling impact, and not scaling organizations, almost all of them depend, nonetheless, on the existence of a strong organization, whether it be an intermediary, a technology-based enterprise, or a single nonprofit organization with a very strong policy and advocacy team. So one important line of research to pursue is what distinguishes organizations that are effective in these endeavors from those that are not? What does it really take in terms of strategy, capital, and talent to pursue these extra-organizational strategies for impact?

Second, with all of these strategies, organizations are attempting to achieve impact that is wildly disproportionate to their size. These attempts matter profoundly if we are to make meaningful progress on many of the issues that nonprofits attack. The challenges we confront, in the United States and worldwide, virtually always extend beyond the capacity of any single organization, so finding ways to achieve more leverage is critical. This is why finding ways to scale impact without scaling the size of an organization is the new frontier for work in our field. Put simply, how can we get one hundred times the impact with only a two times change in unit size? Cracking the code on that problem will enable us to affect the most critical challenges and opportunities facing society today.

This Book

This book offers a range of insights into the variety of ways that people are building strong organizations and finding ways to get dramatically more impact. It is exciting to see Duke University taking the lead to bringing this volume together, in an interdisciplinary collaboration between the Fuqua School of Business's Center for the Advancement of Social Entrepreneurship (CASE), which has been doing important work on scale for a number of years, and the new Center for Strategic Philanthropy and Civil Society (CSPCS), based at the Sanford School of Public Policy. It is just such collaborations, across academic disciplines—and across theory and practice—that will pave the way to better understanding the scaling of social impact.

This book comes at a time of openness to pursuing bold strategies unlike any we have seen for several decades. And the need for solutions to our most intractable problems has never been greater. With researchers in the field and the academy helping us make sense of what is working—and what isn't—this book makes a valuable contribution to building not only our understanding of how we scale social impact but also a better world.

Notes

1. The venture capital model also legitimated and supported a sharp increase in the sector's attention to "capacity building"—strengthening the internal capabilities that enable organizations to deliver results. One striking measure of the sea change is the growth of Grantmakers for Effective Organizations, which was launched in 1997 and now has a membership that numbers more than 350 foundations.
2. Based on a sample of over 110 full-time MBA schools in the United States (Aspen Institute, 2005 and 2007).
3. Dees's article in the *Stanford Social Innovation Review* in 2004 is an early exception. More recently, articles by Bloom and Dees (2008) and by Bloom and Chatterji (2009) begin to develop frameworks that link the scaling of both organization and impact. Crutchfield and Grant's book *Forces for Good* (2007) traces several pathways that innovative organizations are using to scale their impact.
4. Civic organizations, such as the Lions, Elks, and Rotary clubs, were another type of organization launched in the early twentieth century that scaled dramatically (Skocpol, 2003).

Contributors

J. Craig Andrews is professor and Charles H. Kellstadt Chair in Marketing, Marquette University

Alexander Berger is a masters student in the School of Education and an Andrea Naomi Leiderman Fellow at the Haas Center for Public Service, Stanford University

Lauren Block is Lippert Professor of marketing, Zicklin School of Business, Baruch College

Paul N. Bloom is adjunct professor of Social entrepreneurship and marketing and faculty director of the Center for the Advancement of Social Entrepreneurship (CASE), Fuqua School of Business, Duke University

Jeffrey L. Bradach is managing partner and cofounder, The Bridgespan Group

Imran Chowdhury is a PhD candidate in the Management Department at ESSEC Business School, Paris

Srikant M. Datar is the Arthur Lowes Dickinson Professor of accounting, Harvard Business School, Harvard University

Minette E. Drumwright is associate professor, College of Communication (Department of Advertising and Public Relations), The University of Texas at Austin

Mercedes Duchicela is a PhD student in the department of advertising and public relations, The University of Texas at Austin

John Elkington is cofounder and executive chairman of Volans

Marc J. Epstein is Distinguished Research Professor of management, Jones Graduate School of Management, Rice University

Pamela Hartigan is director of the Skoll Centre for Social Entrepreneurship, Said Business School, Oxford University, and founding partner and non-executive director of Volans

Ronald Paul Hill is Robert J. and Barbara Naclerio Chairholder in business, and senior associate dean of intellectual strategy, Villanova School of Business, Villanova University

Jon Huggett is John B. Reid International Visiting Fellow, Centre for Social Impact, University of New South Wales

Alejandro Litovsky is director of the Pathways to Scale Program at Volans

Johanna Mair is associate professor of strategic management, IESE Business School, University of Navarra

Debra E. Meyerson is associate professor of education and (by courtesy) organizational behavior and co-founder and faculty co-director of Stanford's Center on Philanthropy and Civil Society, Stanford University

Scott L. Newbert is associate professor of management and operations, Villanova School of Business, Villanova University

Cornelia Pechmann is professor, The Paul Merage School of Business, University of California, Irvine

Rand Quinn is a doctoral candidate at Stanford University School of Education. He was awarded a University of California President's Postdoctoral Fellowship for 2010–2011 at U.C. Berkeley Graduate School of Education

David T. Robinson is professor of finance and William and Sue Gross Distinguished Research Fellow, Fuqua School of Business, Duke University, and a Research Associate of the National Bureau of Economic Research

Filipe Santos is assistant professor of entrepreneurship, academic director of the Social Entrepreneurship Initiative, and director of the Rudolph and Valeria Maag International Centre for Entrepreneurship, INSEAD

Funda Sezgi is a PhD student in the strategy department, IESE Business School, University of Navarra

Edward Skloot is director of the Center for Strategic Philanthropy and Civil Society, and professor of the practice of public policy, Sanford School of Public Policy, Duke University

Brett R. Smith is assistant professor of entrepreneurship, and the founding director of the Center of Social Entrepreneurship, Farmer School of Business, Miami University

Lauren Trabold is a PhD student in the marketing department, Zicklin School of Business, Baruch College

Kristi Yuthas is associate professor of accounting, and Swigert Endowed Information Systems Management Chair, Portland State University

Introduction

Paul N. Bloom and Edward Skloot

The first steps toward what we now call social entrepreneurship began less than three decades ago. In the early 1980s, Bill Drayton, a former McKinsey & Co. consultant and government official, publicly asked why enterprise couldn't be used to solve social problems. He began to build a global organization—Ashoka—to put such an approach in place. William C. Norris, the thoughtful founder of the Control Data Corporation, an early mainframe computer manufacturer, and his successor, Robert Price, raised the same question from their corporate perch. They used the resources of the company to create business ventures that would answer society's pressing human needs, such as developing inexpensive computer assisted learning and job training programs for disadvantaged, primarily urban Americans.

A handful of others also came at the same question at the same time, from different angles and from different professions. Edward Skloot (a coeditor of this book), an entrepreneur with a nonprofit and government background, opened the first consulting firm to help nonprofit organizations earn income and not remain trapped in endless cycles of fund raising. Richard Steckel, at the time head of the Denver Children's Museum, sold bricks going up the walkway to the building's entrance. Hundreds of donors gladly paid to have their names printed on the bricks, thereby wiping out the museum's financial deficit. Steckel ushered in a new kind of entrepreneurial fund-raising for arts organizations and other nonprofits. In 1982, a conference called "Social Needs and Business Opportunities" was produced by Jerr Boschee, who has stayed in the social enterprise world as a teacher and organization executive. And in academia, marketing experts at business schools, such as Philip Kotler and Alan Andreasen, took their authoritative work on private sector marketing and adapted it to the needs of nonprofits. Indeed, Kotler's definitive textbook *Marketing for Nonprofit Organizations* was published in 1975.

Each of these individuals contributed to the development of social entrepreneurship, though none had it quite clear exactly what might evolve from their efforts. Their efforts, however, had a unifying characteristic. They blended the operating principles of private corporations with the social missions of nonprofit organizations. In that way, they were boundary-crossers, blending parts of one sector into the other for mutual gain. Still, early efforts were isolated and slow to gain traction. This was a decade where the walls of the private, nonprofit (and public) sectors were rarely breached.

By the end of the decade and into the 1990s, the idea of using enterprise to tackle such seemingly intractable issues as entrenched poverty, inadequate health care, and substandard education began to take root. Boundary-crossing, networking organizations were among the first to spring up. For example, the Social Venture Network—pushed along by such socially minded businesses as Ben & Jerry's, Stonyfield Farm, and The Body Shop—spread the word and modeled a socially activist approach for like-minded others. Business for Social Responsibility, founded in 1992, stood for the possibility of a more humane and socially conscious private sector.

On the nonprofit side, an entrepreneurial service organization Teach for America was founded in 1990 by a young Princeton graduate, Wendy Kopp. It offered an option to young people wanting to revive failing public schools: they would serve two years in a national program to invigorate and enhance the teaching profession and simultaneously eliminate educational inequity. Others, including the more business-like Pioneer Human Services (founded in the 1960s) and the Roberts Enterprise Development Fund (REDF), created in 1990 by the consistently insightful advocate-thinker Jed Emerson, demonstrated how private sector models could work directly for social improvement by providing employment, employment training, and product to the consumer. Abroad, in the 1980s and 1990s, an economist with a passion for social equity quietly pioneered new lending paradigms. In founding and building Grameen Bank in Bangladesh, Muhammad Yunus proved the value of microcredit and microenterprise finance focused directly on the "unbankable" poor. Of his clients 95 percent were (and still are) women. In 2006, in recognition of Yunus' now-global impact, he was awarded the Nobel Peace Prize.

In academia, Students for Responsible Business (now Net Impact), founded in 1993, saw its chapters expand to campuses both domestic and international (they now number 230). That same year, investor and statesman John G. Whitehead pledged ten million dollars to start the Initiative on Social Enterprise at Harvard Business School. One year later, Professor J. Gregory Dees, now at Duke University's Fuqua School of Business, taught the first course ever offered on social entrepreneurship. Later in the decade, Stanford University extended the concept of social enterprise by establishing its Center for Social Innovation. In rather quick succession, other universities and organizations, such as the Foundation Center and the Grantsmanship Center, developed curricula, teaching materials, and educational offerings. They spread the knowledge and encouraged experimentation with social enterprise.

Philanthropy, too, began to respond. In 1999, Jeffrey Skoll, the first president (and second employee) of the Internet auction firm eBay, founded the eponymous Skoll Foundation. It embraced social entrepreneurship as a highly promising area to develop and fund. Today, the Skoll Foundation is the most influential philanthropy in this field. One of its signal projects was the establishment (in 2003) of the Skoll Centre for Social Entrepreneurship at Oxford University which, through research, conferences, and awards, has given much visibility and global reach to social entrepreneurship. The Schwab Foundation became active as well, thus helping to promote and legitimize the use of enterprise as a way to tackle deep social and economic inequity. Their efforts were not entirely unique, since the Rockefeller, Surdna, Kellogg, and Hewlett Foundations and the Omidyar Network also poured funding into the field.

By the end of the 1990s social enterprise had gained considerable credibility, legitimacy, and public appeal. While still dismissed by some, it had gradually seeped into the awareness of individuals and organizations. Intent on attacking social ills through proactive, often hybrid approaches that mixed mission and money, "social entrepreneurs" started hundreds of new, often experimental ventures.

In the new century, experiments with entrepreneurial models that could tackle and eradicate social and economic dysfunction were popping up everywhere. Some were revenue generating while others deliberately weren't. The ventures covered all thematic areas, from education to physical disabilities to health care delivery. Collectively, these initiatives began to tilt the scales of acceptance. In 2009, in an impossible-to-imagine event only a few years before, the Obama administration and Congress blessed— and funded—social entrepreneurship through the creation of the small, but more-than-symbolic, Social Innovation Fund. In fact, the core purpose of the Fund is to scale-up social enterprise programs that have been shown conclusively to work.

This edited volume represents another small step in the conceptual development and practical application of social entrepreneurship. It is worth noting that these enterprises have been particularly noticeable in developing countries where the costs of start-up and operations, as well as the availability of "new" technology, such as cell phones, have seemingly offered the opportunity to make a demonstrable impact. To be sure, many of the issues confronting social entrepreneurs in those parts of the world are vast and seemingly intractable. Yet the enterprises they have established and that have flourished, along with those in the industrialized world, surely have much to share and teach each other, as well as the interested public. That is our premise in compiling the original readings found in this book. In the years to come we will see how successful—and replicable—such ventures are, why they have been so, and what impact they will have had in ushering in a more equitable and just world.

In less than thirty years, social enterprises have gained recognition, significant funding, and, frequently, success by combining social mission with businesslike approaches. We are at a moment when both theory and practice need wider exploration and exposition.

A central issue, for example, one that animates all these chapters, is the meaning, opportunity, and cost of "scaling-up" social enterprises that apparently are running successfully. How do we do this? When is the right time? What principles of success can be distilled and shared? We have no clear answers yet, although finding out is surely one of the purposes of the Obama administration's Social Innovation Fund. What we do know is that if system change is to be achieved, then successful but isolated, largely unknown, and smallish ventures—and the ideas that underpin them—will need to grow in resources, operating capacity, and demonstrable impact in order to thrive.

Background on this Volume

In response to the great interest in generating new knowledge about scaling social impact, two Centers at Duke University (the Center for the Advancement of Social Entrepreneurship—CASE—and the Center for Strategic Philanthropy and Civil Society—CSPCS) organized a conference at Duke in November 2008 titled *Scaling Social Impact: What We Know and What We Need to Know.* This event brought together practicing social entrepreneurs, funders of social entrepreneurs, and academics interested in social entrepreneurship for a day and one-half of presentations and discussions about where the gaps in knowledge about scaling seemed to be and what would be the most fruitful directions to pursue in trying to close those gaps. Following this event, attendees were asked to propose research papers they would like to write that would address topics identified during the conference. Twelve papers on a variety of topics were proposed and the authors were asked to complete the papers in time for presentation at the *Second Conference on Scaling Social Impact,* which was held at Duke in November 2009. Ten of the papers were presented at the conference and all twelve are included in this volume.

The twelve essays are divided into five sections or groupings:

1. Framing the issues
2. The pros and cons of scaling
3. Cultivating ecosystem alliances and networks
4. Communicating and branding
5. Guiding funders and supporters

The remainder of this introduction briefly summarizes the essays.

Summaries of the Essays

In the section on "Framing the issues," the essays offer several different frameworks for thinking about the challenge of scaling social impact.

The first chapter by Bloom and Smith introduces the SCALERS model, originally proposed by Bloom and Chatterji (2009), which posits that an organization's success at scaling social impact will be a consequence of its capabilities in seven areas: staffing, communicating, alliance-building, lobbying, earnings-generation, replicating, and stimulating market forces. The model recognizes, however, that strong performance in all of these capabilities will not be necessary for scaling success for all organizations, as certain situational contingencies can make some capabilities more important than others. For example, lobbying (or advocacy) may not be an important driver of scaling for an organization that does not need supportive government regulations or financing. After introducing the SCALERS model, Bloom and Smith go on to report on an exploratory empirical test of the model that they conducted using survey data obtained from a sample of several hundred managers of nonprofit organizations. Their results are supportive of the model, although they acknowledge that much additional research is needed to refine and supplement the data-gathering instrument used to obtain self-assessments about capabilities and scaling success.

The other essay in the opening section by Sezgi and Mair builds on a framework offered by Dees et al. (2004), which identifies different strategic pathways to scale. This framework proposes three dominant strategies for scaling, which are labeled as *branching, affiliation,* and *dissemination.* Sezgi and Mair examine how one organization, the Aravind Eye Care System in India, has deployed all three strategies to help it scale. They provide an analysis of the strengths and weaknesses of each strategy for producing organizational control over processes and outcomes. While their findings apply to a single organization in a single country, insights are provided that have great relevance to scaling efforts in other contexts.

In the second section of the book on "The pros and cons of scaling," the two essays take a highly critical look at two frequently touted success stories in scaling social entrepreneurial impact: the growth of microfinance in the developing world (Datar, Epstein, and Yuthas) and the growth of charter schools in California (Meyerson, Berger, and Quinn). Both essays point out that while much good has come out of the scaling attempts in these sectors, a certain amount of bad outcomes and disappointments have occurred because of the emphasis on scaling and, particularly, because of the emphasis on scaling the size of organizations as opposed to scaling *impact.* The essays raise the important issue of whether rapid scaling should always be the overriding goal of a social entrepreneurial initiative. The authors suggest that sometimes a more cautious, methodical approach to scaling may serve society better.

The third section of the book on "Cultivating ecosystem alliances and networks" contains four essays that analyze the value of not trying to "go it alone" in scaling a social entrepreneurial venture—that is, enhancing the "alliance-building" capability in the SCALERS model. The inclusion of four essays under this heading reflects the importance that alliance-building has been accorded by students of scaling social entrepreneurial impact.

The opening essay of the section by Elkington, Hartigan, and Litovsky makes an especially compelling case for the value of understanding the ecosystem that surrounds the problem you are trying to address and then forming partnerships and alliances within that ecosystem to work toward significant social impact. In presenting a five-stage "pathways to scale" model, they stress the importance of transitioning from the model's stage 3 to stage 4, stating that "moving from individual business models to broader ecosystems requires collaborative forms of leadership...systemically mapping and engaging all key actors in the relevant parts of the economy." They cite several examples of efforts in the solar energy field (e.g., Solar Aid in Africa, Grameen Shakti in Bangladesh, the India Solar Loan Programme) that have had success in scaling impact through employing collaborative approaches that fit the conditions of their ecosystems very well.

The other essays covering alliances stress other keys to successful collaborations. Huggett emphasizes the value of taking an "integrator" approach, which he describes as something in between trying to scale using (1) a centralized "hub" to guide activities and (2) a loose structure of local organizations trying to replicate one another. Integrators are groups of locally based organizations that are linked with one another through having "shared goals for impact," strategy, branding, and "complementarity" in the skills and contributions they make to the network (reducing replication). They are run by effective professional managers and not "heroic" leaders who try to direct "followers" from a central location. Examples of groups that have scaled in this way are Save the Children, World Vision, and Habitat for Humanity.

The essay by Newbert and Hill discusses the importance of conflict management as a determinant of successful alliances. They point out that misrepresentation, opportunism, and hostage are the three main threats to alliances and that avoiding the emergence of these threats (and conflict) requires paying close attention to the history of trustworthy behavior exhibited by potential partners as well as making sure that the partners recognize their strategic interdependence on one another for achieving overriding goals. They report on two different cases, one where a productive alliance was worked out after some setbacks (focused on homelessness) and another where an alliance fell apart (focused on downtown redevelopment).

The last essay addressing alliances is by Chowdhury and Santos. They present a case study of a highly successful partnership between Gram Vikas and the Comprehensive Rural Health Project in India, where Gram Vikas' "Movement and Action Network for the Transformation of Rural Areas (MANTRA)"—an approach to supplying clean water and sanitation to rural communities—has been replicated successfully hundreds of times. A key to the success of this venture has been agreement on the overriding goal of bringing clean water and sanitation to 100 percent (and nothing less) of the people in each community, regardless of caste or wealth.

The section of the book on "Communicating and branding" contains two essays that focus on the role that thinking from the fields of marketing and consumer behavior can contribute to successful scaling. Trabold, Bloom, and Block draw on the social marketing and consumer behavior literature to identify propositions about the types of message themes and media that are likely to be more effective in persuading potential beneficiaries of health-oriented social entrepreneurial efforts to change their behaviors. Achieving behavior change is often a severe obstacle to scaling for organizations trying to get people to eat better, exercise more, obtain screening tests, or take medications. The authors cite examples of organizations that seem to be using the themes and media suggested by the propositions, but determining the true effectiveness of these communications remains a task for further research.

Drumwright and Duchicela also present propositions about approaches that might work more effectively in helping organizations scale their impact. Their ideas are drawn from the literatures in marketing as well as other disciplines and from in-depth interviews they conducted with leaders of social entrepreneurial organizations. They cover, among other things, what is likely to work best in branding (e.g., a stand-alone brand name, open source), message themes (e.g., engaging the heart, simple, compelling visuals), and corporate partnerships (e.g., retailers with numerous locations).

The final section of the book on "Guiding funders and supporters" presents two essays that argue for the importance of providing funders and supporters of social entrepreneurial organizations with carefully developed, accurate, and useful information and metrics about how well organizations are doing at scaling impact. Robinson stresses the importance of having accurate information to allow financial capital to flow to its best uses. He emphasizes the key role that social financial intermediaries (e.g., Acumen Fund) can have, not only in providing information and facilitating matchmaking between funders and organizations, but also in helping to deal with governance and compensation challenges faced by social entrepreneurial organizations.

Last, Pechmann and Andrews stress the value of rigorously conducted evaluation studies to guide funders and managers about what is working effectively at truly creating impact and what is producing disappointing outcomes. They report on the strengths and weaknesses of several large-scale evaluation studies that have been conducted to determine the impact of social programs.

Acknowledgments

This volume would not be possible without the dedicated work of all the chapter authors and several other people who deserve special thanks. Our Duke faculty colleagues, J. Gregory Dees and Joel Fleishman, helped us recruit speakers/authors to the two conferences and, more generally, have consistently provided guidance and inspiration to both of us in our efforts to learn more about social entrepreneurship. We would also like to thank the staffs of our Centers—the CASE group of Wendy Kuran, Matt Nash,

Erin Worsham, Ruth Tolman, Jane Smith, Shu He, and Terri Taylor, and the CSPCS group of Sarah Burdick and Barry Varela—who helped to make all aspects of the conferences run smoothly and competently. In sum, this volume represents the collective effort of more than two dozen people who are committed to building new knowledge about scaling social impact. We hope to add even more new knowledge through future events and publications, including follow-up volumes to this inaugural volume of the CASE Series on Social Entrepreneurship.

I

Framing the Issues

1

Identifying the Drivers of Social Entrepreneurial Impact: An Exploratory Empirical Study

Paul N. Bloom and Brett R. Smith

Many social entrepreneurs and their supporters and funders have now turned their focus on the goal of scaling the social impact of their programs and initiatives (Bloom and Dees, 2008; Bradach, 2003; Dees et al., 2004). In an era when resources for social programs are scarce, the idea of scaling up well-performing efforts so that social problems are mitigated more efficiently, effectively, and widely has become compelling. Investors and grantors want to obtain a good social return on their investment, and managers of social entrepreneurial organizations want to please their funders while also making a big difference in the world. Great interest has developed in finding the drivers of successful scaling of social impact that will allow innovative, smaller-scale social programs to move rapidly and efficiently from helping just a few people to helping more people more dramatically.

Researchers interested in scaling social impact have addressed the issue in a number of ways. For instance, several frameworks have been proposed to help guide practitioners toward more effective strategies for scaling, drawing in part on theoretical thinking and empirical work done in fields such as organizational behavior, strategic management, sociology, and economics (Dees et al., 2004; La France et al., 2006). The empirical work that has been done, specifically to understand the drivers of successful scaling for social entrepreneurial organizations, has been limited, with most of it utilizing comparative case-study approaches (Alvord et al., 2004; Grant and Crutchfield, 2007; La France et al., 2006; Sharir and Lerner, 2005). While this work has generated provocative theoretical insights and hypotheses, rigorous empirical tests of theories and hypotheses have been limited (Sherman, 2007).

In this chapter, we take new theoretical thinking about scaling and begin to explore how that thinking might be tested with empirical data.

We examine the recently developed SCALERS model (Bloom and Chatterji, 2009)—which proposes that the strength of seven organizational capabilities (staffing, communicating, alliance-building, lobbying, earnings-generation, replicating, and stimulating market forces), moderated by certain situational contingencies, drives successful scaling of social impact—and conduct an initial, exploratory, empirical test of several hypotheses drawn from the model. We begin by briefly describing the model and then discussing the methodological challenges associated with trying to test its notions. We then describe a survey-research study that we were able to participate in and that gave us the opportunity to refine measures of some of the model's constructs and determine how those measures related to one another, to other indicators, and to a measure of scaling success. Although the number of items we could include in the survey was limited, and the respondents were not purely social entrepreneurs (many were conventional nonprofits), we think the results obtained from this exploratory study are consistent with the model's character and suggest that a more extensive, more rigorous test of the model could yield very interesting and valuable insights about the drivers of successful scaling of social impact.

The SCALERS Model

Much of the early writing about scaling social impact has focused on how changing the people and policies *inside* the social entrepreneurial organization can lead to growth and greater social impact. This work has emphasized the value of leadership, staying on mission, fund-raising, creating a supportive culture, establishing replicable policies and procedures (e.g., franchising), and obtaining evaluation results (Bradach, 2003; La France et al., 2006; Sherman, 2006). More recently, authors have recognized the value for social entrepreneurial organizations of interacting effectively with various players and forces in their *external* ecosystems, creating alliances to acquire resources and political support (Grant and Crutchfield, 2007; Sharir and Lerner, 2006), building on market incentives to change behaviors of beneficiaries and influencers, and capitalizing on economic and social trends to attract attention and build momentum for their causes (Austin, 2000; Bloom and Dees, 2008). The SCALERS model, shown in figure 1.1, draws on this previous research on scaling, as well as on theoretical notions from strategic management, organizational behavior, and marketing.

The model proposes seven drivers—or organizational capabilities—that can stimulate successful scaling by a social entrepreneurial organization, employing the acronym SCALERS as a label to aid recall. The model also proposes that the extent to which an individual SCALER (i.e., driver or capability) will influence scaling success will depend on certain situational contingencies. There may be distinctive aspects of the organization's "theory of change" or its internal and external environment (e.g., intense *Labor Needs* or weak *Public Support*) that will enhance or suppress a

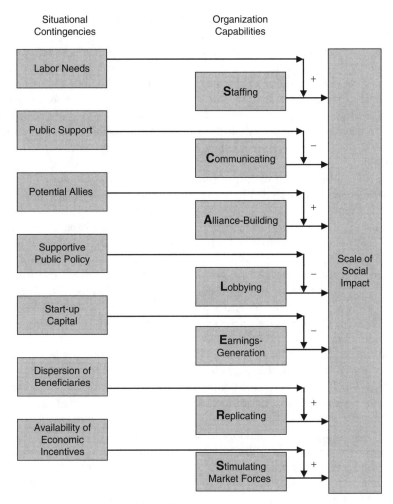

Figure 1.1   The SCALERS model.

SCALER's influence. In some situations, effective deployment of all the SCALERS may be needed for successful scaling. In other situations, strong effectiveness with only a few SCALERS can drive scaling success. Note that, as shown, figure 1.1 depicts only the main relationships or effects of the SCALERS. For simplicity, feedback loops and interactions among the constructs are not shown, although they are hypothesized to exist. A short description of the model's constructs and hypothesized relationships follows.

The term *staffing* refers to *the effectiveness of the organization at filling its labor needs, including its managerial posts, with people who have the requisite skills for the needed positions, whether they be paid staff or volunteers.* A high value on this construct would reflect having little difficulty filling all of its jobs with competent people. The degree to which staffing drives scaling will vary, depending on the situational contingency of the organization's *labor needs*—that is, *the extent to which the organization's change strategy requires it to provide labor-intensive and skilled services to beneficiaries.* When labor needs are high, such as when the organization is providing counseling or health services to indigent patients, staffing will be crucial for successful scaling. But when labor needs are less severe, either because the organization's theory of change is not based on service provision or because the services can be provided by machines or less skilled workers, then other SCALERS may determine scaling success more than staffing.

Without adding arrows to the figure, the authors point out that effectiveness at staffing can lead to improved effectiveness at all the other SCALERS and, conversely, effectiveness at communicating, alliance-building, and earnings-generation can lead to improved effectiveness at staffing. For example, the recruitment of a formidable fundraiser can help improve communicating, alliance-building, and earnings-generation, which can, in turn, help to provide the persuasive messaging, contacts, and funding needed to attract other talented staff members. Undoubtedly, there are likely to be effects of the SCALERS on one another, as well as synergies among them, that ultimately affect the scale of social impact the organization can achieve.

Communicating refers to *the effectiveness with which the organization is able to persuade key stakeholders that its change strategy is worth adopting and/or supporting.* A high value on this construct would mean that the organization's communications have been successful at: (a) persuading potential beneficiaries to take advantage of organization services and/or to change their behaviors in socially beneficial ways (e.g., becoming more prudent financially, pursuing healthier lifestyles); (b) persuading volunteers and employees to work for the organization; (c) persuading consumers to patronize the earned-income activities of the organization; (d) persuading donors/financiers to provide funds to the organization; or (e) creating favorable attitudes toward the organization's programs among the general public.

There will be some situations where communicating becomes a less important driver of successful scaling. This will occur when high levels exist of the situational contingency of *public support*, or *the extent to which the general public already supports the change strategy of the organization.* This is because "ceiling effects" might occur and there is not much room to shift people's views toward the organization's change strategy—and consequently other SCALERS may be more likely to influence scaling success. Such a ceiling may face organizations pursuing popular causes such as tobacco control or breast cancer prevention and treatment. These organizations may find their scaling success is more dependent on how effective they are at alliance-building, lobbying, and replication.

As is the case with staffing, communicating effectively can make the other SCALERS more effective and also produce synergistic effects on the scale of social impact. For example, signing up a well-known, credible spokesperson to appear in your communications (e.g., President Jimmy Carter speaking for Habitat for Humanity) can help scale your social impact through a host of different synergistic mechanisms.

The capability of *alliance-building* refers to *the effectiveness with which the organization has forged partnerships, coalitions, joint ventures, and other linkages to bring about desired social changes.* A high value on this construct would mean that the organization does not try to do things by itself, instead seeking the benefits of unified efforts. Some social entrepreneurial organizations may face the situational contingency of being low on *potential allies*, or *the extent to which other organizations and institutions are potentially available to work with the organization to achieve social change.* Some organizations may pursue causes that are controversial (e.g., gun control, legalization of drugs, right to choose) and finding allies may be difficult. In those cases where it is necessary to operate in a more solo fashion, other SCALERS may be more important for achieving scaling success.

Still, forming a relationship with a great partner—just like finding that great fundraiser or the super spokesperson—can uplift the effectiveness of all the SCALERS. Think, for example, of how much Timberland Corporation has helped City Year become successful at encouraging thousands of young people to spend a year working on social welfare projects in inner cities (Dees and Elias, 1996).

The capability of *lobbying* is defined to mean *the effectiveness with which the organization is able to advocate for government actions that may work in its favor.* The term "lobbying" is used loosely here and does not refer just to efforts employing registered lobbyists that could jeopardize an organization's tax-exempt status. A high value on this construct would mean that the organization has succeeded in getting the courts, administrative agencies, legislators, and government leaders to help its cause. A situational contingency that can moderate the effect of lobbying is *supportive public policy*, or *the extent to which laws, regulations, and policies that support the organization's social change efforts are already in place.* For some social entrepreneurial organizations, public policy is basically neutral or mildly positive, and the potential impact of lobbying on scaling is likely to be minimal. Other SCALERS will drive scaling success more dramatically. But many social entrepreneurial organizations can benefit greatly from shifts in public policy.

Once again, the model suggests that having some special success with this single SCALER (e.g., getting a generous government budget allocation)— just like acquiring a special fundraiser, spokesperson, or partner—can make all the SCALERS more effective.

The capability of *earnings-generation* refers to *the effectiveness with which the organization generates a stream of revenue that exceeds its expenses.* A high value on this construct would mean that it does not have trouble paying its bills and funding its activities. Earnings-generation emerging from earned-income efforts (e.g., selling ad space on a website), donations, grants, sponsorships, membership fees, investments, or other sources will primarily have their social impact through how they allow the social entrepreneurial organization to increase the effectiveness of their staffing, communicating, alliance-building, lobbying, replicating, and stimulating market forces. Indeed, there are probably reciprocal relationships between earnings-generation and the other SCALERS for most organizations. For example, effective staffing can cause increased earnings-generation and vice versa. Of course, which drives the other may be unclear as many chicken-egg situations might exist. Regardless, earnings-generation can still have an impact on its own (as the model shows), in that the organization that is financially healthy should have more legitimacy and persuasiveness with various influencers of social change.

A situational contingency that could affect the impact of earnings-generation is *start-up capital*, or *the extent to which the organization is starting its scaling efforts with an ample pool of financial resources committed to it*. Scaling success will be driven more by the other SCALERS in situations where the organization has ample financial resources to draw upon when scaling.

The capability of *replicating* reflects *the effectiveness with which the organization can reproduce the programs and initiatives that it has originated*. A high value on this construct would mean that the services, programs, and other efforts of the organization can be copied or extended without a decline in quality, using training, franchising, contracting, and other tools to ensure quality control. The influence of replicating can be moderated by the situational contingency of *dispersion of beneficiaries*, which is defined as *the extent to which variation exists in the people the organization is trying to serve, including demographic and geographic variation*. If there is little dispersion of those being served, there may be little need to set up new organizational entities to scale up, as growing the "home" organization may be sufficient. Indeed, such an organization might accomplish more by trying to scale "deep" rather than "wide," and by therefore putting its emphasis on SCALERS such as staffing, communications, and alliance-building. Being outstanding on this single SCALER can, again, help to make many of the other SCALERS more effective.

The final capability of *stimulating market forces* covers *the effectiveness with which the organization can create incentives that encourage people or institutions to pursue private interests while also serving the public good*. A high value on this construct would mean that the organization has been successful at creating markets for offerings (i.e., products and services) such as micro-loans, inexpensive health remedies, inexpensive farming equipment, or carbon credits. The extent to which stimulating market forces will encourage scaling will depend on the situational contingency of the *availability of economic incentives,* which reflects *the extent to which the organization operates in a sector where economic incentives motivate people's behavior.* For example, organizations involved with providing financial services would be higher on this dimension than those involved with encouraging physical activity.

Methodological Challenges

Ideally, we would like to test the SCALERS model on data obtained from a broad cross-section of social entrepreneurial organizations that have had a wide range of positive and negative experiences with scaling social impact. The data would provide perceptual and archival measures of how the SCALERS and other variables performed at various points in time, allowing for tests of causal relationships. Although the measurement, data collection, and analysis problems associated with creating such a data base are daunting, we believe that a research program dedicated to this task, patterned in part after the PIMS (Profit Impact of Market Strategies) program that received so much attention in the field of strategic management (Buzzell, 2004), would be worthwhile. The field of entrepreneurship has also benefited from the development of cross-organization data bases (Griffin, 1997; Griffin and Page, 1996).

Recognizing the challenges ahead, we have embarked on a research program to create such a data base about social entrepreneurial organizations. Thus far, we have developed a set of scale items that could be used to obtain self-reports from managers about how well their organizations have performed in scaling social impact and in deploying the individual SCALERS. We have tested these items with an available sample of nonprofit managers and obtained initial readings on the reliability and validity of the multi-item scales, which are reported here. In the future, we hope to do further tests of the reliability and validity of refined versions of these scales, as well as of new scales that capture the situational contingencies faced by these organizations, using: (1) a more representative sample of managers of social entrepreneurial organizations and (2) data obtained from other informants and archival sources (to look for convergent validity and to test for "common method bias," which can lead to correlations among constructs because they are measured with similar scales, see Podsakoff et al., 2003). Ultimately, we hope to be able to conduct rigorous tests of the causal and interactive relationships that the individual SCALERS have with each other and with the scale of social impact an organization has achieved, while also showing how certain situational contingencies moderate the effects of the SCALERS. Uncovering the effects of the situational contingencies is extremely important, since not controlling for these contingencies may make it very difficult to form accurate judgments about the effects of the SCALERS when dealing with an extremely heterogeneous sample of organizations. Including the situational contingencies in the analyses is a way to compare apples to apples in the analyses to see what drives scaling, and not apples to oranges.

Methods and Hypotheses

Three outfits that serve the interests of social entrepreneurs and managers of social venture organizations are Community Wealth Ventures, the Social Enterprise Alliance, and REDF. Recently, they decided to collaborate on a survey exploring the state of the art in social enterprise and contacted us for technical assistance. We agreed to help them in exchange for the opportunity to include twenty-five Likert-type items in the survey questionnaire. The sampling frame used in the survey was the mailing lists of the three organizations, plus a list provided by Guidestar, with all the members of the lists being contacted. Admittedly, this created a sample tilted toward an emphasis on social enterprise (i.e., creating revenue-generating businesses under the organization's umbrella), rather than on social entrepreneurship (which can be done without social enterprise). A total of 5,965 members were sent emails requesting their participation in the study (i.e., completion of a SurveyMonkey online questionnaire), with the email reaching 5,424 (because of bouncebacks and opt-outs) and with a total of 1,008 responding, 601 completing our twenty-five items, and 591 of those reporting that they worked for nonprofit organizations. Respondents were offered an incentive of entrance into a lottery where they could win free registration at an upcoming conference. Although we believe for-profit organizations can pursue social entrepreneurial ventures, we decided that in this exploratory study it would be preferable to restrict our analysis to only the nonprofit managers, cutting down some heterogeneity.

The twenty-five items are reprinted in the appendix and descriptive statistics on composites of these items and on several other measures for the nonprofit respondents are reported in table 1.1. Four items were used to measure "scaling social impact" and three each were used to measure the seven individual SCALERS. The survey also collected measures of the year the organization was founded and the degree to which social enterprise was supported by the organization's board and staff. Besides examining the validity and reliability of the multiple-item scales, we used these data to examine the following hypotheses:

Hypotheses 1a–g: For each SCALER'S capability, higher scores on "scaling social impact" will be reported for those who score high on that capability than for those who score low on that capability.

We would expect these results for all the seven SCALERS, even though the model suggests that under certain situational contingencies a particular SCALER may not have much influence on scaling success. However, on average, we would expect high performers on any capability to report

Table 1.1 Correlations, descriptive statistics, and reliability coefficients

Variables	1	2	3	4	5	6	7	8	9	10	11
1. Year founded											
2. Staffing	-0.04										
3. Communicating	0.01	0.34**									
4. Alliance-building	-0.12**	0.25**	0.24**								
5. Lobbying	0.17**	0.19**	0.27**	0.25**							
6. Earnings-generation	0.05	0.42**	0.44**	0.22**	0.24**						
7. Replicating	0.01	0.32**	0.28**	0.22**	0.18**	0.36**					
8. Stimulating market forces	-0.04	0.36**	0.35**	0.21**	0.23**	0.51**	0.41**				
9. Scaling social impact	-0.12**	0.39**	0.37**	0.20**	0.19**	0.51**	0.40**	0.43**			
10. Attitude of board	-0.09*	0.11*	0.21**	0.13**	0.13**	0.29**	0.22**	0.44**	0.26**		
11. Attitude of staff	-0.15**	0.12**	0.15**	0.16**	-0.02	0.21**	0.19**	0.30**	0.18**	0.67**	
Mean	5.41	10.10	10.58	11.31	9.01	9.73	10.41	10.21	14.61	4.66	4.67
Standard deviation	2.78	2.29	2.23	2.50	2.40	2.42	2.46	2.46	2.92	1.92	1.87
Reliability coefficient		0.61	0.71	0.82	0.63	0.60	0.79	0.76	0.73		

Note: $n = 516$ for attitude of board; 547 for attitude of staff; 586 for year founded; 591 for all other variables.
$* p < .05; ** p < .01$.

greater scaling success than low performers on that capability. In a similar vein, we would expect the following:

Hypotheses 2a–g: When regressed on "scaling social impact" in a multiple regression, each of the SCALER'S capabilities will show a positive, significant effect.

Moving beyond the consequences of the SCALERS, we are also interested in beginning to understand their antecedents. From the data available, we develop two initial sets of hypotheses related to how the attitudes of the stakeholders of the organizations are related to the development of the organizational capacities of the SCALERS. Specifically, we focus on the attitude of the board and the attitude of the staff toward social enterprise. Prior research by psychologists generally suggests a positive relationship exists between attitudes and behaviors (for a review, see Eagley and Chaiken, 1993). Building upon this logic, we expect the attitudes of the stakeholders to be related to the development of organizational capabilities of the SCALERS. As such, we examined the following sets of hypotheses:

Hypotheses 3a–g: When regressed on each of the SCALER'S capabilities, the attitude of the board toward social enterprise will show a positive, significant effect.

Hypotheses 4a–g: When regressed on each of the SCALER'S capabilities, the attitude of the staff toward social enterprise will show a positive, significant effect.

Results

Scale Validity and Reliability

To examine their validity, the measures of the SCALERS were assessed by confirmatory factor analysis (CFA). The CFA contained twenty-five items, three for each of the seven SCALERS capabilities and four for scaling of social impact. For each of the SCALERS, we used formative rather than reflective measures, where the items "cause" the construct (Diamantopoulos and Winklhofer, 2001). The results of the CFA analysis indicated an acceptable fit with the data ($\chi^2 = 837.70$, $p = 0.001$; GFI = 0.90; RMSEA = 0.06; NFI = 0.92). The standardized factor loadings were large and significant at the 0.05 level ($t > 2.0$). There was also evidence of discriminant validity because in each case the construct intercorrelations were less than one ($p < 0.001$). To assess common method variance, we used Harman's one-factor test to determine whether a single factor accounted for most of the covariance in the relationships between the independent and dependent variables (Podsakoff and Organ, 1986). After performing a factor analysis on all twenty-five items, eight factors with eigen values near or greater than one emerged and no single factor accounted for more than 26 percent of the variance. As such, common method variance was not likely to present a serious problem in our study.

Examination of Hypotheses

T-tests and linear regression were used to test our hypotheses. Table 1.1 presents the correlations, descriptive statistics, and reliability coefficients for each construct. The date the organization was founded was positively and significantly related to lobbying ($r = 0.17$, $p < 0.01$), suggesting older organizations tend to engage more in lobbying. The date the organization was founded was also negatively and significantly related to alliance-building ($r = -0.12$, $p < 0.01$), scaling of social impact ($r = -0.12$, $p < 0.01$), attitude of board ($r = -0.09$, $p < 0.01$), and attitude of staff ($r = -0.15$, $p < 0.01$). This pattern of results suggests length of time since founding affects the SCALERS, as well as the antecedents and consequences of the SCALERS.

Our first set of hypotheses (H1a–g) predicted a positive and significant difference between high and low SCALERS on the scaling of social impact. Table 1.2 presents t-tests comparing differences of high and low SCALERS on scaling of social impact. For each of the seven SCALERS, we compared the scaling of social impact of organizations that scored low and high, based on median splits for each of the SCALERS, on the different organizational capabilities. Across each of the SCALERS, we found a positive and significant difference between low and high SCALERS on the scaling of social impact (t ranged from 3.40 to 10.33). While the greatest difference was found for stimulating market forces and the smallest difference for alliance-building, all seven of the SCALERS provided evidence of differences at the 0.001 level, supporting each of our first set of hypotheses.

Table 1.3 presents hierarchical linear regression results regarding scaling social impact. Our second set of hypotheses (H2a–g) predicted SCALERS

Table 1.2   T-tests of differences between low and high SCALERS: scaling social impact

Variables	Low mean (s.d.)	High mean (s.d.)	t-Statistic
1. Staffing	13.81	15.64	7.93***
($n = 332$ for low; 259 for high)	(2.82)	(2.71)	
2. Communicating	13.94	15.64	7.20***
($n = 357$ for low; 234 for high)	(2.87)	(2.68)	
3. Alliance-building	14.17	14.99	3.40***
($n = 273$ for low; 318 for high)	(3.08)	(2.72)	
4. Lobbying	14.19	15.18	4.14***
($n = 337$ for low; 254 for high)	(2.87)	(2.88)	
5. Earnings-generation	13.40	15.67	10.26***
($n = 275$ for low; 316 for high)	(2.84)	(2.55)	
6. Replicating	13.71	15.61	8.36***
($n = 309$ for low; 282 for high)	(2.76)	(2.76)	
7. Stimulating market forces	13.50	15.79	10.33***
($n = 304$ for low; 287 for high)	(2.74)	(2.63)	

Note: $n = 591$; *** $p < .001$.

Table 1.3   Results of hierarchical regression analyses for scaling social impact

Variables	Step 1	Step 2	Step 3	Step 4	Step 5	Step 6	Step 7	Step 8
Control variable								
Year founded	−0.12**	−0.11**	−0.11**	−0.10**	−0.12**	−0.14**	−0.14**	−0.13**
Independent variables								
Staffing		0.38**	0.30**	0.28**	0.28**	0.17**	0.14**	0.13**
Communicating			0.26**	0.25**	0.23**	0.11**	0.10*	0.09*
Alliance-building				0.07+	0.05	0.03	0.01	0.01
Lobbying					0.08*	0.06	0.05	0.04
Earnings-generation						0.37**	0.33**	0.28**
Replicating							0.21**	0.18**
Stimulating market forces								0.13**
Δ R²	0.02**	0.14**	0.06**	0.01+	0.01*	0.09**	0.04**	0.01**
Total R²	0.02**	0.16**	0.22**	0.23**	0.24**	0.33**	0.37**	0.38**

$^+ p < .10$; $^* p < .05$; $^{**} p < .01$.

would be positively related to scaling of social impact. After controlling for year founded, we find evidence of a positive relationship between the SCALERS and scaling of social impact. As each of the SCALERS is entered into the stepwise regression, each one is positively (β ranges from 0.07 to 0.38) and significantly related to scaling of social impact, although alliance-building is only marginally significant. A comparison of beta coefficients suggests earnings-generation has a relatively stronger effect than the other SCALERS. We find individual support for the effects of staffing, communicating, lobbying, earnings-generation, replicating, and stimulating market forces on scaling of social impact. We also find marginal support for effect of alliance-building on scaling of social impact. When all SCALERS are entered into the model, alliance building and lobbying become insignificant. Taken together, the SCALERS explain 38 percent of the variance in scaling of social impact.

Table 1.4 presents regression results of the antecedents of attitude of board and staff on SCALERS. With respect to the antecedents of attitude of board and attitude of staff, we find 13 of the 14 relationships are positive and significant. Consistent with our third set of hypotheses (H3a–H3g), attitude of the board is positively (β ranges from 0.11 to 0.44) and significantly ($p < .05$) related to each of the SCALERS. Consistent with our fourth set of hypotheses, attitude of the staff is positively (β ranges from 0.12 to 0.30) and significantly ($p < .01$) related to each of the SCALERS except lobbying. Collectively, these results generally support the idea that the attitude of the board and staff are important antecedents to the SCALERS. In this way, these results begin to establish some evidence for nomological validity of the SCALERS constructs.

Table 1.4 Regression analysis of antecedents of (a) attitude of board and (b) staff for SCALERS

Variables	Staffing	Communicate	Alliance	Lobby	Earnings	Replicate	Stimulate
(a)							
Control variable Year founded	−0.02	0.03	−0.12**	0.21**	0.09*	0.04	0.01
Independent variable Attitude of board	0.11*	0.21**	0.12**	0.14**	0.29**	0.22**	0.44**
Total R^2	0.01	0.04	0.03	0.06	0.09	0.05	0.19
(b)							
Control variable Year founded	−0.01	0.03	−0.08+	0.20**	0.09*	0.05	0.01
Independent variable Attitude of staff	0.12**	0.15**	0.15**	0.02	0.22**	0.19**	0.30**
Total R^2	0.01	0.02	0.03	0.04	0.05	0.04	0.09

$^+ p < .10$; $^* p < .05$; $^{**} p < .01$.

Discussion

The purpose of this study was two-fold. First, this study sought to empirically test a model of factors, termed SCALERS, related to scaling of social impact. As such, we were interested in testing the validity and reliability of the SCALERS constructs, testing the predictive ability of the SCALERS on scaling of social impact, and testing the antecedents of the SCALERS. Perhaps the most important contribution of this research is the identification and testing of some initial factors that are related to the scaling of social impact, arguably the most important dependent variable in the domain of social entrepreneurship. Our results indicate staffing, communicating, alliance-building, lobbying, earnings-generation, replicating and stimulating market forces are all important predictors of scaling of social impact. Even though alliance-building and lobbying no longer remained significant when all the SCALERS' capabilities were entered into the regression analysis, we think this may have reflected the character of the organizations in our sample. On average, these organizations may have operated in situations where there were (a) few opportunities for allies and/or (b) supportive public policy that did not leave much room for additional lobbying success. Future development of measures of the situational contingencies should allow the testing of these alternative explanations.

Second, this study sought to respond to the call for large scale quantitative studies in the field of social entrepreneurship. While much has been gained by the use of the qualitative case-study approach to the field, this study sought to complement this approach by using a large scale quantitative study of nearly six hundred social enterprises. Although the nature of the data collection has some limitations, this study is one of the first of its kind to address the scaling of social impact in a large scale quantitative manner. In this way, the findings of this study may better generalize to a larger population of social entrepreneurial ventures than previous studies and may contribute to the relatively sparse quantitative empirical work in the domain of social entrepreneurship. Looking forward, there is much work to be done on several different fronts and several challenges that make the research task daunting.

Limitations and Future Research

One important area for future research is scale development. In this study, we took advantage of an opportunity to collect data from a large sample of social enterprises but we were also restricted in the number of questions we could ask. While confirmatory factor analysis provides some evidence of acceptable measures, a more comprehensive approach to scale development is needed. In future work, the scale development process of the SCALERS could more closely adhere to the paradigms for measure development (Churchill, 1979; Gerbing and Anderson, 1988). Specifically, the generation of a larger sample of items and the purification of the measure may provide more valid and reliable measures for the SCALERS. Future research is also needed on both the SCALERS and the situational contingencies. In the current study, we were not able to collect data on the theorized situational contingencies that are an important part of the SCALERS model. Research that begins to specify under what conditions the SCALERS capabilities are related to scaling of social impact individually and collectively is an important next step. In addition, additional research that uses newly developed SCALERS measures is needed to continue the process of construct validation.

An additional measurement issue for future research is the development of the dependent variable of scaling of social impact. In the current study, we measured the scaling of social impact through the collection of self-report data. Despite the use of Harman's single factor test, such an approach raises the issue of common method variance. While future research could address this issue in a number of ways (see Podsakoff et al., 2003), one promising approach is to bifurcate the collection of data of the independent and dependent variables between different people. For example, if data were collected from a single organization with multiple branches, data on the independent variables could be collected from the branches and data on the dependent variable could be collected from the parent company. In addition, similar to suggestions for research in commercial entrepreneurship, multiple measures and dimensions of performance could be collected (Murphy et al., 1996) including objective measures of scaling.

Another important issue for future research in the area of social entrepreneurship is the development and use of appropriate samples. In our study, we made a small but important step in the development of empirical work through the use of large scale data collection. Similar to the methodological issues in the domain of entrepreneurship, future research will need to begin to collect data on large scale cross-sectional and longitudinal samples to begin establishing causality between the variables (Low and MacMillan, 1988). In addition, the sampling of social entrepreneurial ventures will also need to address the survivorship bias of sampling only successful social ventures. In entrepreneurship, some approaches to address this issue include event-history analysis, research on failures, and panel data for in-gestation organizations [e.g., see Reynolds (2000) for an explanation of the Panel Study of Entrepreneurial Dynamics]. These and other approaches will be important to advance our understanding of the processes and causal mechanisms of scaling social impact.

While we have identified a number of important directions for future research, the challenges to pursue these directions are indeed great. The identification of social entrepreneurial ventures is often difficult particularly while they are in the process of organizing. The relative incidence of social entrepreneurship is still likely smaller than that of its commercial counterpart. As a result, a substantial amount of funding may be needed to develop a database of in-vitro social entrepreneurial organizations and follow them over time. While work is emerging in the area of social return on investment, a common measure of performance of social value creation is still lacking thereby complicating comparison of social impact across different organizations. Many social entrepreneurial organizations are resource constrained in terms of both money and time. As a result, the accessibility to social entrepreneurial organizations may be difficult. These are but a few of the challenges that complicate this important stream of research.

Conclusion

The effective and efficient scaling of social impact holds much promise for addressing some of world's most intractable social problems. Yet, our understanding of the factors that lead to scaling is rudimentary. This study offers an exploratory empirical test of a model of organizational capabilities—SCALERS—which influence the scaling of social impact. While exploratory, we hope this study motivates future research on the scaling of social impact.

Appendix

Thinking about *the last three years* of operations of your organization, please indicate how strongly you agree or disagree with each of the following statements, assuming each statement starts with the following phrase:

Compared to other organizations working to resolve similar social problems as our organization...

I. *Scaling Social Impact*
1. we have made significant progress in alleviating the problem.
2. we have scaled up our capabilities to address the problem.

3. we have greatly expanded the number of individuals we serve.
4. we have substantially increased the geographic area we serve.

II. *Staffing*
1. we have been effective at meeting our labor needs with people who have the necessary skills.
2. we have an ample pool of capable volunteers available to help us meet our labor needs.
3. we have individuals in management positions who have the skill to expand our organization, program, or principles.

III. *Communicating*
1. we have been effective at communicating what we do to key constituencies and stakeholders.
2. we have been successful at informing the individuals we seek to serve about the value of our program for them.
3. we have been successful at informing donors and funders about the value of what we do.

IV. *Alliance-building*
1. we have built partnerships with other organizations that have been win-win situations for us and them.
2. we rarely try to "go it alone" when pursuing new initiatives.
3. we have accomplished more through joint action with other organizations than we could have by flying solo.

V. *Lobbying*
1. we have been successful at getting government agencies and officials to provide financial support for our efforts.
2. we have been successful at getting government agencies and officials to create laws, rules, and regulations that support our efforts.
3. we have been able to raise our cause to a higher place on the public agenda.

VI. *Earnings-generation*
1. we have generated a strong stream of revenues from products and services that we sell for a price.
2. we have cultivated donors and funders who have been major sources of revenue for us.
3. we have found ways to finance our activities that keep us sustainable.

VII. *Replicating*
1. we have a "package" or "system" that can work effectively in multiple locations or situations.
2. we find it easy to replicate our programs.
3. we have been successful at controlling and coordinating our programs in multiple locations.

VIII. *Stimulating Market Forces*

1. we have been able to demonstrate that businesses can make money through supporting our initiatives.
2. we have been able to demonstrate that consumers can save money through patronizing our products and services.
3. we have been able to trust market forces to help resolve social problems.

2

To Control or Not Control: A Coordination Perspective to Scaling

Funda Sezgi and Johanna Mair

The question of how social initiatives can effectively scale their impact to reach individuals and communities that benefit from their innovations has received increasing attention over the past few years. A number of scholars adopt a strategic perspective and investigate the mechanisms to scale social *organizations* (Bradach, 2003; Oster, 1996), while others argue that scaling organizations is not necessarily sufficient to scale *impact* (Uvin, 1995; Wei-Skillern and Anderson, 2003). The latter group of authors argues that scale is not a particularly good proxy for the effectiveness of the programs (Frumkin, 2007), and that becoming large is only one of the many other possible ways of expanding impact in terms of the number of beneficiaries served (Edwards and Hulme, 1992; Uvin et al., 2000). These authors emphasize that instead of focusing on growing organizations, we need to turn attention to more effective and inclusive ways to address social problems.

Current discussions on scaling predominately concentrate on how to enhance social *impact* and include a broad spectrum of activities:

> expanding the quantity and improving the quality of the services provided directly by [the focal] organization; enabling other organizations to provide a higher quantity and quality of direct services; changing the political, cultural, or economic environment to reduce the need or problem; attracting more or improving the productivity of resources devoted to addressing the need or problem. (CASE, 2006: 9)

In this chapter we deliberately assume a narrow view and adopt an organizational perspective on scaling. This allows us to reengage with an important stream of literature that has emphasized the role of control in organizational achievements. Although the level of control exerted differs from one organizational setting to another, control is essential in any type of organization to coordinate organizational members toward coherent goals. In this chapter we analyze an eye care system, representing a tightly controlled setting, in order to disentangle the mechanisms underpinning coordinated efforts toward scaling.

Scholars define three modes for scaling social innovations: branching, affiliation, and dissemination. Accordingly, an awareness of the potential options help social entrepreneurs in specifying the core of the strategy for scaling their organizations' social impact. While we know that moving along a continuum, from dissemination to affiliation to branching, organizations require larger amounts of resources and an increasing degree of control (Dees et al., 2004), we know little about how such control is exerted. A better understanding of how organizations scale, the mechanisms they put into use for achieving differing degrees of control under different organizational modes, can help both organizations and entrepreneurs align their strategies with appropriate design features. In order to shed light on the mechanisms at play, we investigate Aravind Eye Care System,[1] a nonprofit organization based in India providing eye care services to poor people. Aravind serves as a unique setting for zooming inside organizational modes since it is a rare example of an organization that applies the three modes simultaneously. Based on our interview data as well as on longitudinal data for a number of past and ongoing scaling efforts that employ different organizational strategies and structures, we identify the mechanisms employed by Aravind under the three organizational modes. It is our hope to provide social entrepreneurs with the know-how to design the tools they need for exerting differing degrees of control once they decide on the organizational mode for scaling their social impact.

Scaling Social Impact: An Organizational Perspective

Recently, there has been an increasing interest among organizational scholars to conceptualize the strategies that social organizations pursue in their scaling attempts (Bradach, 2003; Dees et al., 2002,2004; Uvin, 1995; Uvin and Miller, 1996; Uvin et al., 2000; Wei-Skillern and Anderson, 2003). Three dominant organizational modes for scale are described in the nonprofit world as branching, affiliation, and dissemination. A case study survey on social enterprises reveals that 77 percent of the organizations investigated for the study employed branching, 41 percent affiliation, and 36 percent dissemination as their scaling strategy (La France Associates, 2006).

Accordingly, *branching* is a direct activity (Uvin et al., 2000), where all units are legally part of one organization: a setting analogous to company owned stores (Dees et al., 2002). This mode is the closest one to 100 percent replication of the original model as it involves only a few adaptations. In *affiliation* mode, independent legal entities are tied with the founding structure through a formalized contract that specifies the procedures and practices to be shared by all sites (Dees et al., 2002). Organizations employing this mode can increase impact both directly—by delivering services to a larger number of people—and indirectly—by inducing partners to undertake new activities that are geared to enlarging the overall impact (Uvin et al., 2000).

Finally, *dissemination* typically relies on contractual agreements and the focal organization actively shares information with the recipient organization for the adoption of the model (Dees et al., 2002: 5). Frequently referred to as diffusion, spread, or political scaling out, the dissemination mode is an indirect means for greater impact, where "non-profits that are capable of learning the lessons from their operational programs diffuse the resulting knowledge through training, information sharing, consultancy and advice whether to other non-profits, governments, or international donors" (Uvin et al., 2000: 1414). While the process of spreading ideas or knowledge is not amenable to a great deal of control (Frumkin, 2007), dissemination mode is advantageous in that it not only allows nonprofits to increase their impact without expanding in size (Uvin et al, 2000), but is also a prerequisite for learning which elements of the program are relevant to be routinized for expansion through large scale operations (Korten, 1980).

Dees et al. (2004) suggest that all these organizational modes—branching, affiliation, and dissemination—should be considered as a continuum in terms of increasing degree of central coordination and resource requirements toward branching. The authors argue that dissemination is the simplest and usually the least resource intensive mode since "the originating organization has at most a short-term agreement to provide technical assistance to those who would use this information to bring the innovation to a new locale" (Dees et al., 2002: 5). However, according to the authors, the disseminating organization has little control over implementation in new locations (Dees et al., 2004). Dees and his colleagues (2004) argue that branching, at the other end of the spectrum, offers the greatest potential for coordination and commonly requires the greatest investment of resources by the focal organization.

In this chapter, we seek to go beyond static descriptions of organizational modes adopted by social enterprises in their attempts to scale social impact. We seek to contribute to the organizational perspective on scaling impact through a systematic analysis of the mechanisms employed by a nonprofit organization to activate varying degrees of control in three organizational modes. By unpacking the "nuts and bolts" of a successful initiative, we hope to provide tools for social enterprises in determining the design features of their organizations to achieve fit with their intended strategies.

Organizational Control

Control is one of the main pillars of organizational design. Tannenbaum (1968) defines control as "any process in which a person (or group of persons or organizations of persons) determines or intentionally affects what another person, group, or organizational will do" (p. 238). Control can be conceptualized as how much power an organization has over its other resources and subunits (Floyd and Lane, 2000; Jaeger and Baliga, 1985; Kirsch, 1996; Tannenbaum, 1968), or as the processes by which the firm coordinates the activities (Lebas and Weigenstein, 1986; Ouchi, 1979, 1980; Tushman and Nadler, 1978). To date, scaling scholars have focused on the former perspective and analyzed the degree to which organizations can control the implementation of its practices in new locations. In this chapter, we adopt the latter perspective and investigate the mechanisms that enable coordination within and between subunits once the organization chooses the organizational mode(s) through which it scales its impact.

Control is crucial in ensuring that organizational members direct their efforts toward the attainment of organizational objectives (Olsen, 1978). In designing the control system, it is important to keep coherence with the strategy, and to implement features that ensure progress toward desired organizational and social outcomes (Chenhall, 2003). A study on social enterprises replication efforts supports these arguments suggesting that one of the key questions to be addressed in a replication strategy is "what level of control does the social enterprise want to have over replicated entities?" (UnLtd Ventures, 2008). Accordingly, the degree of control the organization seeks to exercise is important in ensuring that the appropriate structure is chosen for replication of the social innovation in new locations. However, understanding how much control the focal organization can employ is not sufficient. We need a better understanding of the design features that enable the activation and maintaining of the level of control the organization seeks to exercise under various organizational modes.

This study is based on an instrumental case study research design. Our research setting, Aravind, uniquely combines three modes of scaling discussed in the popular literature on scaling, namely branches, affiliation, and dissemination. The mission of the organization is to eliminate needless blindness by (1) providing compassionate and high quality eye care for all in its branch hospitals, (2) working with socially committed partners in underserved areas of India and other developing countries in its affiliated hospitals, and (3) providing teaching, training, capacity building, advocacy, research, and publications in its dissemination mode.[2] As suggested by the literature, all those modes/strategies require different levels of resource commitments and control properties. In the rest of the chapter, we provide an analysis of how the focal organization in this study coordinates its activities around the sub-purposes mentioned earlier. We build on longitudinal archival data as well as interviews and observations from multiple field trips to conduct a comparative analysis on the specific coordination mechanisms characterizing each mode.

Aravind Eye Care System

Aravind was founded in 1976 with the objective of overcoming preventable blindness in resource-poor settings, India being the initial target. According to World Health statistics,[3] as of 2009, there are about 314 million visually impaired people worldwide, of which 45 million are blind. Geographic distribution of people with visual problems is not even: approximately 87 percent live in developing countries. In India, in particular, over 12 million people—of which 63 percent are cataracts—are visually handicapped (IndiaStat, 2004). It is estimated that more than 6 million operations are needed per year to tackle the rising incidence rate (Bhandari et al., 2008). Infrastructure deficiencies in India to meet this need energized Dr. Govindappa Venkataswamy—known to many as "Dr. V."—to start Aravind Eye Care System.

The initial goal of the organization was to provide quality eye care surgeries at reasonable cost. Over time, however, Aravind built a self-sustaining business model, where the quality of eye treatment combined with compassionate care and the efficiency of operations are its main strengths. Aravind charges below-market prices for patients who can afford the surgery and cross-subsidizes the income generated therein for the patients who cannot afford to pay. Today, approximately 60 percent of the all operations at Aravind are provided for free or at a low cost (Bhandari et al., 2008).

The ability to provide free and/or low cost surgeries to poor people while being financially self-sustaining is due to the efficiency achieved at Aravind. Two key components of the innovative Aravind model are among the many things that help explain the level of efficiency achieved: cost cutting through establishment of Aurolab, the lens manufacturing division of Aravind, and the large volume of surgeries thanks to the flow of operations. From its establishment until 1992, intraocular lenses needed for cataract surgeries were donated by American manufacturers for Aravind to fulfill its social mission. However, the fast growth in the number of surgeries proved the model based on donations infeasible. To overcome the dependence on other parties in its operations, Aravind established Aurolab in 1992 and started producing its own lenses for ten dollars each while the market price for the same variety was two hundred dollars in the United States.

The other key component of the Aravind efficiency model is the "serial production model" inspired by the McDonald's food chain model (Bhandari et al., 2008). Young girls hired from villages are trained for two years to become mid-level ophthalmologists (MLOPs) who can fully prepare patients for operation. The doctor, having two operating tables one next to another, takes solely six minutes to perform a cataract surgery and has the next patient ready by the time he finishes one operation. These two examples illustrate many of the innovative dots of the Aravind business model through which it sought to increase productivity at the lowest cost possible, and hence to serve as many people as possible.

Efficiency is the key to success in this type of setting, and Aravind puts utmost effort into maintaining quality while providing large volume of eye care service. The organization emphasizes "treating rich and poor people alike" as the core principle of the organizational culture, and is driven by values such as modesty, sincerity, dedication, teamwork, conservatism, growth, spirituality, discipline, and energy to help the poor sector. According to the founders, commitment to the value system established at Aravind is vital to the sustainability of the model over years and across contexts.

Since its inception, therefore, Aravind is faced with two major conflicting challenges that are common to many social enterprises: (1) How to scale up their innovative health service business model to build capacity for achieving their strategic objective of delivering one million eye surgeries per year by 2015? (2) How to cultivate and maintain value consistency across the system throughout expansion?

Organizational Evolution

Having started off with an 11 bed capacity, Aravind increased its number of cataract surgeries from a total of 29,928 in 1988 (Natchiar et al., 2008) to 269,577 in 2008, performed at five branches. Today, Aravind Eye Care System is the largest provider of eye care in the world: the organization performs approximately 270,000 surgeries per year and serves over two million patients in its branch and affiliated hospitals; it has provided consulting and capacity building services to 216 hospitals across India, South East Asia, and Africa.[4] Figure 2.1 provides an overview of the evolution of the organizational modes adopted by Aravind over time.

As figure 2.1 suggests, Aravind expanded only through branches in *Phase 1*. After expanding its capacity to 250 beds in Madurai, the organization built its Thenni branch in 1985 and Tirunelveli in 1988. By the beginning of the 1990s, Aravind had obtained "proof of concept" through its hospital in Madurai and the successful replications of the main hospital in two other Indian cities. The success of the Aravind model attracted the attention of other organizations that sought to collaborate with it in different ways. *Phase 2* started with Lions Clubs International Foundation

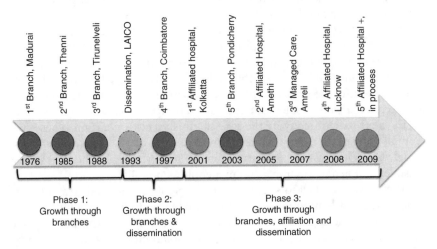

Figure 2.1   Timeline and phases of the Aravind Eye Care System evolution.

approaching Aravind to join forces for overcoming blindness. Lions had raised money to fight cataract blindness and the organization decided to use the fund for improving poorly performing hospitals around India instead of building new ones. Leveraging the knowledge base it accumulated over years, in 1993 Aravind standardized its practices and created templates for strategies to generate demand, provide low cost high quality services, and achieve financial viability. In 1996, Lions Institute of Community Opthalmology (LAICO) was officially established through which Aravind started disseminating knowledge by training healthcare and managerial personnel in the development and implementation of efficient eye care services. *Phase 3* started in 2001 when Aravind, for the first time, was approached by a third party organization to establish affiliated hospitals. From then onward Aravind has been expanding its impact through a combination of all three organizational modes mentioned in scaling literature: branching, affiliation (a.k.a. managed care in Aravind terminology), and dissemination (a.k.a. consulting and capacity building projects through LAICO).

Today, Aravind has five branch hospitals with nearly 4,000 bed capacity, four affiliated units and plans of reaching a target of 25 affiliated hospitals and 1 million surgeries by 2015, and has provided capacity building services to 216 hospitals and indirectly helped them increase their performance significantly. Figure 2.2 provides an illustration of the performance data on Aravind branch hospitals. Social impact achieved through these direct (branching and affiliation) and indirect ways of scaling (dissemination) is evident: the evolution described has played a major role in increasing the cataract surgery rate in Tamil Nadu (from 2,039 in 1988 to 7,633 in 2005) and in India as a whole (Natchiar et al., 2008).

However, as mentioned earlier, since its inception, Aravind has endeavored to fulfill dual objectives simultaneously: scaling social impact to overcome blindness and keeping value consistency within the system throughout expansion. In the rest of the chapter, we illuminate the key mechanisms at play under the three organizational modes employed by Aravind to

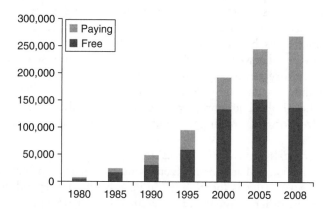

Figure 2.2   Number of surgeries performed in branches over years.

demonstrate its efforts to serve those dual purposes. As suggested by previous research on scaling, we also observe that Aravind has greatest control over its resources in branches and decreasingly so toward the dissemination mode. However, our analysis pushes the thinking on control issues in social enterprises by providing a coordination perspective where we systematically investigate the mechanisms enabling the functioning of a complex system encompassing three organizational modes simultaneously.

Mechanisms at Play

Our data reveal that in trying to maintain consistency across the system in terms of practices, procedures, and values, Aravind uses patterns of coordination activities that are organized under four mechanisms: *training, mobility, communication,* and *sharing of knowledge through templates*. That is to say, the organization attempts to: (1) train organizational members in order to teach them skill and cultivate values, (2) rotate organizational members to cultivate values in newly established hospitals and maintain values in existing ones, (3) ensure communication between the hospitals mainly to monitor performance measures and also to reinforce the other two mechanisms, and (4) provide up-to-date templates reflecting its best practices to be shared with third party hospitals. However, as the following analysis demonstrates, differences between organizational modes in terms of their subgoals determine whether a mechanism is employed by an organizational unit and, if yes, to what extent.

Training

Training is necessary in establishing control because while providing organizational members with the necessary abilities to be functional in the organization, it allows the organization to communicate and cultivate its expectations (Jaeger and Baliga, 1985). At Aravind, there is a strong emphasis on training. Especially in branches and affiliated hospitals where Aravind seeks to establish tight relationships with its partners, training serves as a mechanism to establish and maintain consistency not only in terms of operations but also in terms of values and culture. Differences remain, however, between branches and affiliated units since affiliation mode limits the organization's span of control. At the other end of the spectrum, Aravind provides training services mainly to share its best practices with other hospitals. Therefore, training is less intensive in terms of duration and levels of organizational members involved from the third party hospitals.

More specifically, in the *dissemination* mode, clinical and management staff from clients, and managers from funding agencies receive training mainly at LAICO that is located at the base hospital. Depending on the need, however, other branches also get involved in training of the consulted hospitals under dissemination mode. While the standard version of the training provided in this mode is a one-week vision-building workshop, depending on the demand from the client, duration of the training ranges from several days up to a year.

Training in affiliated units and branches, however, goes beyond short- to long-term workshops. In the case of *affiliated hospitals*, clinical and management staff get trained in the responsible branch, although for slightly shorter periods than the staff that are employees of branches. Doctors of affiliated units are sent to Madurai for three months: two months for organizational orientation and one for surgical training; and the duration of the MLOP training varies between six months to one year, while locally recruited doctors and other medical staff receive bundled training in various branches for one to several months. Aravind puts great effort into going beyond teaching operating skills through their training programs in affiliated hospitals. According to one of our interviewees, operating skills are easy to learn; what makes the difference is the "attitude toward patients" that organizational members acquire throughout training.

In *branches*, same as affiliation units, all clinical and management staff gets trained; however, training in this mode takes place only at base branch. This centralized approach ensures the highest level of homogeneity possible. In branching mode, training of the branch staff is considered to be an ongoing activity, as the organization considers branches as the originating points for disseminating the original business model and the staff there is considered to be learning-by-doing on a continuous basis. Moreover, training takes more time in this mode. For instance, MLOP training is two years instead of one in branches. Our informant responsible for the training of the staff explains that the first year of branch MLOP training includes teaching skills and values, and the second year is for "molding" them for Aravind culture.

Table 2.1 compares branches, affiliated hospitals, and dissemination mode in terms of their use of mechanisms. As shown, training gets more intensive toward branches. Drawing from the literature on control mechanisms and our observations, we expect that organizational subunits that are subject to more intensive and centralized training are likely to be more coordinated with the original model.

Communication

Communication is also crucial in establishing and maintaining control, because as Stacey (1993) puts it: "control operates through self organization: through the spontaneous formation of interest groups and coalitions around specific issues, communication about those issues, cooperation and the formation of consensus and commitment to a response to those issues" (p. 242). In other words, communication is a means to control and helps build commitment. Although at varying degrees among branching, affiliation, and dissemination modes, communication is extensively used by Aravind as a mechanism to monitor various performance outcomes in its lightest form, and to be aware of changes taking place in different parts of

Table 2.1   Coordination mechanisms at use under different organizational modes

	Branches	Affiliated hospitals	Dissemination
Training	• Centralized • Longer	• Decentralized • Shorter	• Decentralized–centralized • Shortest
Communication	• Larger scope in terms of levels of staff involved • Higher frequency	• Smaller scope in terms of levels of staff involved • Lower frequency	• Smallest scope in terms of levels of staff involved • Lowest frequency
Mobility	• Larger scope during establishment • Larger scope and higher frequency at established hospitals	• Smaller scope during establishment • Smaller scope and lower frequency at established hospitals	• Smallest scope • No repetition, merely visits
Templates	No templates	In process	Extensive use of templates

the system, to be informed about emerging problems, to harmonize problem solving efforts, and to acknowledge accomplishments.

Under the *dissemination* mode, communication is limited. While the heads of client hospitals and involved funding agencies receive reports from Aravind regarding the general outcomes of consulting projects, in return, they provide Aravind with monthly standardized reporting on financial and outcome measures.

In *affiliated units*, standardized performance reports are produced and shared with the branches. Moreover, subjective reporting on outcomes and quality are exchanged on an individual basis between hospital heads and AMECS staff at the headquarters. There is also ongoing emailing and telephone calls on a nonstandardized basis between management, clinical staff (doctors and nurses) with senior staff from branch in charge. One of our interviewees explains that he meets with doctors at the end of the month to discuss the reasons for the complications, how they handle them, and how they could be overcome. Moreover, every six months all supervisors gather to have an interaction with one of the founding members and discuss what they have been doing. In these meetings, information is presented to the vice chairman and is then spread throughout the system.

Within the *branches*, there is continuous exchange of information and experience between staff at all staff meetings. Moreover, communication is more frequent and the tools used more elaborate in comparison to affiliation units. Other than the standardized and comprehensive reporting agendas on finance, performance, and quality measures, there is ongoing teleconferencing, internal mailing lists, internal newsletters, and journal clubs to share experiences, frequent meetings of hospital, clinical, and nursing heads at the base hospital, and semiannual auditing team visits that are still to be standardized. One of the hospital administrators interviewed explained that every change made in the branch hospitals is communicated to the main branch, and that the change is integrated into the system if it is considered valuable to the system.

As table 2.1 suggests, in branch hospitals, communication is more frequent and covers a larger scope of staff levels. As we move along the continuum, however, smaller numbers of staff levels get involved in coordinating the activities and communication channels are less frequently utilized. Therefore, while in the case of branching communication serves as a strong mechanism to ensure coordination and consistency across units, in the dissemination mode, it barely has positive effects on the performance of the consulted hospitals.

Mobility

One distinctive practice employed by Aravind to ensure consistency throughout the system is the continuous movement of organizational members. This mechanism is predominantly evident in managed care and branch hospitals. The rationale behind this mechanism is to establish commitment to organizational values in newly established hospitals, and to maintain Aravind value system across the already existing hospitals. Mobility is effective in maintaining consistency across the system because it goes beyond formal training methods by teaching values through role models. Value training or socialization is an interpersonal process of informally or implicitly teaching organizational values and behavioral expectations to organizational members to bring them in line with what is required for successful participation within the organization (Etzioni, 1961; Jaeger and Baliga, 1985). The use of this mechanism varies significantly across organizational modes at Aravind.

In the *dissemination mode*, clinical and management staff from hospitals involved in capacity building projects visit Aravind hospitals to observe the functioning of the system, only for short durations though.

In *affiliated units*, both clinical staff (doctors and nurses) and management staff (hospital and department administrators) rotate on a temporary basis. Especially during the establishment of the affiliated units, senior clinical staff and one hospital administrator move temporarily to the unit until the system is in place. This generally takes about two years. Moreover, for their training purposes, MLOPs visit the branch associated with the affiliated hospital they will eventually settle down in. MLOP training used to take four months in the making of the affiliation mode; however, it is now increased to one year to enhance learning. Nurses interviewed confirm that spending time in branch hospitals is key to understanding the Aravind-way-of-doing-things. However, this process is not repeated after the training period is over. Once the best practices are settled and core values cultivated, an unsteady circulation of the senior level staff or high potential candidates starts from branches to affiliation hospitals. This is the main distinction between mobility of staff in affiliated hospitals and branch staff, although senior management is currently considering standardizing the ongoing rotation of the former to reenergize them periodically.

In the case of *branches* there is a *steady* circulation of clinical staff and management staff. All clinical and administrative members take on duties in various branches before they settle down to one. The chief training officer for MLOPs explains that rotation during and after training ensures that branch members experience at least three hospitals before they settle in. Moreover, any organizational member can be called on duty when a new branch is to be established. So, establishment of branches involves not only senior executives, but also all levels of hospital staff, including housekeepers, MLOPs, operation theatre nurses, and so on. During the establishment of one of the branch hospitals, for instance, out of 150 people needed for the new hospital, 130 were transferred from other branch hospitals to ensure that the value system was in place. One of the informants highlights that they started employing local people only after the system was settled in that new branch hospital, and when the established system could absorb those newly hired within a short period of time.

As table 2.1 demonstrates, dissemination lies at the far end of the continuum: only hospital heads are involved in the process and they visit Aravind hospitals for only short periods of time to observe the functioning of the system. In branch hospitals, during start-up of new hospitals and ongoing operations, mobility covers the largest scope of employee levels and is most frequent. Although differences remain between branches and affiliated hospitals, people in branches and affiliated units are mobilized for ensuring that they learn the Aravind-way-of-doing-things through firsthand experience; and they are expected to serve as role models committed to Aravind values when they settle in a hospital. Therefore, while employed at varying degrees, mobility at Aravind serves a strong mechanism for establishing and maintaining consistency across the system.

Templates

Organizational literature suggests that templates are useful for sharing codifiable practices with other organizations (Jensen and Szulanski, 2007; Jensen et al., 2003). Although having access to a template does not ensure that the template is used by the recipient unit, it helps the focal organization to communicate its practices and serve as a means to reproduce the complex set of interrelated organizational routines necessary when setting up a site for independent production or for improving the practices of an existing organization. At Aravind, generating templates is related both to the size of the operations of organizational modes and to the depth of content Aravind coordinates with other hospitals. Accordingly, template use becomes more salient when the focal organization seeks to coordinate the activities with a larger number of hospitals and when it seeks only to coordinate practices rather than to transfer tacit knowledge that is embedded in individuals (Nonaka, 1994; Polanyi, 1966).

Hence, template is the mechanism that is mainly used by *dissemination* mode. To share its knowledge base on human resource management, infrastructure, systems, and procedures built over time at the branches, Aravind has prepared extensive templates related to demand generation, quality, and financial viability. Having standardized the mainstream activities that are considered to have a positive effect on performance in terms of number and quality of surgeries and hospital performance, and having prepared simplified checklists out of them, Aravind has shared knowledge with 216 eye hospitals across India, South East Asia, and Africa to date.

There are no templates available for the *affiliated units*, although the senior management at Aravind considers having templates for this mode as an emergent necessity. One of the interviewees highlights that mistakes that were made during the making of affiliation mode might not be affordable with intended scaling efforts through this mode (i.e., reaching the target of one million surgeries per year via twenty-five affiliated hospitals to be established by 2015). Another informant also confirms that standardizing the process and generating templates simplify the scaling efforts as it prevents the organization from reinventing the wheel and helps in focusing on novel tasks.

"In the branches there is almost zero documentation: mind wise, it's more like that," says one of the senior managers regarding the use of templates in *branches*. Another informant explains that branches do not need templates due to the accumulated knowledge in humans. In other words, in trying to maintain full consistency across its branches, Aravind relies more on the other three coordinating mechanisms mentioned earlier rather than on template use.

As table 2.1 suggests, templates are mainly used in the dissemination mode for sharing practices. Since Aravind seeks to coordinate values as well as practices in branches and affiliated hospitals, to date, templates have not been utilized under these two modes. However, the need for standardizing activities becomes more salient as the affiliation mode evolves to become a larger subsystem. Therefore, templates are in process to ensure that the basics of the complex Aravind model are shared with newly established units via templates, and higher order coordination is to be maintained through the support from the other three mechanisms.

Organizational Modes, Coordination, and Scaling

The analysis presented in this chapter allows us to go beyond a brief description of the level of control implemented through different organizational modes and demonstrates the mechanisms the organization has available to activate the level of control it seeks to exert on third parties. Table 2.2 provides a comparison of the three organizational modes in terms of their use of the discussed mechanisms. The difference between modes in terms of use of mechanisms arises from the level of coordination Aravind seeks to achieve under different modes.

Table 2.2 Intensity of coordination mechanisms used under organizational modes

	Branches	Affiliation	Dissemination
Training	+++	++	+
Communication	+++	++	+
Mobility	+++	++	0
Templates	0	In process	+++

In the dissemination mode, Aravind merely shares strategies and best practices with consulted hospitals and does not seek to impose its value system on the recipient units. Hence, mechanisms used under this mode are mainly to transfer operational knowledge and coordinate the activities of the consulted hospitals with that of Aravind. In branching and affiliation, however, Aravind seeks to go beyond replicating best practices, although differences remain between these two modes. Full ownership of its branch hospitals allows the organization to fully concert the efforts of its organizational members toward the achievement of the organizational mission, which is scaling social impact while maintaining value consistency throughout the system for Aravind. Although the same level of consistency is intended for the affiliation mode, full coordination in the mode is contingent upon the extent to which Aravind has control over its partner organizations.

These observations suggest that when the organization seeks also to ensure value consistency together with operational consistency across branches and affiliated units, there is higher reliance on informal coordination mechanisms such as training, communication, and mobility. When the objective is to coordinate only practices and procedures, as is the case in the dissemination mode, there is higher reliance on formal coordination mechanisms such as templates (although this mechanism is also enforced through communication and training). Informal mechanisms help establish a base of attitudes, habits, and values that foster cooperation and minimize the divergence of preferences among group members by exerting culture control through socialization instead of formal performance evaluations as control mechanisms (Govindarajan and Fisher, 1990; Pascale, 1985). Formalizing through templates, on the other hand, helps to share knowledge on good practices at larger scale since they are codified, standardized forms of knowledge (March and Simon, 1958) that coordinate activities without stretching human resources and at lower cost.

These observations are helpful for understanding the design features that are relevant for differing degrees of control exercised under different organizational modes. Depending on (1) the level of control a social entrepreneur seeks to exercise and (2) what it seeks to coordinate an organization needs to employ various combinations of coordination mechanisms at varying degrees. However, it should be noted that choice of mechanisms to

Table 2.3 Type of coordination mechanisms appropriate for varying degrees of coordination and scale

	Coordination of...	
Scale	Practices only	Practices and values
High	Formal mechanisms	Informal and formal mechanisms
Low	Formal and informal mechanisms	Informal mechanisms

exert differing levels of control across organizational modes is not a static decision. As the organizations evolve to scale further, they might need to revise their structural components since increasing number of employees intensifies the need for coordination in the organization (Blau, 1970). For instance, at Aravind, at its initial stage, affiliated hospitals were intended to be fully aligned with branches (to the extent that the partners' values are consistent with Aravind's). However, as the organization moved toward higher number of affiliated units, the need to generate templates for establishing and maintaining new hospitals arose.

Therefore, when the objective is to coordinate practices only, formal mechanisms are useful. Higher reliance on informal mechanisms is advisable when the organization seeks to achieve value consistency together with coordinated practices. However, as the scale of operations increases, there is a tendency to include formal mechanisms in the formula. Table 2.3 summarizes our conclusions related to coordinating mechanisms in terms of scaling and coordination considerations.

Conclusion

The difficulties around scaling and replicating good practices have been discussed widely and these difficulties are evident in the many failures to replicate new business models in different contexts. Therefore, by studying the main features of the innovative Aravind business model we seek to provide insights into the main challenge of scaling social impact while maintaining core values. Zooming in on the organizational modes employed by Aravind, we provided a systematic analysis of the mechanisms underlying the organizational structure. We identify the practices to establish and maintain differing degrees of control depending on the organizational subunit purposes. Linking our observations to "what the organization seeks to coordinate" and the scale of operations under each organizational mode, we then offered suggestions as to the types of mechanisms appropriate for organizational strategy, objectives, and structure. By systematically unpacking the "building blocks" of a successful initiative, therefore, we hope to have provided know-how and possible tools for social enterprises in determining the design features of their organizations to achieve fit with their intended strategies.

Notes

1. Hereinafter referred to as Aravind.
2. Source: Aravind Eye Care System Activity Report (2008–2009).
3. http://www.who.int/mediacentre/factsheets/fs282/en/index.html (last access: October 22, 2009).
4. See www.aravind.org.

II

The Pros and Cons of Scaling

Enamored with Scale: Scaling with Limited Impact in the Microfinance Industry

Srikant M. Datar, Marc J. Epstein, and Kristi Yuthas

In many ways, the microcredit industry is a scaling success story. With fewer than 10 million clients a decade ago, the industry now serves approximately 150 million clients and continues to grow, even through the economic downturn. In part, this growth is made possible by the very nature of microcredit—it is a service that clients both need and are able to purchase, enabling donated funds to be recycled many times. In addition, the industry as a whole has served a critical role in catalyzing growth. Cooperative efforts among industry stakeholder groups have led to the development of information exchanges, rating systems, and research efforts that have rapidly improved efficiency and professionalization of microfinance. Nonetheless, mission drift has become a real concern, and the industry has reached a point where additional scale does not guarantee increased social impact. Some markets are saturated and hyper-competitive, while enormous demand remains unfulfilled in difficult-to-serve markets and among clients whose credit needs fall beyond the narrow range of products currently offered. Continued questions about microcredit's poverty-reducing potential continue to plague the industry, and high rates of client defection and over-indebtedness provide cause for alarm. Without significant changes in microfinance institution (MFI) management and business models required to serve client needs, further growth may harm the very clients the industry seeks to serve.

This chapter tells two coexisting, but very different, stories. The first depicts the microcredit industry as a model for effective scaling. The industry has worked with individual MFIs to make effective use of critical levers that have catalyzed growth and enhanced financial sustainability. The second paints a different picture, one in which microcredit fails to deliver on promises of social impact, leaving many clients with little change in their poverty status, disillusioned, and mired in debt. The chapter closes with suggestions for how the industry can use its proven assets to scale social impact by increasing both the depth and breadth of outreach.

Industry Background

The microcredit industry began with experimental programs during the 1970s in Bangladesh, Brazil, and elsewhere. The well-known Grameen model was able to lend small amounts of money to poor women who could not access formal credit by developing a group lending model in which borrowers served as co-guarantors. The model was a success—the poor were able to access financial services for the first time, and high repayment rates enabled the funds to be used for repeat loans. Many MFIs opened in Bangladesh and elsewhere using similar models and experienced similar success.

Since the 1970s, microcredit has grown dramatically. The Microcredit Summit Campaign (2009) reports that the number of clients served by microfinance grew by more than 1,300 percent in the decade between 1997 and 2007, and that during 2007 alone, more than one hundred million clients received loans worldwide. And there is ample room for future growth. Estimates suggest market penetration rates of about 10 percent, leaving most of the market still untapped (Deutsche Bank, 2007). Even among the very poor, microcredit reaches less than 50 percent in well-developed Asian markets and less than 10 percent in Africa and the Middle East (Daley-Harris, 2006). In addition, the industry has focused primarily on business loans to existing microenterprises leaving market gaps in areas such as long-term housing loans and short-term consumption loans. The industry has received funding from a broad range of donors and investors, including foundations and NGOs, development agencies, and, increasingly, individual and institutional investors. Money has continued to move into microfinance through much of the global economic downturn, and an estimated ten billion dollars is now invested in microfinance (Reille et al., 2009).

Scaling Social Enterprise

Scaling has been an increasing focus of research and writing on social enterprise, and a number of authors have identified levers that have promoted effective scaling in microfinance and other industries. Learning to replicate programs that produce results in new locations and markets is perhaps the most basic of these levers. Bradach (2003) argues that to replicate, an organization needs a clear theory of change that identifies actions to be taken and how they translate into social benefits, along with standardized and documented operating practices and a clear strategy for growth. LaFrance et al. (2006) focus in addition on the importance of organizational structure, culture, and leadership, recognizing that, particularly in social organizations, these elements of the organization are critical in attracting and motivating commitment from key stakeholders.

In addition to organizational factors, external levers such as developing networks and working with affiliates (Bradach, 2003), sharing leadership and activities with supporters, and engaging in advocacy can be essential in creating scale and leveraging impact (McLeod et al., 2007). Such activities enable social organizations to change the environments within which they operate by mobilizing participants and developing new institutional arrangements (Bloom and Dees, 2008). Social entrepreneurs also need to develop strategies for achieving scale, such as sharing information and technical assistance, forming networks and affiliations, and establishing new branches within the existing organization (Dees et al., 2004). In addition, they need to understand their resources and readiness for scaling activities as well as the risk that problems such as improper implementation and lack of market readiness will result in failure to achieve the desired impact (Dees et al., 2004).

Bloom and Chatterji (2009) have developed a framework that collapses scaling drivers into a set of seven critical capabilities: staffing, communicating, alliance-building, lobbying, earnings-generation, replicating, and stimulating market forces. The authors highlight the role of situational contingencies that influence the importance of these capabilities in driving successful scaling. They examine organizations involved in poverty alleviation, and argue that depending on the theory of change held by these organizations and the situational factors limiting their growth, emphasis will be placed on the subset of scaling levers that can most effectively address the scaling problem.

Drivers of Scale in the Microcredit Industry

The microcredit industry has been successful in developing the capacity to effectively use all of the internal and external levers and strategies identified in the social scaling research. Bloom and Chatterji (2009) note that "in many ways, the social entrepreneurial organizations involved with capital provision serve as the 'guiding lights' of the field" (p. 128). The basic microcredit model is key in this success; clients borrow money and repay with interest, enabling funds to be recycled and outreach to be enhanced. Also critical is the support MFIs receive as a result of cooperative engagement among practitioners and other stakeholder groups in the industry. In microfinance, rapid scaling cannot be attributed to an individual MFI or to a small handful of high-growth firms, although Grameen, BRAC, and others have certainly been key contributors. In this industry, made up of some ten thousand participating organizations, collaborative, industry-wide efforts have been critical both in developing internal practices and strategies as well as influencing public opinion, regulation, and other features of the external environment. Several of the most significant drivers of scale in microfinance are summarized here.

It is important to note that in the discussion of these drivers, the term "scale" primarily refers to scale of "outreach" rather than to scale of "impact." In the microfinance industry scale is typically measured using the number of clients served, or corollary measures of the number of loans granted, total dollar amount of loans granted, or the size of the outstanding loan portfolio. For some, the goal of microfinance is simply to provide the poor with access to financial services. How they use those services and how use of those services affects their lives and businesses is left up to them. The general perception of microfinance, and the stated objective of many of the largest microcredit providers, is to raise the poor out of poverty by providing loans that promote income generation and economic development. The subsequent discussion focuses on levers that have been effective in expanding outreach; the question of impact is addressed in the latter half of the chapter.

Microcredit model

The microcredit model developed in the 1970s and still used today is one in which funds are lent to microentrepreneurs who invest in their businesses and repay using profits from their investments. The industry's primary goal was to alleviate poverty through economic development. Using market-rate loans rather than grants helped minimize disruptions to ongoing market relationships and helped ensure that funds were used for productive investments. From the MFI's perspective, the model helps ensure that interest paid by clients covered most or all of the organization's costs, allowing the MFI to recycle repaid funds multiple times.

Loans to individual borrowers are often secured with collateral such as land or fixed assets. But the majority of clients seeking microcredit services lack sufficient collateral to secure loans, and may reside in shanty-towns or other temporary living arrangements, which make them high credit risks. Group lending schemes, in which a group of borrowers serve as co-guarantors for each other, enabled MFIs to lend to these clients. Group members helped screen potential investments, and group knowledge of member business and personal characteristics was used in place of cash flow projections and business plans to ensure the funds would be put to productive use. The group model also proved very effective in ensuring repayment—microfinance has higher repayment rates than SME loans in developed countries, with some organizations reporting rates as high as 99 percent (Economist.com, 2009). Thus the basic model alleviates a great deal of the financial pressure facing many social enterprises because the financial needs of the company are largely served through the normal process of providing loans to clients. In addition, the model has proven to be appealing to a broad variety of donors and investors because it provides aid critical to efforts toward poverty eradication while working within basic capital market mechanisms.

Industry-wide organizations

Industry-wide collaboration within and among stakeholder groups in microfinance has been very strong and has contributed in many ways to the scaling success of the industry. Several organizations have played key roles. The Microcredit Summit Campaign has provided a forum for bringing together microfinance organizations along with donors and financial institutions to promote interaction and sharing of best practices across the industry. The Campaign currently has over 7,000 member institutions and holds one or more conferences each year, with hundreds and sometimes thousands of attendees from numerous industry groups. It has focused directly and intensively on promoting scale. In 1997 it set a goal of serving 100 million of the poorest clients in the world. That goal has been achieved and the Campaign has now increased that goal to 175 million by the year 2015 (Microcredit Summit Campaign, 2009).

The Consultative Group to Assist the Poorest (CGAP) was launched in 1995 by a group of donor agencies including the World Bank, and has now become a service center for the industry. The CGAP seeks to improve institutional capacity and service quality by developing technical tools and providing technical and strategic assistance to microfinance practitioners. It also provides tools for donors to enhance their ability to support and promote effective MFIs. The CGAP has also invested heavily in efforts to promote effective regulation and supervision in the industry as well as transparency through products such as the Microbanking Bulletin, which provides financial benchmarking data. It also supports the Microfinance Gateway, a forum for sharing microfinance research and industry publications and announcements. The Gateway hosts a database of over seven thousand online documents that provide information and support to a broad range of stakeholders.

The Microfinance Information Exchange, Inc. (MIX) provides an online forum, the MIX Market, for sharing and comparing financial and social data across nearly fifteen hundred practitioner firms in the industry. It also collects and disseminates data on other industry members, including donors and investors as well as service providers such as rating agencies. Its purpose is to promote the comparability and transparency that can strengthen practice in the industry.

Microfinance providers have worked with a variety of service agencies to further ensure effectiveness and transparency through the development of rigorous evaluation standards and techniques. Standard tools such as ACCION's CAMEL instrument have been developed to monitor and evaluate key financial and managerial performance indicators in microfinance firms. A variety of microfinance rating agencies such as MicroRate and PlaNet finance provide private ratings of fiduciary and credit risk as well as governance and management. The ratings produced by these agencies as well as the indicators available through the MIX Market have enabled industry stakeholders to make more informed resource investment decisions.

All of these industry organizations and services have contributed to the industry's growth. Together, they enable microfinance practitioners and other industry participants to pursue strategies and to invest resources in a manner that promotes effectiveness and efficiency and strives to continually increase the industry's outreach to impoverished populations.

Communication
Industry organizations have been instrumental in broadly communicating developments and successes in the microfinance industry. The industry's basic message—that microfinance is a key element in economic development and poverty reduction—has been repeatedly and broadly communicated within and outside the industry. The industry has also been effective in linking microfinance success to achievement of the Millennium Development Goals, and has received attention and support from a variety of organizations and agencies instrumental in promoting these goals.

Muhammad Yunus of Grameen Bank is perhaps the most well-known spokesperson for microfinance. He speaks regularly on behalf of the entire industry, spreads the message of microfinance through a variety of venues, including best-selling books, interactions with international media, and broad participation in meetings and conferences related to international development and poverty. His message about the relationship between microfinance, prosperity, and peace resulted in his receiving the Nobel Peace Prize in 2006. This award generated increased interest from the international press on the role that microfinance could play in addressing global challenges.

Lobbying and alliance-building
The microfinance industry has been very successful working with governmental and quasi-governmental agencies to further policies and investments supportive of microfinance. Many agencies, such as USAID, have developed large microfinance initiatives, aimed at providing financial and technical support and engaging in research, planning, implementation, and evaluation activities to improve the practice of microfinance. The Microenterprise Best Practices program has studied numerous leading MFIs and collected best practices in a series of reports that have been widely disseminated throughout the industry. Another project —Assessing the Impact of Microenterprise Services—has developed guidance on defining and evaluating performance of microfinance services. Such contributions have greatly enhanced the ability of the industry to attract new entrants and to grow.

Industry organizations have also been effective in advocating for pro-microfinance policies such as interest rate liberalization. For example, RESULTS, a parent organization for the Microcredit Summit Campaign, lobbied for passage of the Microfinance Results and Accountability Act of 2004. This legislation directs half of USAID's microfinance assistance toward the very poor, and mandates development of poverty indicators. Microfinance industry associations in a number of countries with active microfinance practitioners have promoted pro-poor and pro-microfinance legislation in those countries. The Small Enterprise Education and

Promotion (SEEP) Network helps establish and connect industry associations throughout the world.

Donor sophistication

Donor support has been essential in providing the funding to fuel the dramatic growth in the industry. For much of its history, the majority of funding for not-for-profit firms came through donations. Donor funding continues to play a critical role in microfinance, with contributions of approximately $1.5 billion in 2008 (Reille et al., 2009) from bilateral and multilateral development agencies and ministries as well as foundations. Scaling up of donor funding is expected to continue throughout the economic downturn, with few donors reporting significant changes to planned donations for 2009.

Donor agencies have worked together to improve their effectiveness in not only providing funding, but in developing characteristics and processes to support MFIs in delivering financial services. For example, the Consultative Group to Assist the Poorest developed a peer review process to enhance donors' ability to clarify strategic objectives, enhance staff capacity, account for results, manage knowledge, and use appropriate financial instruments. At least seventeen agencies have already participated in peer reviews. Such collaboration helps donor agencies identify and develop their unique strengths and to match them with microfinance markets in need of support (Duflo et al., 2004). This is an impressive level of sophistication that helps to ensure that donor funds aren't all targeted toward the largest or most well-known MFIs. Instead, donor funds are channeled toward practitioners whose needs and performance profiles are most compatible with the guidelines and objectives of the donor agency.

Organizational practices

Scaling in the microfinance industry has been supported by the adoption of standardized, replicable processes and practices by many firms. The process of providing loans to the poor can be quite complex, costly, and risky, but the industry has standardized on several processes that reduce costs and risks and are generalizable across a wide range of clients and locations. A number of industry organizations provide support and training for effective practice. As noted earlier, USAID provides a series of Best Practices studies to spread innovations and promote proven approaches. The Boulder Institute offers regular courses on a wide range of microfinance topics to support microfinance administrators in addressing a host of problems and opportunities.

As a result of information sharing and practitioner interaction, the industry has largely standardized on a set of common lending practices. For example, loan officers are generally hired from the locations in which the MFIs wish to operate. These loan officers are familiar with the region, as well as with the language and culture of the area, and are often familiar with businesses operating in these regions. Within MFIs, many practices are carefully defined and often scripted, ensuring that inexperienced staff can quickly gain the knowledge and skills needed to perform their jobs effectively and contribute to organizational growth. For example, when lending to clients new to microfinance, loan officers engage in "sensitization" activities prior to granting loans. These activities introduce potential clients to microlending processes and debt management, prepare them for receiving loans and managing them effectively, and help them form borrowing groups. Such activities have proven effective and have become widespread within the industry.

Products in the microfinance industry also tend to be standardized. The standard product is a business loan, targeted toward investment in inventory or small improvements in an existing business. Loans typically have four–twelve-month repayment periods, and require a proportion of the loan to be held in savings to secure the loan. Repayment begins immediately and the loan is repaid in small frequent increments that are thought to support repayment discipline among clients. The initial loan offered to a client is quite small, and loans are gradually increased as clients demonstrate repayment behavior.

Performance indicators are likewise standardized, and designed largely to enhance financial performance and reduce default risk. The most commonly used measures are portfolio size and the percentage of the portfolio at risk (PAR) or in arrears. Together, these policies help promote efficiency in loan delivery and repayment and have resulted in very high repayment rates across the industry.

Earnings-generation
Microfinance institutions have focused intensely on carefully managing costs and generating earnings through normal lending practices. The ultimate goal of many MFIs is to become donor independent, first achieving operational sustainability or the ability to cover all expenses through operating activities, and then achieving financial sustainability—the ability to cover both operating expenses and the cost of debt at market rates of interest. Ledgerwood (1999) refers to the current approach to microfinance as the "financial systems" approach. This approach, she says, is based on the belief that below-market rates of interest undermine development efforts, and that financial sustainability is essential for institutional efficiency as well as longevity. And although the morality of Compartamos' excessive profitability has been questioned, many agree that financial sustainability is essential for donor independence and the key to growth in the microfinance industry (Cull et al., 2009).

Among 451 firms reporting full financial data to the MIX market for 2008, median reported financial sustainability was 105 percent, indicating that on average, revenues were 5 percent higher than expenses. These firms are likely more profitable than non-reporting firms in the industry, with typically smaller and less sophisticated information technology and other organizational systems. Nonetheless, if accurate, this number suggests that the industry has made large gains in profitability. Two recent papers have confirmed that many MFIs are now sustainable and that a significant proportion of microfinance clients are served by these institutions (Cull et al., 2009; Gonzales and Rosenberg, 2006). Profitability in one firm, Banco Compartamos of Mexico, was so high and investor interest in microfinance so strong that the bank held an IPO that was oversubscribed by thirteen times, and raised $450 million in equity for 30 percent of its shares and thus a market capitalization of approximately $1.5 billion (CGAP, 2007).

Today, Banco Compartomos is one of three public microfinance organizations, along with Bank Rakyat Indonesia and Equity Bank of Kenya. At least one other large microfinance organization, SKS, has been very effective in attracting investment funding and may be the next MFI to go public. In fact, equity investors have become very interested in the industry and foreign capital investment in the industry now exceeds $10 billion (CGAP, 2008). In addition to standard investment funds, a variety of microfinance investment vehicles (MIVs), including private equity funds, structured finance vehicles, fixed income funds, and holding companies, have been developed to support the diverse needs of investors and MFIs.

For-profit commercial banks have also become interested in the microcredit sector. DFID (2005) demonstrates the business case for microfinance and provides case studies of six commercial banks that entered this market for social and regulatory reasons but have stayed because they were able to operate profitably in the space. The DFID report notes that microenterprises and SMEs employ between 20 and 80 percent of workers in developing countries, providing a strong incentive to the formal financial sector. The report further argues that commercial firms have potential advantages in the market because they can leverage existing infrastructure and expertise.

Failure to Scale Social Impact

Despite the industry's remarkable success in scaling up the number of clients served through microfinance and size of the outstanding loan portfolio, serious questions remain about whether the industry is producing improvements in social impact that are commensurate with its financial growth. And, increased focus on economic performance that financial sustainability and commercialization requires have increased concerns about mission drift. The industry has long used anecdotes about the success of individual clients to substitute for rigorous evidence of social impact, which it argues is difficult or impossible to obtain in this field (see Armendariz de Aghion and Morduch, 2000, for a discussion of these difficulties). But evidence that many clients exit after only one or two small loans suggests that success is not common to the majority of microfinance participants. Further, the subprime crisis in the United States has caused many to speculate that a credit bubble exists in microfinance as well (Gokhale, 2009). Thus questions about social impact have increased attention to potential failures in social performance.

Mission drift

Even among those who believe that microcredit is a powerful solution for addressing global poverty, there is serious concern that firms are drifting away from their social missions in the scramble for financial performance (Copestake, 2007). While achieving financial sustainability is considered to be a fundamental necessity for MFIs seeking to achieve rapid growth and scale (Christen and Drake, 2001), the tension between the desire for social impact and the demands for financial performance can be intense, and balancing the two is a significant managerial challenge (Epstein and Yuthas, 2009). And if rapid scaling does cause the MFI to lose sight of its poverty-alleviation mission, there is currently no reliable metric to detect that shift (Hishigsuren, 2008).

Although many MFIs are now sustainable, the majority still operate at a loss, causing experts to question whether it is possible to effectively serve the poor, even at scale, without charging higher-than-market interest rates (Morduch, 2000). Research confirms that in order to be sustainable, MFIs reduce their depth of outreach—shifting their portfolios away from the poorest, least profitable clients toward clients who can manage larger loans. Thus, to the extent that scaling is driven by financial sustainability, pressures to shift away from social missions are unlikely to abate (Hishigsuren, 2007).

Poverty alleviation

There has long been debate surrounding the impact microfinance has had and can potentially have on economic development and the alleviation of poverty. For example. Karnani (2007) has argued that microcredit doesn't work because microbusinesses cannot provide significant economic growth, and lenders should target SMEs instead. In the past decade, several attempts have been made to explore the impact of microfinance empirically under tightly controlled circumstances to determine whether microfinance can be proven to contribute to the alleviation of poverty. Microfinance has been demonstrated to have significant positive impacts on women's empowerment and nutrition (Hashemi et al., 1996; Pitt and Khandker, 1995; Pitt et al., 2003). And there is also convincing evidence that microcredit can help reduce vulnerability of the poor (Morduch, 2000). But despite these promising results, empirical research on microfinance has not produced convincing evidence that microfinance alleviates poverty (Goldberg, 2005).

Even in Bangladesh, where microcredit has been available for decades and reaches a large proportion of poor households, one study (Zaman, 2004) shows that microfinance impacts poverty alleviation only for wealthier clients. There are several potential reasons for this lack of impact. For example, geographic features and infrastructure make poverty-reduction in Bangladesh very challenging. Nonetheless, failure to achieve widespread demonstrable results in a country with some of the most well-respected and advanced MFIs in the world leaves questions about developmental potential for microfinance in other countries.

Two new studies provide the most carefully controlled scientific evidence on microfinance impacts to date. These studies find some positive and promising impacts, but fail to convincingly conclude that microfinance is a cure for poverty. Banerjee et al. (2009) conducted randomized control trials in villages that were otherwise very similar but had differential introduction to microfinance. The study found some evidence of increased business profits, with wealthier clients more likely to open a business and shift spending from unnecessary consumption on goods such as snacks toward durables with income generating potential. The study found no significant results, however, on a number of important impact indicators, including household spending, women's empowerment, and healthcare and education expenditures.

Karlan and Zinman (2009) studied entrepreneurs in Manilla and found that although they shifted borrowing from informal sources to MFIs when those lending options became available, they did not experience significant increases in profitability or spending. Clients did experience some social benefits, such as increased trust and access to loans from family and friends, but they also reduced spending on labor and household improvements, possibly as a result of business investments or repayment difficulties. These long awaited scientifically controlled studies suggest that the verdict is still out on whether microcredit reduces poverty.

Most of the research on poverty-related impacts focuses on the average impact on clients relative to non-clients, and finds that clients are not significantly better off. What remains unstudied is how microfinance impacts those that are worse off after the microfinance intervention. While it is possible that the majority of clients are not significantly impacted, it is also possible that one group of clients experiences significant improvements in well-being while another experiences significant decreases. Thus, a lack of change in overall poverty status does not mean that the impact of microcredit is neutral. The potential negative effects are worthy of greater study.

Overindebtedness

There is increasing evidence that in some regions, clients are taking multiple simultaneous loans from different MFIs (Kamath et al., 2008; Srinivasan, 2009). In some cases, this can be due to the restrictive nature of loans. MFIs often control risk by requiring that clients begin with small loans and gradually increase the size as repayment capacity and business needs suggest. Thus clients often take multiple loans to make the investments they need.

In other cases, however, clients engage in "overlapping" or "recycling." Overlapping is the process by which a client secures a new loan to repay the loan already outstanding. It occurs because clients tend to have repayment difficulties, especially during the latter period of loan repayment. They seek alternative sources of borrowing when this occurs, relying on short-term loans from group members, family and friends, or local loan sharks to obtain the cash needed for loan repayment. Overlapping places the client in a cycle of debt that may be difficult or impossible to escape.

Even when clients do not overlap, they may cycle through the borrowing process without any real progress in building a business or accumulating wealth. Some clients regularly and repeatedly take loans of the same size and term from an MFI, using microlending as a source of revolving credit that boosts short-term consumption but fails to provide other significant benefits, eventually leaving the client cash-strapped in the latter part of the loan cycle as she struggles with the burden of heavy principal and interest payments.

Even in traditional lending situations, borrowers may take on too much debt, either because of their own or the MFIs inability to predict the outcomes of their investment opportunities, or because of opportunistic behavior on the part of one of the parties. Contrary to popular arguments, timely debt repayment does not signal a successful business because clients regularly make extraordinary efforts such as working excess hours, selling off assets (Gonzalez, 2008), or even reducing food consumption (Brett, 2006) to make the required payments. Even with these efforts, repayment rates under competitive conditions are not as high as commonly believed. For example, Grameen Bank, which pioneered many of the methods adopted broadly within the industry, experienced significant repayment difficulties in some regions where as many as 32 percent of its clients had fallen far behind their repayment schedules (Perl and Phillips, 2001).

Client defection

Client defection, or "exit," is a significant problem in microlending and has often been called the "achilles heel of the microfinance industry" (Copestake, 2003). One of the few industry studies to examine this phenomenon found that almost 50 percent of all microfinance clients left the MFI within one year (Pawlak and Matul, 2004). Because it is highly unlikely that a client can make significant wealth gains after only one or two small loans, the exit of a client prior to the second year suggests the MFI has failed to provide a positive benefit to the client (Simanowitz, 2000). When questioned about the reasons for exiting, clients give a variety of answers. In one study, more than 60 percent of the dropouts were attributable to product design and institutional processes, while market demand and idiosyncratic shocks accounted for most of the remaining dropouts (CHIP, 2005).

Both reasons point to potential failures on the part of the MFIs. Product design exits occur (Copestake, 2007; Pagura, 2004) because borrowers need lower interest rates and longer repayment terms to successfully build their businesses and repay their loans. Studies recording detailed financial transactions among the poor have shown that difficulties in loan repayment are distressingly common. Some repayment difficulties arise from income shocks. Although some shocks are unpredictable, many such as illness and festival costs are commonly occurring events. If the heavy debt burden forces the client to exit when such an event occurs, it signals an unmanageable level of risk or debt, potentially because of inadequate knowledge and skills to assess the capacity to manage debt.

The cost of default to the individual client, the borrowing group, and to the MFI can be quite high. When customers default they may be removed from the group by the other group members who are responsible for paying the loan, or by the loan officer on behalf of the MFI. For clients, default may mean reduced access to future borrowing from formal and informal sources, and it may result in significant social sanctions from group members forced to cover the debt. This puts an extra financial burden on group members and, in addition, requires them to quickly replace the defaulting member with another client to ensure the viability of the group. For the MFI, customer acquisition is costly, and new clients have higher default and defection rates than mature ones.

These clear signals of failure have raised concerns about whether microcredit, as currently implemented, can make significant inroads into poverty reduction. Further scaling under the current model may not provide social benefits, and can potentially result in negative impacts for clients and MFIs. But enormous market gaps remain. Further scaling efforts must systematically address underserved microcredit markets and must be supported by rigorous efforts to measure and manage the social impact.

Solutions for Scaling Social Impact

Social enterprises exist to meet needs that cannot be effectively met by markets. But microfinance now finds itself competing directly with commercial firms in some markets, serving the same clients and offering the same products at similar prices. The microfinance industry has been enormously successful in developing the models and methods to effectively serve many clients that were previously unable to access financial services. These processes have become so efficient that commercial enterprises can and do step in to serve these clients (DFID, 2005). In some cases, MFIs continue to serve their most profitable clients—typically urban clients with larger loans—as a way to cross-subsidize loans to very poor clients whose businesses are not as profitable. But there is also evidence that MFIs are moving up-market toward more profitable clients and leaving the poorest behind (Olivares-Polanco, 2005).

MFIs are also attempting to scale their businesses in highly competitive and commercially unprofitable markets. They regularly and systematically expand into markets that are already served by other MFIs. MFIs may need this scale to increase efficiency or increase access to funding sources. But unless this results in client benefits by way of reduced interest rates or enhanced services, such scaling efforts will not result in commensurate increases in social impact. Developed microfinance markets, such as major urban centers, have been saturated by competition among MFIs. This can lead to reduced sustainability or even failure of socially motivated MFIs that seek to provide greater depth of service relative to financially motivated MFIs and commercial banks (McIntosh and Wydick, 2005).

MFIs may enter these markets believing they are increasing access for underserved clients. These MFIs may reach clients that had previously been cautious about entering into debt agreements but have viable investment opportunities. Other MFIs, however, intentionally direct their marketing efforts toward existing clients of competing MFIs (McIntosh and Wydick, 2005). The processes of acquiring and screening clients, forming borrowing groups, and educating clients on debt management principles are very costly. When an MFI can "steal" an existing borrowing group from another MFI, it avoids those costs and greatly enhances profitability. Shifting clients from one MFI to another in this manner does not add to industry scale or efficiency. Instead, MFIs need to develop specializations in client cultivation that results in greater outreach to previously underserved clients. Certainly, competition among MFIs can result in reduced rates and better services for clients. But the commoditization of MFI products provides the client with few real options, and the lack of transparency regarding interest rates leaves clients unable to make accurate decisions about pricing.

Increasing Breadth of Outreach

To provide real gains in social impact, MFIs need to expand both the markets they target and the range of products they offer. Despite extraordinary rates of growth in recent years, gaps in financial access are significant. In rural India, for example, only 20 percent of households have loans (Basu, 2006) and in much of Sub-Sarahan Africa, access to loans is even lower (Demirgüç-Kunt et al., 2008). Capital flows are not matched to poverty-related needs, and Africa and East Asia have had very low levels of foreign investment due to concerns about regulatory and managerial risks (Forster and Reillie, 2008).

Rural areas in many countries lack financial services. These areas are less densely populated than urban areas, and population dispersion and infrastructure issues make these markets difficult and costly to access and serve. As a result, MFIs are concentrated in urban centers, and may resist expanding into rural markets. New developments in technology, such as the use of truck-mounted mobile banks and electronic mechanisms for making payments, makes it easier to operate in previously undesirable markets.

Microfinance also fails to effectively serve the "core" poor in many markets, focusing instead on wealthier clients. It is sometimes argued that the very poor do not need financial services, but as Matin et al. (1999) point out, this group does require financial services, and in fact relies on a wide variety of informal arrangements to address their needs. Yet this group lacks access to financial services, in part, because the current rigid loan products do not effectively fit their needs. The business activities of these clients provide lower and more variable incomes than those of wealthier clients. They therefore need loan products with longer terms, or with the flexibility to skip payments during low-income weeks. Although MFIs avoid these clients because they see them as unprofitable, MFIs have little real information about their costs (Morduch, 2000). While evidence suggests that MFIs that serve core poor clients can achieve financial sustainability (Churchill, 2000; Khandker, 1998), there is often clearly a trade-off between financial sustainability and service to the poor.

Commercial institutions that use market-based funding options are significantly less likely to serve very poor clients than are donor-supported institutions (Annim, 2009). Likewise, these commercial institutions serve fewer women customers (Cull, et al. 2009). Because the push toward commercialization is gaining strength some MFIs need to focus on serving the very poor and not be tempted by financial sustainability to drift away from this mission.

Increasing Depth of Outreach

A common problem associated with scaling is the potential that the social enterprise reduces the level of service offered to individual clients in order to provide service to a greater number of clients. There is some evidence that this has occurred in microcredit. Datar et al. (2008) suggest that rather than cutting services to clients, MFIs need to offer additional services, such as business development services, if they hope to support clients in their efforts to increase their business income.

The microfinance industry uses the term business development services (BDS) to encompass a wide variety of services to support profitability and growth of small entrepreneurs. Among the services most widely adopted by MFIs are training programs, especially for the poorest clients. Microfinance institutions that offer these services train borrowing groups during the regular repayment meeting, or during supplemental meetings. Training includes business-related topics such as financial literacy, basic business management, and entrepreneurship, or focuses on other critical aspects of poverty such as family health, HIV/AIDS, domestic relationships, or education.

But training is costly and requires a different skill set from the one required for basic lending. Some critics argue that training detracts from the central mission of the MFI and is best accomplished by firms focused exclusively on training. Moreover, some argue that training is not valued by clients unless they purchase training services on the market. The inability to motivate clients to attend training sessions and to apply these learnings in their businesses sometimes discourages MFIs from providing more training.

This results in clients who have very little understanding of the most basic business principles needed to successfully manage a microenterprise, and who would benefit greatly from training programs designed to provide them with these skills (Karlan and Valdivia, 2006).

Value-chain services can also provide significant benefits to clients. Many clients lack the capacity to organize activities with peer organizations or to work collaboratively with customers and suppliers. Yet such efforts have the potential to enhance productivity across the supply chain and to provide competitive benefits to all participants. USAID, SEEP, and other organizations have provided detailed guidance for how MFIs can support their clients by strengthening the value chain.

Other services that can enhance depth of outreach include loan products that meet nonbusiness needs of clients. Although the majority of micro-credit is earmarked for use in productive business investments, in reality, MFIs rarely engage in follow-up activities to ensure that borrowed funds are invested in income-generating activities. It is well-known that clients divert as much as a third of the credit obtained for consumption (Feder et al., 1990). Yet few MFIs provide products specifically designed to meet consumption needs. As a result, clients lie about the purposes of their loans, take loans that have payment terms ill-suited to consumption resulting in excessive interest and/or a crushing debt. Other products such as fixed asset and housing loans are also of great interest to microfinance clients. Current loan structures are primarily geared toward working capital investments that can generate the payoffs for immediate and regular repayments. Short-term loans are not designed to support investments in equipment and other fixed assets that require longer repayment schedules but have the potential to generate more substantial profits.

Although beyond the scope of this chapter, a full range of financial services such as savings, insurance, or remittances could be offered to clients as a supplement to or as a substitute for microcredit. Much has been written about the poverty-reducing potential of these instruments, yet many MFIs are unable or unwilling to offer these services to their clients.

Measuring and Managing Social Impact

As firms develop new strategies for serving their clients, they must also gain expertise in measuring and evaluating social impact. MFIs have long been satisfied with using small loan size and large number of clients as prox-ies for social impact. However, some MFIs are more impact-focused than others. Grameen, for example, has long used a ten-point rating system to evaluate the poverty status of its clients. The rating evaluates core poverty indicators such as quality of client housing, nutrition, healthcare, and education. The organization has been active in promoting the development and use of the "progress of poverty index" (PPI). The PPI uses country-specific economic and income data as a basis for developing tools for measuring poverty status relative to one and two dollars per day purchasing power parity standards. PPI tools are now available for many countries and provide one way for MFIs to assess social impact.

Other poverty measurement tools are available and have been used for a variety of governmental and developmental purposes. USAID and CGAP, for example, also have standardized poverty measurement tools that have been validated and used by the microfinance industry. Such tools provide the means for evaluation of individual performance over time as well as comparison across MFIs.

Despite the availability of poverty measures, the industry has, to date, been much more proactive in promoting financial sustainability than social impact. More recently, however, there has been greater interest in establishing industry averages and benchmarking data for social impact. The Social Measurement Task Force, a group of leaders from MFIs, donor agencies, technical experts, and other stakeholder groups, has worked toward development of an industry-wide reporting framework for social performance. This framework has resulted in the development of a twenty-two-item questionnaire that is being managed by the Microfinance Information Exchange, the clearing house organization for microfinance trade data. The questionnaire, which covers measurements relating to client poverty movement, product design, and institutional performance, has already been pilot tested and is being used to gather data from the more than thirteen hundred MFIs that participate in the exchange.

Concluding Remarks

As an example of scaling social enterprise, the microcredit industry has done many things exceptionally well, achieving a ten-fold growth in the number of clients served within a decade. In large part, this success is due to the effective use of industry-level scaling levers developed through collaborative efforts among individual practitioner firms, donors, and service providers. Key levers include organizations for collaboration and information sharing, effective communication of the microfinance message, building alliances to lobby for and improve the microcredit climate, promoting donor sophistication, developing standardized and replicable practices, and carefully managing earnings. The microfinance industry has been extremely effective in supporting the scaling of microfinance by providing opportunities for sharing information and leveraging resources.

But despite its sophistication and effectiveness on these dimensions, the microcredit industry has made the same mistake as countless other social enterprises: it has failed to hold social impact paramount during the push for financial sustainability and growth. As a result, some MFIs have emphasized and pursued growth in a manner that has caused them to drift away from their social missions. Increased professionalism and efficiency have not guaranteed improved results for clients, and it is still unclear which clients are benefitting from microfinance and how they are impacted. MFIs routinely churn rapidly through clients for whom the value proposition is lacking. And in the race to increase their portfolios, MFIs may be pushing clients to take on debt they cannot afford.

It is time for the industry to put the mechanisms that have been so effective in scaling the volume of lending to work in scaling up social impact for clients. There is much to be learned about the process through which loans are translated into business profits and social outcomes but there are few systematic attempts to monitor and manage these processes and outcomes. The industry has begun to focus on social performance measurement, which is a critical first step. Organizations seeking to reduce poverty through microcredit can use this as a foundation to scale their efforts in a manner that truly improves the lives of their clients.

4

Playing the Field: Implications of Scale in the California Charter School Movement

Debra E. Meyerson, Alexander Berger, and Rand Quinn

This isn't McDonald's [where everything can be controlled and quality is simply a matter of doing the same thing every time]...The process of replicating a good school isn't easy or predictable.

—Nelson Smith, President and CEO of the National Alliance for Public Charter Schools

Whether the aim is to slow global warming, reduce poverty, or improve urban education, social entrepreneurs and philanthropists seek scalable solutions to the pressing social problems of our time. More recently, however, academics, nonprofit leaders, and consultants have questioned the emphasis on scale on two counts. First, a number of scholars have shown that organizations can significantly grow their impact without growing in size (Dees et al., 2004; Uvin et al., 2000; Wei-Skillern and Marciano, 2008). Second, social entrepreneurs and their observers have documented the challenges associated with scaling social change organizations.

Furthermore, the effect of a single organization's growth on others within the same collective movement and thus on the movement as a whole has not been fully explored. This chapter begins to fill this void by raising questions about the benefits and unintended costs of scaling from the perspective of organizations and the movements to which they belong. Our observations are based on a synthesis of relevant research and preliminary observations from a multiyear study of the charter school movement in California, a significant reform effort to which educational entrepreneurs and philanthropists have been drawn. To situate our contribution, we begin with a brief overview of some of the current debates on scaling social impact organizations.

Prior Studies of Scaling

Social entrepreneurs, philanthropists, policymakers, and analysts agree that nonprofit scaling offers huge opportunities for progress on major social problems. There is far less agreement, however, on what scaling is or how to achieve it. Discussions of "going to scale" by nonprofit leaders traditionally focus on growing an organization or the number of people organizations serve (Foster and Fine, 2007; Uvin, 1995; Wei-Skillern and Anderson, 2003). Authors working within this broad conception of scaling tend to focus on ways of overcoming the challenges of replicating social change programs and organizations (Ahlert et al., 2008; Bradach, 2003; Campbell et al., 2008; Oster, 1996; Racine 2003).

In contrast, a number of articles point to strategies organizations use to extend their social impact that do not entail significant organizational growth (Alvord et al., 2004; Dees, et al., 2004; Taylor et al., 2002; Uvin, 1995; Uvin et al., 2000). Organizations rely on building their impact through strategic collaborations and network alliances (Alvord et al., 2004; Uvin, 1995; Wei-Skillern and Marciano, 2008) or by disseminating lessons learned and innovations in addressing a social problem (Dees et al., 2004; Taylor et al., 2002). These are important contributions that raise a number of questions about implementation and measurement of impact, to name a few. They do not, however, illuminate how the actions of one organization or group of organizations can indirectly or unintentionally affect others within the same social movement.

The chapter proceeds as follows. By way of background, we begin with a brief description of the charter school movement and an overview of the study that generated the observations on which this chapter is based. We then review the benefits and challenges of organizational scaling as identified by leaders of charter schools and prior research on charter school scaling. As our point of departure, we shift to a social movements perspective. Drawing from our study and prior research, we identify some of the benefits and unintended consequences of rapid scaling for other organizations within the same social movement. We conclude the chapter with implications and cautions for social entrepreneurs aspiring to effect change within the context of a social movement with an array of interdependent actors.

Charter Schools and the Study

Charter Schools

Public schools are embedded in a bureaucracy in which grade levels, graduation requirements, curricula, textbooks, teacher certification, and in many cases, instructional methods are dictated by a central district office, the state, and the federal government. Few substantive decisions are made at the school or classroom level. While this uniformity has its benefits, it is not without drawbacks; public schools have come to be seen as overly bureaucratic and factory-like, unable to effectively address the various needs of local communities or individual students. Charter schools emerged as a response to these concerns.

Charter schools are publicly funded, privately managed schools of choice. Modeled after the seventeenth-century charters between the East India Company and English explorers, school charters detail the educational vision, mission, and goals of the new school and the responsibilities and support provided by the chartering authority (typically the local education authority/school district; Budde, 1989). The idea behind charter reform is to develop a system in which teachers with nontraditional "teaching methods, technologies, [and] organizations of time and human resources" receive permission and funding to implement innovations (Shanker, 1988).

In 1991, Minnesota became the first state in the nation to authorize charter schools. Charters are now a rapidly growing sector in education. In 2006, approximately 1.2 million students across 40 states and the District of Columbia were enrolled in a charter school (National Center for Education Statistics, 2009). Yet charter schools remain a comparatively small portion of the entire K-12 education field, with a mere 2.5 percent of all students nationwide enrolled in a charter school in 2006.

Under the charter system, states grant charter schools regulatory freedom from portions of the education code in order to allow for experimentation with curriculum, teaching style, and structure. In exchange, charter school operators are held accountable for the academic performance of their students and the financial solvency of their organizations and they receive per pupil funding that varies by state.[1] Since state legislatures determine the parameters of charter school laws, there exists significant variation across states. For example, in 2009, no more than 120 schools were allowed to operate in Massachusetts, whereas California's limit was 1,350 schools. In Arizona, charters were authorized for a maximum of fifteen years, while in California the maximum length of a charter was five years. In Michigan community college and public university boards could charter but in California only boards of education—local, county, and state—held the authority to grant charters.

California was the second state to pass a charter school law.[2] Originally, the statutory limit on the total number of operational charters statewide was 100, but after significant lobbying the cap was raised to 250 for the 1998–99 school year with a stipulation that the cap increased by 100 charters each year after that. (To date, the yearly increase in the cap has more than accommodated the actual growth rate of charter schools in the state.) For the 2008–09 school year, there were 746 charter schools serving 285,617 of the state's approximately 6.25 million K-12 students (California Department of Education, 2009).

The California charter school field has been populated by a variety of different types of organizations (see Meyerson et al., 2009, for a detailed typology). The most common form has historically been the "standalone" charter school. We define standalones as single schools, typically founded by parents, educators, or other advocates for the benefit of a local neighborhood or community. Often, the primary goal held by leaders of these charters was to provide underserved families an alternative to their neighborhood schools. Over time, some standalone charter schools developed loose connections with other schools or launched additional schools. In addition to standalones, charter schools are incubated and operated by *for-profit* education management organizations (EMO) and *nonprofit* charter management organizations (CMO). For the purpose of this analysis, we define CMOs as operating three or more schools, having an unambiguous goal to scale by expanding organizations or programs, and having centralized components of education, operation, or culture. These management organizations profess the broad goal of increasing decentralization, autonomy, and choice in public education (Meyerson et al., 2009) and, to varying degrees, they aim to transform public education. While the percentage of students enrolled in an EMO-operated school has been on the decline in California, the percentage of students enrolled in a CMO-operated school has been rapidly increasing. During the 1999–2000 school year, a mere 0.7 percent of all charter school students in California were enrolled in a CMO-operated school. By the 2006–07 school year, the proportion had grown to 12.6 percent.

The Study

Because of the state level variation in the charter school regulatory environment, we chose to examine the charter school movement within a single state. California was an ideal site for our study because of the maturity of its charter laws, the density of charter organizations, and the presence of institutional actors such as large-scale charter school funders and technical assistance organizations.

Our analysis drew from three sources of data collected from 2004 to 2009 by a team of researchers. (For a detailed description of the study, see Meyerson et al., 2009.) First, we conducted in-depth, semi-structured interviews with fifty-two informants involved in the California charter school movement, including founders and key staff members of charter management organizations (CMO) and standalone charter schools as well as senior personnel from foundations. Second, members of the research team participated and observed in numerous charter school forums, conferences, and meetings across the state. And third, we relied on multiple sources of archival data to understand the growth trends of the charter movement in California and trends in philanthropic funding to charter schools, including data from the California Department of Education, the U.S. Department of Education, and the Foundation Center.

Scaling in the Charter School Field

Despite the quiet skepticism about a narrowly organizational perspective of scale and limited discussions by policymakers about the rapid growth of the charter school movement (e.g., Harvey and Rainey, 2006; National Charter School Research Project, 2007), the majority of charter school leaders and foundation representatives we interviewed talked about scaling from the perspective of their focal organization. Here we describe the costs and benefits of scaling that surfaced in these discussions and our review of the literature before examining the implications of scale for the charter school movement.

Benefits of Scaling Charter Schools

The charter school leaders we interviewed offered a wide variety of reasons for seeking to scale their organizations. First and foremost, they felt compelled to offer more students access to the education offered by their schools. In some cases, the charter schools were dramatically oversubscribed, forcing the leaders to turn away students who had entered the lottery. A number of charter leaders told us how difficult it was to turn away students who could benefit from their schools. Even with the rapid growth of charter management organizations, demand for their schools continued to far outstrip the supply (Harvey and Rainey, 2006), and many of the leaders of charter management organizations felt that they had an obligation to meet this demand.

Second, expansion through a centralized management organization offered the internal benefits of a stronger brand and economies of scale. An organization's brand tends to become stronger as it grows because more sites attract more attention from the media and local elites, especially if the organization is already considered successful. In many cases, a strong brand has proved invaluable for CMOs. Aspire Public Schools, a CMO that operates charters throughout California, found that as it grew and continued to receive positive media coverage, it faced less resistance from districts in which it sought to operate schools. Powerful local support was available from parents who wanted an "Aspire school" for their kids. A strong brand also gave Aspire greater credibility with the foundations that were financing its expansion. The rapid growth of KIPP (Knowledge is Power Program), a national network of college-preparatory charter schools that serves disadvantaged communities,[3] was made possible by a widely publicized "60 Minutes" segment that helped build its brand when the organization was comprised of only two schools (Colby et al., 2005). According to a number of other CMO leaders, strengthening their brands through organizational growth enabled them to attract talented people to their schools, central offices, and boards, which in turn enhanced the quality of the schools.

Third, growing to scale also provided economic efficiencies by enabling charter organizations to spread fixed costs over a larger number of students.[4] CMO business plans regularly identified "break-even" points, a size at which CMO schools could, in theory, be sustained on public funding alone (based on per pupil allocations that vary dramatically by state). Economies of scale also made it economically viable for CMOs to hire specialized staff dedicated to improving operations and instruction, resources that standalone schools could rarely afford.

A fourth benefit of growth cited by CMO leaders was the possibility of learning through experience. The founders of standalone charter schools climbed a steep learning curve when they launched their schools, but they rarely had the opportunity to take advantage of the lessons they learned in the process. In contrast, CMO founders who opened multiple schools were able to leverage their accumulated expertise. As one leader explained, "Look, if we're going to do one, why not spread that learning out over a number of schools?" In addition to learning how to open schools more efficiently, CMO leaders mentioned that their size enabled them to experiment with a reform or new curriculum in one school and then implement the lessons learned in subsequent schools.

A national survey found similar motivations for scaling throughout the nonprofit sector. Like the charter school leaders we interviewed, the primary motivation for expansion among nonprofit leaders was the unmet need of their constituencies (Wei-Skillern and Anderson, 2003) followed by the possibility of achieving economies of scale and a stronger brand. The nonprofit leaders reported that they did not usually achieve the cost savings they had hoped for, but the benefits of building their organizational brands consistently exceeded early expectations. While organizational learning was rarely given as a motivation for expansion, leaders of nonprofits also recognized learning as one the most important benefits of growth (Wei-Skillern and Anderson, 2003).

Challenges of Scaling Charter Schools

Growth also created significant challenges for a number of charter organizations. The push to grow quickly at times rushed school openings and community building efforts that compromised relationships with local stakeholders. When a San Francisco-based charter management organization opened a charter in a predominantly Latino district of San Francisco, linguistic barriers became significant impediments in their efforts to garner local support. Because the CMO needed to open schools quickly with limited resources, they had neither the time nor the capacity to translate marketing materials and admissions documents into Spanish, an understandable compromise that may have led to the school's under-enrollment during its first few years since charter schools depend on parents to voluntarily enroll their children.

Inhospitable local political climates also caused problems for a number of CMOs that attempted to scale quickly. The Big Picture Company, a national CMO, started out by launching schools in areas where its leaders had personal connections. Over time, however, they discovered that political opposition could not be overcome with just a few friends, and they changed their site selection process to choose areas that were more politically amenable to CMOs (National Charter School Research Project, 2007). Building local relationships takes time, and trying to shortcut these efforts can lead to challenges and costs in the long term for other charter schools.

Another persistent challenge that charter schools have faced in their efforts to scale has been finding the right level of model specification and ensuring compliance with it (Lake, 2007; National Charter School Research Project, 2007). Variations on this concern have been articulated in studies addressing the challenge of scaling other educational reforms (Coburn, 2003; McLaughlin and Mitra, 2001) and nonprofit organizations (Ahlert et al., 2008; Bradach, 2003; Campbell et al., 2008; Oster, 1996; Racine, 2003). CMOs vary in the extent to which they standardize and centralize control over curriculum and operations (Colby et al., 2005). For example, San Diego-based High Tech High began as a voluntary network with a highly specified educational model. After some schools in the network began deviating from its model, High Tech High became a charter management organization with the authority to impose compliance. KIPP had a less specified model than High Tech High based on five shared principles and a commitment to autonomy for school leaders, but it also began providing more support and oversight to local schools after concerns surfaced about inconsistencies in quality across KIPP schools (Education Sector, 2009).

Along with model compliance and local support, virtually all of the CMO leaders we interviewed suggested that sustaining an aggressive rate of growth to achieve scale posed significant organizational challenges. Some leaders reported that they had to hire teachers and school leaders with minimal experience because they needed to open a school by a certain date and did not have a sufficient pipeline of candidates. In addition, the demand to open new schools in crowded urban areas meant that CMOs sometimes had to rely on inadequate facilities or invest considerable resources into bringing the sites up to a reasonable standard. One CMO leader explained how his organization was forced to lease warehouse space and convert it at great cost in order to have a building by the opening of the school year. Even with that investment, the building remained a suboptimal facility for the school and was only a temporary solution. As a result of these and other challenges associated with rapid growth, maintaining the quality and capping the costs of new charter schools has proven to be much more difficult than early CMO advocates had envisioned (Harvey and Rainey, 2006).

We consider next the benefits and unintended costs of charter school scaling from the vantage point of other interdependent organizations within the charter movement. Because our analysis is informed by prior research on social movements, we briefly review relevant findings from that literature.

Scaling within a Social Movement

Social movements are "mobilized attempts of groups, organizations, and individuals acting in some coordinated way to change policies, social structures, and the concrete distribution of goods and services" (Zald, 2004: 26). Movements take many forms and advance different types of agendas. In the United States, the Civil Rights and Women's Movements are among the most celebrated and successful contemporary movements. But scores of others, including the anti-drunk driving and antitobacco movements, have achieved success in changing policies and norms over the past few decades. Although they differ in their objectives and effectiveness, social movements are mobilized efforts to challenge and transform the status quo.

Examining the effect of scaling by a focal organization on a broader movement requires considering the impact of an organization's growth on movement's goals and on other organizations within the movement. Such an account presumes that organizational actors within a movement are interdependent; the activities of one set of actors can affect the positioning or practices of others. For example, social movement scholars have written about the "radical flank" effect in the Civil Rights Movement, whereby the transgressive actions of radical organizations enabled moderate organizations to receive financial support (Haines, 1984). In the 1960s, as Black nationalist organizations became an increasingly prominent force within the movement, moderate organizations, such as the NAACP and the National Urban League, came to be seen by those in power as relatively reasonable and legitimate, thereby strengthening their base of support and funding. Although the Black nationalist organizations were rarely successful in accomplishing their own goals, their radical actions made possible the reforms championed by moderate organizations.

In a similar vein, Andrew Hoffman's research (2009) reveals the interdependencies among disparate organizations involved in the environmental movement. According to Hoffman, the environmental movement has been dominated by two camps of actors: "dark greens" and "bright greens." Dark green environmental nongovernmental organizations (ENGOs) are typically confrontational with corporations while bright green ENGOs are more likely to partner with corporations in pursuit of their goals. Based on a network analysis of the largest U.S.-based ENGOs, Hoffman finds that the choice to engage or not engage with a corporation is a strategic one that may open or close off opportunities with the general public, the media, policymakers, and other actors:

> In the late 1990s, for example, the Sierra Club decided to oppose all logging on federal lands, an action that isolated them from negotiations with the government on that topic. But it opened up opportunities to appeal to a broader public by voicing a strong ideological position on the issue. As a result, other ENGOs gained the power to bargain with the government and corporations on logging on federal lands. (p. 49)

Hoffman's research demonstrates how the positioning, perception, and influence of a focal organization within the environmental movement depends on its relationship to neighboring organizations within the same movement. "It all comes down to the constituency an ENGO is trying to reach and the network of other players who are working on a particular issue" (Hoffman: 49).

From the perspective of a collective movement, the activities of any one organization are understood to be embedded in and interdependent with a broader network of organizations. This notion is consistent with the work of scholars that urge organizations in the nonprofit sector to attend to impact rather than size (e.g., Dees et al., 2004). However, that research tends to focus on ways to maximize the impact of a focal organization rather than the efficacy of a collective comprised of heterogeneous and interdependent organizations. Furthermore, with a few exceptions (e.g., National Charter School Research Project, 2007), charter school researchers, funders, and proponents tend to restrict their discussion of scaling to how best to extend a focal organization's impact with limited consideration of the effects of an organization's growth on other organizations. These considerations may be particularly important in the context of social movements comprised of networks of interdependent actors with distinct strategies and resources (Hoffman, 2009).

Organizations within the charter school movement share the overall aspiration of providing an alternative to traditional public schools, however they diverge in form (e.g., standalone, EMO, CMO), goals, ideology, and access to critical resources (King et al., forthcoming; Wells, Grutzik, Carnochan, Slayton, and Vasudeva, 1999; Wells, Lopez, Scott, and Holme, 1999). The movement also includes organizations that support and invest in charters, state, federal and local policymakers that establish the regulatory context, charter school associations that identify and advance charter schools' collective interests, and new organizations that prepare professionals for charter schools and charter management organizations.

Intended Benefits of Scaling for the Charter School Movement

As discussed earlier, scaling enables an organization to increase its own impact by serving more people, developing a stronger brand, lowering costs, and learning from experience. Organizational scaling can also serve broader movement objectives in a number of ways.

Rapid growth by charter management organizations was motivated in part by the movement's objective of transforming traditional educational institutions (National Charter School Research Project, 2007; Smith and Peterson, 2006). Leaders within the movement regularly referred to "tipping the system," a term made popular by Malcolm Gladwell (2000) to refer to the moment in which a system is poised to undergo significant change. Charter leaders and funders used the term loosely and they differed in whether they sought to "tip" a district, state, or national education system. According to some CMO leaders, tipping the system required building sufficient scale and market share to force an institutional response. Mike Feinberg (2008), cofounder of KIPP, articulated this view by drawing parallels between his organization and FedEx:

> We want to have the same effect on public education the way FedEx affected the Post Office...And we really like that analogy because...the U.S. Post

Office, which was another government monopoly, stopped making their own *"Yes, buts."* You know, *"Oh, that delivery is impossible. It's too expensive. It's not possible"*…They stopped making their *"Yes, buts"* and they started doing Next Day Air as well…FedEx really didn't hurt the Post Office, they actually made it better.

In a similar fashion, KIPP attempted to reach scale in key urban school districts to induce institutional change. In a recent commentary published in Forbes.com, Feinberg explained, "We hope KIPP's expansion will spur healthy competition and cause school districts nationwide to raise the quality of educational offerings for young people."

In addition to tipping the public system through market pressure, the charter school movement has attempted to build political capital by growing to scale. With sufficient political influence, coordinated action among organizations within the movement can influence public policy in ways that will advance the charter movement's objectives, such as eliminating statutory limits on the total number of charter schools or changing credentialing regulations. One CMO leader determined that at approximately fifty schools, his CMO would be equivalent in size to the fifth largest school district serving a high percentage of low-income students in California, and large enough to have earned "a seat at the table." Steve Barr, another charter school leader and founder of Green Dot Public Schools, argued that the tipping point for them came when local political pressure, mobilized around Green Dot's previous success in Los Angeles, forced the district to turn over one of its failing high schools and ultimately partner with his CMO:

> I think the political tipping point for us was not just building charter schools, it was when we took Locke High School, because that sent shock waves through the system. What I see as a political tipping point is when a district has no other option but to work with you on your grounds or terms. I think it starts when you take $26 million away from the school system. (Quoted in Chang and Meyerson, 2008)

In short, the movement stands to gain influence in public policy deliberations as the organizations within it grow in size and legitimacy, particularly if member organizations act in a coordinated fashion. If, however, organizations diverge in their goals and strategies, the larger ones, especially those that have used their scale to gain political power, may inadvertently thwart the influence of smaller actors and, in effect, channel the movement toward their objectives. We will discuss this concern further in the next section.

Finally, the growth of one network of organizations within a movement can help spur the growth and legitimation of organizations in complementary networks and overlapping movements. With the rapid increase in the number of CMO-operated charter schools, the charter movement has gained momentum and legitimacy, which in turned helped fuel the growth of complementary organizations, including entrepreneurial human capital organizations that have built alternative pipelines to recruit and prepare teachers and principals, such as Teach for America and New Leaders for New Schools (Meyerson et al., 2009). CMOs lacking an adequate supply of desirable candidates for teacher and principal positions within their expanding portfolio of schools have developed programs to recruit and prepare professionals. High Tech High, for example, launched its own fully accredited graduate school to train and credential teachers for its schools. Institutional sociologists have long noted that the creation of novel organizational forms within established fields (the charter school form within the education field, for instance) generates employment opportunities that legitimate new classes of professional actors (DiMaggio and Powell, 1983).

These alternative human resource pipelines and credentialing organizations share many of the objectives of the charter movement. They compete with and aim to transform traditional educational institutions that have had a hold on professionalization and credentialing, such as teacher unions and university-based schools of education. While waged by different organizations, the effectiveness of this challenge to traditional institutions has been spurred, in part, by the increase in scale and legitimacy of charter schools.

Unintended Consequences of Scaling for the Movement

Although the strength of the charter movement and the effectiveness of its challenge may depend partly on its scale, the rapid growth of charter schools has created a number of unintended consequences. The concerns we raise in the following paragraphs are based on tentative observations combined with and informed by prior research. We offer them as topics for further investigation.

The desire to scale has increased CMOs' dependence on philanthropic support, which in turn appears to have heightened pressure to scale. With varying degrees of enthusiasm for the objective, virtually every CMO leader we interviewed had felt pressure to scale. Some charter school founders who had not originally planned to develop multiple schools understood that cultivating an aggressive plan to scale had become an essential criterion of funding. One CMO founder explained, "We had to raise some money locally. So where was the money? The money was in scale." Other CMO leaders echoed this sentiment: "They won't fund us unless we can show a plan to open 25 new schools." Thus, getting to scale became a perceived condition of funding for the charter management organizations we studied. The resulting commitment to scale their organization, in turn, reinforced their dependency on continued foundation patronage.

Social movement researchers have debated the effects of this dependency on a movement's goals and activities. On one hand, some have argued that the effectiveness and sustainability of social movements hinge on their access to critical resources. According to the resource mobilization strand of social movement theory, access to resources enables collective engagement in social conflict (McCarthy and Zald, 1977). On the other hand, researchers have shown that dependence on philanthropic patronage tends to channel movements away from radical activities toward more conservative goals (Jenkins and Eckert, 1986). This occurs, in part, through selection processes whereby foundations favor professional organizations. Others have found that foundation funding leads organizations to professionalize over time by creating incentives for them to display symbols of professionalism and hire professional staffs (Jenkins and Halcli, 1999). As others have demonstrated, professional expertise has come to be equated with managerial expertise and standards, credentialed through business experience and MBA degrees (Hwang and Powell, 2009), and displayed through a variety of symbols, such as strategic plans and corporate job titles.

The CMO sector of the charter school movement appears to have followed this course. CMOs tend to be led and staffed by professionals with business credentials along with education professionals, and all of the organizations we studied had developed a strategic plan that mapped out a growth strategy (Meyerson et al., 2009). While these symbols of professionalization can provide a number of benefits, prior research suggests that professionalization channels the movement away from radical activities and distances it from grassroots and community-based objectives. This raises the possibility that, over time, CMOs will steer charter organizations toward the activities and goals that sustain them and away from activities that challenge traditional institutions and methods.

To the extent that CMOs have been subject to these channeling forces, we would expect their dependence on philanthropic funding to discourage innovation. In other words, we surmise that organizational efforts to satisfy foundations' requirements with regards to scale and professionalism would, over time, lead to standardization and isomorphism within the field, a pattern that has recently been noted (Cuban, 2006). According to some critics, the movement had failed to live up to its promise of fostering innovations in curriculum, pedagogy, or organization despite the autonomy afforded by charter legislation and the emphasis on innovation in early justifications of charter schools (Lubienski, 2003). Future research can help identify the conditions under which charter schools encourage versus discourage innovation.

In addition, organizational growth within a social movement can result in a shortage of critical resources, fueling competition between organizations within the same collective movement (Soule and King, 2008; Zald and McCarthy, 1980). More specifically, charter school organizations within the same region often compete over a limited supply of funding, talent, and facilities.

Charter schools compete for philanthropic support, particularly in states with relatively low per pupil funding, such as California. Over the past decade, however, the majority of philanthropic dollars spent on charter schools in California have been allocated to CMO-managed schools. According to the Foundation Center, between 2002 and 2005, grants to

California CMOs totaled $81,439,000 while foundation spending on non-CMO charter schools over the same period amounted to $5,890,000.[5] One leader of a standalone charter summarized the implications of this funding gap: "We are like a small fish in a big pond when it comes to the charter school movement. And not having the resources...restricts the development that can occur at the school."

In addition, charter school expansion has fueled the competition for qualified teachers and principals. A number of CMO leaders suggested that the opportunities for professional development and mobility they were able to offer their staffs made them more attractive in the human capital markets. Assuming CMOs can continue to secure resources to offer superior professional development, we conjecture that CMO-managed schools would become more attractive employment targets than most standalone charter and traditional public schools, which should contribute to their effectiveness.

Finally, charter school growth within urban regions has exacerbated the competition over limited school facilities, one of the most serious bottlenecks constraining the expansion of charter schools in California. The competition over school sites has also driven up the prices for facilities (particularly in states that do not require districts to provide adequate building sites), which in turn imposes a cost on the movement and favors charter organizations with the deepest pockets. Informants admitted that the "mom-and-pop" standalone schools could not compete against the "Starbucks."

In one example, a successful standalone charter school serving African American and Latino students in Los Angeles was given a few months' notice that it would need to find a new location because its facility had been purchased by a growing CMO. The only affordable building the leaders could find on short notice was a temporary facility in a suburb forty-five minutes from the original site. To continue to serve its students, the charter school invested in improving the temporary facility and bussing its students to the new site. However, because of the lengthy commute time and the diversion of resources to transportation expenses, student involvement and the school's investment in extracurricular and community-based programs—which had been core to its mission—had to be significantly curtailed.

Some might argue that, overall, these competitive dynamics may serve as an efficient means of weeding out underperforming charter schools. But in the example offered, the quality of the school was not the deciding criteria. On any number of metrics—graduate rates, college readiness, and college acceptance to name a few—the school had achieved strong results. Yet its capacity to sustain and expand its core educational program had been put at risk.

Implications and Conclusions

After reviewing the benefits and challenges of scaling from the perspective of charter school organizations, we offered observations about the perceived benefits and unintended consequences of scaling for the charter school movement. Some of our observations and predictions were based on findings from prior research on social movements that has shown, for example, the effects of social movement organizations' dependence on foundation support (e.g., McCarthy and Zald, 1977; Jenkins and Halcli, 1999). Other observations, such as the effects of scaling on competition between organizations, surfaced in the course of our study and point to the need for additional research. So too are the dynamics of cooperation between and within different charter types of charter school organizations. In a subsequent study, we explore the competitive and cooperative dynamics generated by rapid growth of charter schools in a concentrated, resource-constrained region.

This chapter also contains a number of implications that extend beyond the charter school movement. First, our description of the pros and cons of organizational scaling from both the organizational and movement perspectives makes salient the differences between these views and highlights the importance of considering the intra-movement dynamics that can result from organizational decisions with regard to scaling. Thus, when thinking about scaling an organization, leaders and funders would be well advised to attend to the broad array of contributions and consequences at both the organization and movement levels.

Second, our observations of movement dynamics raise questions about how scaling by one set of actors enhances or undermines the possibility of coordinated action by different movement actors. To the extent the growth spurs competition, what kind of competition is productive for a movement? What forms of competition are counterproductive, and on what criteria do we differentiate?

Third, does competition fueled by scaling inevitably favor organizations with the resources required to scale and squeeze out organizations that are effectively serving local constituencies? Is it important to sustain local, grassroots organizations as part of the ecology of a social movement? How do local "mom-and-pop" organizations sustain themselves in a market dominated by high-growth organizations, and what is lost if and when local grassroots organizations disappear from movements?

In the case of charter schools, a reform movement that originated with an explicit aim to encourage localism and community ownership of its schools, the trends driven by an emphasis on scaling and the resulting intra-movement competition can be seen in different lights. A recent report by the National Charter School Research Project (2007) characterizes the growth of CMOs as a response by the charter movement to the failure of standalone charter operators to maintain quality or reach an adequate scale for collective impact:

> By 2001, the charter school movement had no choice but to shift its strategy to intensive growth. Quality required work; without quality the movement would stall, not grow. Future growth would depend on nurturing a pipeline

of qualified operators...The frontier "land rush," in which new operators were welcome even if they were undercapitalized, financially primitive, politically naive, or educationally unprepared, was over. (16)

Others value the preservation of standalone community-based schools and see the trend toward scaling as troubling for the movement and the communities it serves. The cofounder of a standalone charter school reflected:

In order for [the charter school movement] to develop fully and to maximize its impact, there has to be room for schools run by those who are indigenous to the community. You have charter organizations that are coming in with great intentions, but [often] they're not coming from the community.

As these examples indicate, the advantages and disadvantages of scaling depend in part on an organization's goals and ideology as well as the organization's conception of its broader impact. Those organizations that aim to generate change as part of a collective movement would be well advised to consider the consequences—intended and otherwise—of its actions on others within that movement. We hope that our chapter provides some questions for future research and urges charter leaders, social entrepreneurs, funders, and policymakers to consider movement implications of their actions, and particularly the effects of one organization's expansion on others within the same movement.

Notes

We thank the participants of the Second Conference on Scaling Social Impact at Fuqua School of Business for helpful comments. Megan Tompkins-Stange and Carrie Oelberger provided valuable assistance in the research and are coauthors of related articles.

1. California financing of charter schools (and district schools) is notoriously low. In 2008, for example, charter schools in California received approximately $7,100 per pupil, roughly 69 percent of district allocation, as compared to charter schools in New York that received, on average, $12,200 per pupil from the state.
2. California Charter Schools Act of 1992, California Education Code §47600 *et seq.*
3. Although KIPP schools are comparatively independent, they meet our CMO criteria because of the high degree of cultural consistency across school units.
4. This point was emphasized repeatedly by CMO leaders and highlighted in the November, 2009 report on charter school scaling published by Education Sector (p. 13).
5. Foundation Center Grants Database. Grants of at least ten thousand dollars awarded between 2002 and 2005 to California charter schools. (See Meyerson, Quinn, Tompkins-Stange, 2009, for elaboration of these data.)

III

Cultivating Ecosystem Alliances and Networks

5

From Enterprise to Ecosystem: Rebooting the Scale Debate

John Elkington, Pamela Hartigan, and Alejandro Litovsky

It is basic human nature to want less of bad things—and more of good ones. In relation to the latter challenge, the New Economy era taught us to think in terms of replication and scaling of solutions (Kelly, 1998). For even the perfect solution to a great global—or local—problem will create little or no value unless it can be scaled effectively in good time and at reasonable cost. Meanwhile, achieving systemic social change is a growing concern for governments and for social investors, although to date—with few exceptions—efforts to scale solutions to global social, environmental, and governance challenges have not had the desired impact. It is time to take a closer look at scaling and—though there will never be instant, black box recipes—to begin to build the "Scaling 101" tools needed by social and environmental entrepreneurs and intrapreneurs.

Currently, investor, media, and academic interest in social and environmental forms of entrepreneurship tends to focus on extraordinary individual innovators and entrepreneurs and on their solutions, whereas increasingly we need to look beyond, focusing more attention on the barriers and blockages that stall their progress.

A key step, we believe, is to use an "ecosystem approach" (Volans, 2009). In what follows, we review the "scaling" debate in relation to social entrepreneurship, then widen the focus to look at the current context within which scaling is (or is not) happening, and conclude with an exploration of some early applications of the Pathways to Scale model, which shifts the spotlight from individual enterprises to broader ecosystems of institutions. The focus here is increasingly on the interconnectedness, networks, alliances, and collective leadership needed to achieve system change.

This is far from virgin territory. And much of the work done to date confirms that scaling is a complex challenge, with few—if any—guaranteed solutions. When two of the current authors investigated the scaling challenge in their book *The Power of Unreasonable People* (2008), they ended up agreeing with Jeffrey Bradach (2003) of Bridgespan that the dynamics of replication and scaling call for "anything but a cookie-cutter process." One key factor, they noted, "is whether an enterprise has a strong theory of change, which uses systems thinking to map cause and effect among different parts of the system it is attempting to change."

Other important success factors, they noted, include "the growth model that the [enterprise] adopts, the market opportunity it targets, the sources of funding available to it, and the extent to which the broader business culture and operating environment catalyzes and supports entrepreneurial activity" (Dees et al., 2004). Clearly, picking the right problems to attack is critical, too: choose the wrong market or field, or the wrong solution, and scaling is much harder to accomplish.

The importance of such factors is illustrated in the growth of the environmental industries. Growing concerns about issues related to energy, climate change, and water, for example—and the prospects of higher risks and costs to mainstream businesses in those sectors—are ensuring that *environment*-oriented markets (as in "cleantech") are evolving faster than those for *social* solutions—particularly at the base of the pyramid. Interestingly, however, the cases we explore at the end of this chapter show how environment-related innovations such as solar energy are being cross-applied to challenges of poverty, redrawing the boundaries between the two agendas.

In what follows, we successively (1) review the ways in which the scaling agenda has increasingly cross-cut the worlds of social entrepreneurship and social investment; (2) lay out some of the key lessons learned to date; (3) explore the wider context in which social change is taking place—and introduce a five-stage model of change; (4) describe some of the ways in which the model is already being tested in areas such as solar energy and ecosystem services; and (5) offer our conclusions.

Scaling Social Change

Over the last decade, one of the most frequently repeated concerns among social entrepreneurs, philanthropists, investors, and public sector leaders has been the dearth of locally developed solutions to social and environmental problems that have been able to massively and successfully expand to have large scale impact. This concern has now become a clarion call to action in the face of ever-increasing threats to people and the planet wrought by climate change—including pandemics, water and food shortages, and energy crises—coupled with the poverty and human misery that ensue. Former president Bill Clinton specifically expressed the challenge of scale in reviewing school reform initiatives during his presidency noting that "Nearly every problem has been solved by someone somewhere. The frustration is that we can't seem to replicate [those solutions] anywhere else" (Olson, 1994).

Indeed, if one reviews the key selection criteria for the most widely known entities that search and select promising social entrepreneurs and their organizations, among the most important is "an explanation of how the organization will reach national or global scale" (Draper Richards Foundation, 2009) so that it improves the lives of significant numbers of people.

Despite E.F. Schumacher's famous book *Small is Beautiful* (1973), no one would doubt that the size, breadth, and scope of an organization is directly related to its impact—both positive and negative. To get some perspective of what "big" can mean, we only need to look at the world's leading company at the time of this writing, which, according to the *Financial Times*, is ExxonMobil. This oil and gas giant operates in over two hundred countries on an annual budget of five hundred billion dollars. As much as we may question this multinational's business ethics and environmental responsibility, the company has a significant impact on our lives and the environment in which we live.

Fortune 500 companies have influenced our mental constructs of what "scale" needs to represent for social entrepreneurial ventures and those of us working to support them. It predominantly has come to mean growing one organization from a locally spawned start-up to a multi-country entity, preferably operating across continents.

But as we increasingly are coming to realize, these companies only have been able to bloat out to "ExxonMobil-esque" size in large part because of the infrastructure or ecosystem—legal and fiscal—that governments have put in place to support their mega size, not to mention the critical involvement of financial markets including shareholders and consumers without which companies could not survive.

Visionary Wealth

Additionally, our ideas of what scale means has also been influenced by New Economy entrepreneurs. Over the last two decades, we have witnessed a period of enormous accumulation of wealth, power, and technology, mainly in the North. The last century and the beginning of the twenty-first have been characterized by the triumph of market economics. Business entrepreneurs made millions and shaped the aspirations of a worldwide public who dreamed of emulating them.

These entrepreneurial giants and their companies became household names practically overnight—Bill Gates, Richard Branson, Warren Buffett, George Soros, Ted Turner—followed by a younger generation that includes Jeff Skoll, Pierre Omidyar, Sergey Brin, Larry Page, and others. But the wealth generated benefited primarily educated and skilled populations. The New Economy was unable to bring in the majority of the world's population.

Fortunately, the most successful architects of the New Economy also had a social vision. Indeed, they are a main reason that social entrepreneurship has emerged on the global stage with such force and fanfare. How these moguls went about implementing their respective visions is well detailed in Matthew Bishop and Matthew Green's book, *Philanthrocapitalism: How the Rich Can Save the World and Why We Should Let Them* (2008). They describe how these pioneers are using their entrepreneurial skills and some of their capital to make a difference. And there is much to be celebrated as a result of their efforts, not the least of which is the practically viral global spread of the notion of entrepreneurship for social value creation.

Naturally, in seeking to tackle insurmountable social and environmental problems, these hugely powerful and wealthy individuals turned to the experience of growing their own companies to achieve their current global reach and impact. Hence, initially, conversations about achieving scale for impact were characterized by an emphasis on growing a single organization.

But the last few years have seen a substantive shift in that conversation. While the importance of scale is still at the forefront of many discussions—reinforced by publications such as this book—what has changed is the recognition that there are different ways to strengthen and spread a successful social innovation. The corporate model may not apply to scaling such innovations.

For one, success in the business world equals owning and selling a great product or service and being better than one's competitors at delivering them. And while a small or medium sized company can certainly be profitable, if you want to grow profits in the business world, you have to dominate market share through size. Just consider Microsoft, Wal-Mart, Toyota, Coca Cola, Shell, Starbucks, McDonald's, The Gap, and even The Body Shop.

Picking the Central Unit of Analysis

As Filipe Santos (2009) points out, one of the salient differences between social and commercial entrepreneurs is that the former are primarily driven to create value for society and the latter is primarily focused on appropriating value for shareholders and managers (albeit Santos notes that each must do some of the other—a wholly social value creating venture will not be sustainable, and a wholly value appropriating venture will not be legitimate).

As a consequence, the central unit of analysis for commercial business is the company because it is the locus of appropriation of rents through residual control rights over resources. This is not the case for social entrepreneurs. The central unit of analysis is not the organization—it is the sustainable solution and its underlying business model. The point is that one can scale a social venture to huge size and not make a dent in the issue. It is this realization that has triggered our conception of what "achieving scale" actually means in relation to systemic social change.

Santos' point of view is reinforced by history. The massive social changes that have taken place have never been solely attributed to a single organization. For example, the environmental movement, the women's movement, the civil rights movement, and the 2008 election of U.S. president Barack Obama—plus, unfortunately, the terrorist movement—have not occurred because a single organization grew to huge scale. These movements occur because of a coming together of many who united around a common cause. We see interesting parallels in the world of the humble—but extraordinary—slime mold (see box 5.1).

Box 5.1   Enter the slime mold

Nature also provides some brilliant examples of how sustainable change works. Enter a humble single-celled, amoeba-like organism—the slime mold. As Stephen Johnson (2001) notes, "For scientists trying to understand systems that use relatively simple components to build higher level intelligence, the slime mold may someday be seen as the equivalent of the finches and tortoises that Darwin observes on the Galápagos Islands."

As you read this, you may think you have never come across slime mold. But if you have taken a walk through the woods and come across a rotting log covered with a substance that looks like a dog got sick, what you are observing is slime mold in collective action. Slime mold feeds on decaying matter in nature.

Imagine a single-celled slime mold moving through the forest and coming across a rotting log. The log is massive in comparison to the miniscule slime mold (it is one-celled, after all). So altering the amount of cyclic AMP, a pheromone substance, triggers a "crowd aggregation" process released by the slime mold. If the slime cells emit enough cyclic AMP, clusters of cells form. Other slime mold cells begin following the pheromone trails, creating a positive feedback loop and drawing more cells to join the cluster. When the rotting log has disappeared, so too has the swarm of slime mold. Mission accomplished. The slime mold swarm disbands. Indeed, slime mold spends much of its life as one of thousands of distinct single-celled units, coming together only when the right conditions exist, that is, when there is a problem to tackle that it cannot do as a single-celled creature.

The interesting bit is that for years, scientists studying slime mold kept looking for the "elite" pacemaker cells that called the others to action. But they couldn't find them. It took a molecular biologist, Evelyn Fox Keller, teamed up with an applied mathematician, Lee Segel, to map out how simple agents following simple rules can generate amazingly complex structures. In sum, the slime mold cells were organizing themselves.

As Johnson (2001) notes, "We are naturally predisposed to think in terms of pacemakers, whether we're talking about fungi, political systems, or our own bodies. Our actions seem governed for the most part by the pacemaker cells in our brains, and for millennia we've build elaborate pacemaker cells into our social organizations, whether they come in the form of kings, dictators or city councilmen. Much of the world around us can be explained in terms of command systems and hierarchies." The central question here: How can we learn to apply similar principles to the scaling of social and environmental solutions in tomorrow's markets?

Meanwhile, if social media and open source innovation models are any guide to how the discourse on scale is moving, then we are in for an exciting time in shifting power dynamics. The corporate model for the last two hundred years has been based on a logic of organizational dominance and control as a means to appropriate as much value as possible. But the logic of social entrepreneurial ventures is about massively spreading their model so that it triggers the systemic social change sought. That intention, coupled with the scarcity of financial and human resources that characterize social entrepreneurial ventures, propels social entrepreneurs to seek alliances and partnerships as a way of scaling their transformational models. In contrast to the commercial enterprise, we might say that to be successful, social entrepreneurs need to give up control of their models and enthuse others with adopting them.

The Case of New Leaf Paper

Jeff Mendelsohn and New Leaf Paper are a perfect example of how giving up control of the business model is essential to achieving scale. Mendelsohn set out to transform the paper industry, one of the most polluting and resource intensive industries in the world. It is responsible for over a third of worldwide timber harvest and over 40 percent of all landfill waste in the United States. To change that behavior, he founded New Leaf Paper as a for-profit social enterprise in 1998.

The company embedded its social and environmental values into every product line and every business relationship. New Leaf Paper's innovative strategy is solving the classic "chicken or the egg" dilemma in the paper industry, in which both the supply side and the demand side of the market are unable to change their behavior. Leveraging the strength and clarity of the company's mission, New Leaf Paper developed a market for truly environmentally responsible papers and served this market through leading product innovation. Just over a decade later, New Leaf Paper's sales are over thirty million dollars.

What's more, New Leaf Paper items are manufactured 100 percent with renewable energy, making it the first paper company in the United States to adhere to this practice. Jeff notes that paper is one of the most visible purchases businesses make, and paper made with wind power and biogas energy helps reduce customers' carbon emissions footprint in a measurable way.

New Leaf is an unusual company in many ways, including its business model. It is essentially a distributor, but most distributors simply sell standard mill brand product while mills do all the branding and marketing. New Leaf does all the branding, and all the specifications of its products as well as its distribution.

The company develops mostly white paper, creating product lines that look like any other paper. The difference is in the ingredients. There is a hierarchy of preferred fibers that New Leaf clearly articulates, based on environmental impact. Post-consumer waste is at the top of the list, followed by agricultural products, which include cereal straws and corn stalks that are otherwise burned. Pre-consumer waste is next on the list, including unsold magazines and mill scraps. Sustainably harvested virgin fiber is last, including Forest Stewardship Council certified wood and nonwood sources such as hemp and kenaf.

New Leaf Paper set out to model the behavior it hopes to see in its competition and in the paper industry in general. Jeff acknowledges that New Leaf' is a "David" in comparison to the "Goliaths" of mainstream paper multinationals. But his strategy is one of continuous leadership and innovation in driving better and better environmental specifications in its products without losing sight of meeting the demands of the marketplace. Ultimately, scaling the business model through its appropriation by mainstream companies will prove to have far greater impact than growing New Leaf as an organization, even if it means achieving scale through self-immolation. Note that this outcome would be anathema for commercial companies whose success depends on achieving scale through their organization's market dominance.

Scaling to the Issue

Yet there are multiple challenges involved in moving the scale discourse from one that focuses on the organization as the unit of analysis to one that zeroes in on the issue and the business model. For one, the "scaling to the issue" approach means giving up "ownership" of the issue, and that is a tough call given the existence of egos. But more importantly perhaps is the reality that for the most part, philanthropists and investors fund organizations, not movements. That tendency drives social entrepreneurial ventures to work hard to differentiate themselves from others doing similar or complementary work—even when the issues addressed are huge. To go back to the slime mold, as a single-celled organism, eating through a rotting log is impossible. Joining up with others to do it is efficient and highly effective.

Then there is the ever-present challenge of capital. While social entrepreneurial ventures are set up as for-profit and nonprofits, every entrepreneurial venture begins as a nonprofit, whether intentionally or not. For those set up as nonprofits "on purpose," the "philanthrocapitalists" have provided the critical capital to stimulate the initial growth of highly promising innovative ventures—capital that no risk averse, profit-seeking individual or group would have provided. The problem is that just as these highly successful entrepreneurs would have never scaled their companies on philanthropy alone, it is also evident that enterprises that set out to drive systemic social change will be hard pressed to achieve their goals on the back of philanthropic funding. Consequently, supporting nonprofit social ventures seeking systemic change is about supporting the "ecosystem" that will underpin viral spread of the model through alliances and partnerships.

Donors, too, need to let go of the ego and recognize that they have to form alliances and partnerships to fund and support the change they seek.

Conversely, investors seeking some financial return on a social investment must be immensely patient and in it for the long haul. So far, social investors seeking financial returns are looking for the "next microfinance." Will it be the emerging clean tech industry? Perhaps base of pyramid markets? What people tend to forget is that the first IPO in microfinance took place more than thirty years after the industry first began to form, and that trail was pioneered by initially small social enterprises that kept perfecting their business models. These industries don't emerge in a New York minute, much as everyone would like.

Make no mistake. Scaling an organization is tough. But scaling the entities involved in the supporting ecosystem that makes change happen is immensely harder, as noted by a recent Monitor Group study (Karamchandani et al., 2009). Most emerging markets today are caught in a dilemma of how to implement models that promise strong economic growth, underpinned by a social vision that incorporates their poor millions into the system and its benefits without doing further environmental harm. The study's authors conducted extensive research into hundreds of market-based solutions in emerging markets around the world, with a particular focus on India. As they report, the most successful pass two tests: they are self-funding and they operate at sufficient scale to make a difference to masses of poor people.

The report identifies seven business models that the authors believe have the best chances of success. None of those models would work without extensive networks for backward and forward linkages and partnerships to improve distribution, customer education and awareness, credit provision, human capital, and sharing fixed costs. Few entities can organize entire value chains as BRAC and the Aravind Eye Care Hospital have done. For both, it has taken much time and it is expensive. As the authors note, "System effects greatly complicate the work of many market-based solutions since in most cases markets are much less developed and there is no surrounding ecosystem to plug into." They go on to note that "effort will be required from other parties, namely commercial investors, impact investors, traditional aid donors and philanthropists and large corporations. Finally, building successful market-based solutions will benefit from support from government in the form of business-enabling policies and regulations, better subsidy regimes, SME policies and other rules of the road."

While almost all foundations and investors are aware to some degree of the futility of band-aid approaches to poverty, few are willing to invest in kick starting the entire ecosystem to dramatically accelerate improvements in livelihoods, governance, and transparency. One of the exceptions is John McCall MacBain, a self-made Canadian billionaire who founded the *Auto Trader* classified advertising empire. In looking how to make a difference in the world, he saw the opportunity to completely reboot a country, in this case Liberia.

The Case of Liberia

So why Liberia? (McCall MacBain, 2009). First, its size—it has around four million people. Ellen Johnson Sirleaf, the country's leader, is bent on reform and has put in place a poverty reduction strategy that is built on peace and security, governance and rule of law, infrastructure and basic services, and economic regeneration. The country has two ports, plentiful natural resources, and a tradition of exporting. Fifty years ago it was second only to Japan in terms of rubber exports. But between 1990 and 2005, Liberia was beset with civil war, despotic rulers, and corruption.

The election of Johnson Sirleaf offered new hope. McCall MacBain sold *Auto Trader* in 2006 and set up a foundation to promote health and the environment in the developing world. But rather than parcel out grants to different entities, he put almost the full force of his foundation into rebuilding the country, its health, and education system.

He also was the main investor behind Buchanan Renewable Energies (BRE), which he set up together with fellow Canadian Joel Strickland. BRE discarded the extractive rubber industry model and set up a power generation arm to build biomass stations to provide energy for the country, attracting a US$112 million loan from the U.S. government funded Overseas Private Investment Corporation (OPIC). BRE also entered into partnerships with thousands of small rubber farmers. Under the agreement, BRE builds the roads to the plantations, removes the old unproductive rubber trees, pays the farmers for them, and helps them prepare the land to plant new saplings grown in a BRE nursery. Because the trees take between five and seven years to produce latex, BRE helps farmers plant cash crops in between the trees that provide an income for the farmers while they wait for the latex to kick in. Additionally, BRE trains and employs around one thousand people.

According to *Time* magazine (Perry, 2009), since May 2008, BRE has repaired six hundred kilometers of dirt roads, leveled thousands of acres of rubber, and identified an additional two hundred and fifty thousand hectares. Meanwhile, BRE catalyzed overseas investment capital to the tune of US$132 million in 2007—and more direct foreign investment is coming in since in iron ore, timber, palm oil, and construction. Schools and hospitals have reopened, and while Liberia's problems are far from over, there is new hope and a new vision for the country where war is not the only job in town.

Catalyzing and supporting the kind of massive systemic change being implemented in Liberia has necessitated an "ecosystem investment" mindset. McCall MacBain took the initial risk but drew in government, entrepreneurs, other investors, multilateral and bilateral development agencies, and most importantly, the farmers and their families into the process, each contributing from their separate vantage points to creating the collective development "swarm." And he and his colleagues are in it for the long haul.

The conversation on scaling is maturing and evolving to a new level, one that acknowledges that while individuals can kick start initial change, systemic solutions to overwhelming challenges need to be tackled collectively and on many fronts. How we continue to pull other essential partners into the task is the current challenge before us.

Pathways to Scale

So how do we engage this central challenge of investing in "ecosystems of change"?

Necessarily, the spotlight is opening out, moving on from the heroic figure of the social entrepreneur or intrapreneur, beyond the solutions he or she may propose, to the wider market and political context in which the solutions compete for survival and success. In the third year of a three-year program funded by the Skoll Foundation for Social Entrepreneurship, we too moved beyond social entrepreneurship (SustainAbility, 2007) and intrapreneurship (SustainAbility, 2008) to consider the wider economic context within which new social, environmental, and governance solutions are advanced, in *The Phoenix Economy* (Volans, 2009).

Drawing on field research, interviews and surveys, we developed a simple, five-stage "Pathways to Scale" model of change (figure 5.1). The model is being coevolved with leaders, entrepreneurs, and investors to chart the trajectory of their efforts toward greater impact.

In the model, Stage 1 is "Eureka!"—the creative moment where new opportunities for innovative solutions become apparent. Stage 2, the "Experiment," is where entrepreneurs test, prototype, fail, learn, and adapt new solutions. It is the early stage venture. Stage 3, the "Enterprise," is where experiments become organizations and initiatives with more developed business models, invested in by a broad range of investors. Stage 3 is about growing a business.

Yet if anything close to system change can begin to happen, there is a need to shift the spotlight from individual enterprises to the wider influence

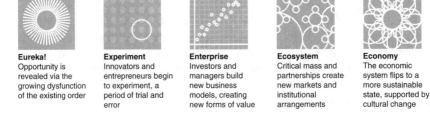

Figure 5.1   Five-stage "Pathways to Scale" model.

in society and markets. Stage 4, focusing on the creation of an "Ecosystem" of change agents, is about creating new markets, incentives, and frameworks for solutions to diffuse and mainstream. Accelerating change is critical to embed the new cultural codes and forms of governance into the mainstream functioning of the "Economy," represented by stage 5.

While stages 1–3 are extremely important, the main focus of our attention is on the transition from stage 3 to 4. Moving from individual business models to broader ecosystems requires collaborative forms of leadership. And addressing the barriers to scaling social innovations necessitates not only investigating the linear value chains of the new business models created by entrepreneurs, but also involves systemically mapping and engaging all key actors in the relevant parts of the economy. No small challenge.

Ultimately, if anything like a truly sustainable and equitable future is to be achieved as the world pushes toward a human population of nine (or even ten) billion, entrepreneurial initiatives will need to scale up further to stage 5 system change—typified by broad-based market and societal adoption of new mindsets, models, and technologies. Success in moving from stages 4 to 5 will involve the transformation of political priorities, governance process, market rules, and cultures.

It is an uncomfortable fact that economic and social systems—like ecosystems—go through periods of convulsive change. Social and environmental entrepreneurs and intrapreneurs may be in the spotlight as never before, but we are seeing a shakeout that will hit both weak and strong organizations. "Down cycles weed out weak players," Jim Fruchterman of Benetech commented in the interviews conducted for our report *The Phoenix Economy*, and, sadly, "some great groups get weeded out because of bad timing." Many survey respondents were increasingly somber, seeing a profoundly challenging period ahead.

This should be of concern to leaders in the public, private, and citizen sectors alike, given that the work of many entrepreneurs spotlights and seeks to address critical issues such as climate change, water scarcity, poverty, disease, corruption, and an expanding array of human rights concerns. Entrepreneurs are worth watching because they are experimenting with new technologies and business models, underscoring the potential for transformational solutions and change (SustainAbility, 2007).

One recurrent problem in change processes is that emergent enterprises have a weaker voice in the relevant politics than vested interests—including incumbent industries and organizations. In what follows, we do not aim to speak for the entrepreneurs who responded to our surveys, but instead to spotlight some of the issues they raised for decision-makers and policymakers. In this spirit we introduced—and are continuing to develop—a "Manifesto" for political leaders, a "Prospectus" for business leaders and investors, and a "Syllabus" for business educators. Box 5.2 highlights some of the things entrepreneurs want from the public sector and governments.

Box 5.2   Toward a scaling manifesto for governments

Here are some of the things governments can do to support the scaling of social and environmental solutions, illustrated by reference to some of the organizations profiled in *The Phoenix Economy*:

1. Redesign spending packages

There is an opportunity—indeed an urgent need—to build public support for scaling social and environmental solutions into the growing number of national bailout plans, "Global New Deal" packages, and spending plans to support industrial redevelopment. Here we welcome the work that the United Nations Environment Programme (UNEP) has been doing toward a "Global Green New Deal" and the efforts of organizations such as the Cleantech Group, Green for All, and Solarcentury to influence the often panicked politics around bailouts and the resulting targets for government spending.

2. Get targets right

To ensure effectiveness and accountability, governments must set, publish, monitor, and report on progress toward ambitious targets on key priority areas such as climate change. Partnerships, once again, will be crucial to help governments understand which targets to set. The highly entrepreneurial Global Footprint Network is building momentum by working with governments around the world to build dashboards of metrics and management systems to include natural assets in national economic accounts; and the governments of Ireland and the United Kingdom are working with AMEE, which calculates carbon footprints, enabling aggregated statistics to be reported.

3. Use procurement as a driver for change

All levels of government can help to drive the transition by adapting their policies in areas such as public purchasing, an approach that has been trialed by initiatives such as C40. Buying green—or more broadly in ways that are "future-friendly"—on a larger scale by aggregating purchasing inexorably drives market transformations. A growing number of examples exist, from police departments requesting the purchase of electric vehicles, to building standards being upgraded, and new green directives being integrated into public purchasing guidelines. Among organizations we are working with on this front is the Paris-based EcoVadis, which is building a range of safety, health, environmental, and human rights standards into supplier management software packages.

4. Improve market governance

Markets are social constructions. Sometimes they just happen, sometimes they are created by design. Public sector efforts are likely to be most effective in providing a platform for scale where they learn from innovators creating a new generation of market governance rules and processes. Such players include the Extractive Industry Transparency Initiative; the Forest Stewardship Council; Healthcare Without Harm; the Roundtable on Sustainable Palm Oil and the Roundtable on Sustainable Biofuels; and the Marine Stewardship Council.

5. Support future-oriented infrastructure

Governments, at all levels, need to think beyond curative solutions and leverage the intelligence of entrepreneurs in the design of innovative and effective policies and interventions, from public health spending to city blueprints. This trend is illustrated by such examples as Better Place and the World Resource Institute's EMBARQ, both working closely with governments around the world on the design of sustainable transport policies and infrastructures for low-carbon solutions. This also applies to sprawling slums where many more people live, an agenda informed by the extraordinary work of pioneers such as Himanshu Parikh.

6. Grow social innovation clusters

Innovation clusters are a forceful expression of the ecosystem approach. Governments have a critical role to play in creating clusters that bring together enterprises with investors and other stakeholders to explore scale, a process that has begun in the United Kingdom with the National Endowment for Science, Technology & the Arts (NESTA). Similarly, MaRS in Canada is a private-public partnership designed to incubate and foster cross-sector collaboration for the development of new technologies in areas such as healthcare. It is also something that the Singapore Economic Development Board (EDB) is working toward in the city-state. Interestingly, EDB has wider, regional ambitions—something that other government agencies could well emulate.

7. Culture change

It's never easy to achieve cultural change, but the world will inevitably undergo a series of cultural transformations in the wake of massive, discontinuous economic upheaval. Here the work of Participant Media (most notable for Al Gore's film *An Inconvenient Truth*) has been inspirational in its use of mainstream media and entertainment to raise awareness of critical societal concerns and encourage a positive paradigm shift in behaviors. The success of Celador Productions' film *Slumdog Millionaire* also suggests ways in which difficult social and environmental issues can be brought to a global audience—on a relative (to Hollywood) shoestring budget. More government support needs to be directed toward such media enterprises, guided by the aspirational goal of Ashoka: to help make "Everyone a Change-maker."

> With a more specific remit, the work of the Oxford Health Alliance on building cultures of preventive health to slow the accelerating global wave of chronic disease has not yet attracted enough support from governments, but nonetheless signals a possible way forward—as do the approaches of others such as Virgance—which exploits the power of social networks to drive change.

Scaling Solar Energy for the Poor

We have reviewed the way in which the scaling debate is evolving, at least from our perspective, and introduced the Pathways to Scale model. Now we turn to the question of how this approach can be applied to a particular challenge: solar energy for the poor. "We want to turn the base of the pyramid into energy producers, not just consumers," explains Nick Sireau, chief executive of Solar Aid, as he lays out his vision of success for providing renewable energy access to the world's poor (Sireau and Leggett, 2009).

It is tall aspiration. An estimated 1.6 billion people in the world live without access to electricity, often relying on kerosene—which is both prohibitively expensive and hazardous. Yet most of them live in the so-called sun-belt, the equatorial regions of the planet where the intensity of sunlight is the highest, suggesting that their energy demand could be met through renewable energy technologies that already exist.

The barriers to scale are massive, well beyond the influence of a single organization. So consider some of the ways in which "solar entrepreneurs" are using the ecosystem approach to overcome some of these challenges.

The Case of Solar Aid

For Solar Aid, whose solution and business model is to help the poor set up small enterprises to make a living out of assembling or selling solar energy devices, the key barriers to scale include disproportionate import tariffs on solar equipment—for example, 40 percent taxes in Malawi; the lack of finance for the poor to buy solar products; and a weak local entrepreneurial culture. Ironically, according to Sireau, some of these problems have been aggravated by the aid mentality and dependency that decades of aid have generated among the poor.

Like most social entrepreneurs, Solar Aid faces an uphill battle against challenging conditions. The main problem is that Solar Aid's entrepreneurial solution is ahead of the market that will support it to scale. "We are creating distribution channels where markets don't yet exist," Sireau explains—a problem that pretty much all social entrepreneurs face.

Since its inception in 2007, Solar Aid has manufactured ten thousand micro-solar products in four production centers in Kenya, Tanzania,

Malawi, and Zambia, employing some forty local people in the production, assembly, and distribution processes. Their ambition, however, is much higher, and involves replacing all kerosene lamps in Africa by 2050 with solar-powered lights. Their micro-franchising model, "Sunny Money," relies on micro entrepreneurs that commercialize the products. Their goal is to have produced thirty thousand units in 2009, and five hundred thousand by 2010.

However, as Solar Aid's practical learning evolves on how to tackle the problem more effectively, so does their business model. In partnership with industrial designers and manufacturers, they are now thinking to mass-produce affordable solar lamps. "We are evolving towards a larger scale model," says John Keane (2009), Solar Aid's director of programs in Dar es Salaam, Tanzania, who recognizes that one of the biggest challenges to scaling up their activities is not only to grow their own impact, but also "to come up with a new distribution strategy by working together with existing distribution networks run by others."

When asked what would these partnerships look like, Keane points to the massive growth of the mobile phone market across Africa, and asks: How are all these phones going to be charged? "We need to generate new business opportunities for solar energy," he says, going on to outline the creating of forward linkages and partnerships in their business model, including "solar recharging stations" and a "pay-as-you-go" model developed by *Sunlabob* in Laos, whose business model relies on selling "hours" of solar light to villagers who wish to recharge energy devices such as lanterns, mobile phones, or radios (Sunlabob Renewable Energy, 2008).

The Case of Grameen Shakti

In Bangladesh, Grameen Shakti has installed 220,000 solar home systems, 6,000 biogas plants, and 25,000 improved stoves, contributing to radically enhance the lives of millions of people. While this is the most impressive success to date, to a large extent its success is due to the link to its sister organization—the Grameen banking model—which has helped Grameen Shakti's ecosystem access loans that enable poor people to afford the costs of the technology.

Grameen Shakti has transformed whole villages, generated thousands of jobs, and prevented hundreds of thousands of tons of greenhouse gases from being released into the atmosphere. In 2009, Dipal Barua, its founder, received the US$1.5 million Zayed Future Energy Prize and declared that it was his dream to create one hundred thousand "green jobs" in Bangladesh.

For Kamal Rijal (2007), an energy policy advisor to the United Nations Development Programme (UNDP), any understanding of the ecosystem approach depends on an understanding of the relevant politics. For him, "scaling up pilot projects requires political commitment." In his view, "reducing the risk to investors and strengthening institutional capacity is one of the keys to achieving scale' where government can play its part."

By setting the rules of the game, governments have the ability to accelerate new markets. These range from targeted taxes and subsidies (e.g., eliminating import tariffs of solar equipment) to the ease and speed of regulatory procedures (e.g., for setting up a business and for customs clearance procedures) or providing incentives and guarantees to commercial banks that can get the financial market in place for solar entrepreneurs and consumers. To a large extent, the success of the Grameen Shakti model also owes much to the lower interest rates guaranteed by the Bangladeshi government.

The Case of India's Solar Loan Programme

Between 2003 and 2007, the India Solar Loan Programme, led by the United Nations Environment Programme (UNEP), invested US$7.6 million to support financing solar home systems in southern India. The alliance involved two of India's major banking groups—Canara Bank and Syndicate Bank—as well as Grameen banks, and a partnership with the UN Foundation and Shell Foundation. The project provided an interest rate subsidy to lower the cost to customers for the financing of solar home systems.

This support to the banking sector provided an incentive for banks to offer lower interest rates, longer payback periods, and smaller deposits. "Asking customers to pay cash for solar systems meant asking them to pay upfront an amount equal to 20 years of electricity bills," explained Jyoti Painuly, a UN senior energy planner. Throughout the program, more than two thousand commercial bank branches participated providing almost twenty thousand loans, with Grameen banks leading the financing in rural areas. Altogether, the impact was a thirteen-fold increase in the number of solar power units being financed within the scheme's area in southern India (BBC, 2007).

The Case of East Africa's Young Solar Entrepreneur Challenge

An example of how the Pathways to Scale model has been applied practically and played out on the ground is the case of solar energy entrepreneurs in East Africa. In partnership with the Tällberg Foundation, a series of workshops in Tanzania–where 98 percent of the population has no access to electricity—brought together solar energy enterprises with youth employment networks, micro-finance providers, training institutions, and large-scale popular media platforms to explore how to address some of the barriers to entrepreneurial business models in order to scale up solar lighting opportunities in East Africa.[1]

Relying on background research conducted by the Volans Pathways to Scale Program, participants discussed the solutions proposed by solar energy enterprises—and considered the barriers they face in their operating environment. The workshop focused on the individual interests of participants: solar enterprises, notably the interest of D.light Design East Africa—a solar light consumer products business—to develop distribution networks and create awareness and visibility for solar lighting. Youth movements, such as YES Kenya and the Tanzanian Youth Coalition, had an interest of creating new, practical solutions to address youth unemployment. The interest of Femina HIP, the mass popular media platform promoting reproductive health, to move beyond health and to communicate livelihood opportunities for poor young people, and those of investors in renewable energy sought to fund innovative, large scale strategies to diffuse the access to renewable energy.

"We've spent 10 years building a media platform to raise the awareness of young Tanzanians on issues of reproductive health and HIV Aids," said Minou Fuglesang (2009), founder and director of Femina HIP, which reaches two million young people through three hundred distribution partnership, adding, "we'd like to use this infrastructure to promote awareness about solar energy enterprises with young people."

A number of bilateral partnerships were brokered between the actors involved, providing linkages to overcome barriers such as the lack of consumer awareness and distribution. Some of these partnerships have already been implemented successfully, creating awareness of solar energy opportunities. Even more importantly, the initiatives have promoted the role-model of the "solar entrepreneur" among young people, potentially with an impact on more than two million young people. In the process, a more ambitious collaborative proposition also emerged: The *Young Solar Entrepreneur Challenge East Africa* to build an extensive new distribution network for solar products by providing unemployed youth with entrepreneurship opportunities. By 2020, the partnership aims to create fifty thousand youth jobs and provide solar lighting to fifteen million people.

The roles of different partners were sketched out along three channels: process channel, support channel, and finance channel, and are summarized in figure 5.2. These include:

- Product suppliers responsible for the availability of products, the functioning of the distribution network, the supply of spare parts, and after sales service.
- Youth network to mobilize, train, and refer organizations to micro-finance institutions. Youth groups to act as small enterprises, carry the responsibility for the loans, and employ peer pressure for loan repayment. Young Entrepreneurs to sell lights on a cash and credit basis.
- Micro-finance institutions to supply credit to youth groups and other SMEs in the scheme.
- Mobile phone operators (under discussion) would be marketing partners and provide a mobile payment system, drawing on their interest to eliminate the

barrier to selling mobile phone airtime credits since people can't recharge their phones.

- Media to lead with awareness building and education, following the early success of the "Solar Entrepreneur" supplements published by Femina HIP.

"We are too comfortable in our own mental models and old ways of working, at individual and institutional levels," commented Carl Mossfeldt (2009), vice president of Tällberg Foundation, when evaluating the success of the media partnership between D.light Design and Femina HIP. "Designing strategic conversations between stakeholders around concrete delivery models and large-scale opportunities is critical for the way forward."

Currently, having already developed media material on solar entrepreneurs for TV and a printed magazine reaching two million young people, D.light Design and Femina HIP, the health awareness NGO, have entered into a formal public-private partnership to spearhead a national campaign.

This new joint initiative, called "The Right to Safe Lights," is focusing on potential youth entrepreneurs, school children, and maternal clinics as well as on the general public to raise awareness about the powerful use of the sun to provide energy access and to eliminate expensive and polluting "killer fuels" such as kerosene.

The partnership was recently chosen by Mary Robinson, former president of Ireland and UN human rights commissioner, to be showcased as

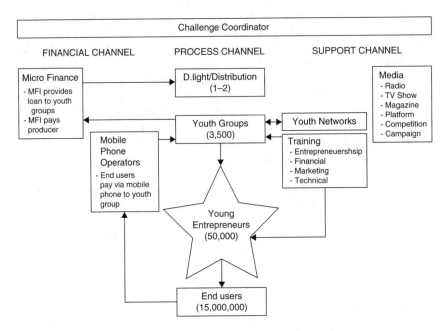

Figure 5.2   The Young Solar Entrepreneur Challenge East Africa.

best practice at a regional deliberation on climate and energy by social impact investors, demonstrating the self-organizing effects that this kind of action can have in the broader ecosystem.

Conclusion

We are in the early stages of a new agenda for social entrepreneurship, one that focuses on the shift from "Enterprises" to "Ecosystems," and where social and environmental solutions and business models to some of the most complex challenges of our time gain traction to reshape markets and political possibilities. The scaling agenda can only become more important as environmental, social, and governance challenges press in ever more urgently.

The metaphor of ecosystems is increasingly used to explore the strategic possibilities for an organization in its environment (Bloom and Dees, 2008). In the innovation literature, Marco Iansiti and Roy Levien (2004) identify firms that act as "keystone" players in an ecosystem. Just like keystone species play a pivotal role in keeping the equilibrium of biological ecosystem, these players provide the organizational links that create the most value within the system, simultaneously ensuring its survival and prosperity. This systemic value creation occurs primarily through "platform leadership." The keystone player develops ways of offering solutions to others in the ecosystem, playing a catalytic role in the acceleration, diffusion and adoption of new solutions.

Solar Aid is a good example of a keystone player. For Jeremy Leggett, chairman of Solar Aid, scale can only be achieved by accelerating connections: "The name of the game is to help networks of entrepreneurs make money by [having Solar Aid] become an enabler of the design and the manufacturing of solar solutions. In shaping the markets for our solutions we need to build on existing movements and platforms as much as we can" (Sireau and Leggett, 2009). The evidence suggests that solar energy enterprises that have found ways of aligning other economic actors behind their proposed business model have had phenomenal success.

The impact investors that have shaped the first wave of social entrepreneurship by backing and betting on the figure of change-makers and heroic individuals have done much to help the field emerge. Now, however, it is necessary to consider investing in efforts that seek to remove barriers from the system, and enable the unleashing of broader markets for social change. Social entrepreneurs and intrapreneurs are likely to keep at the forefront of these efforts. But those that with a catalytic mindset, seeking to realign ecosystems behind proposed solutions and business models, are likely to do better than those that stick to the growth of their individual enterprises. The incentives that investors provide to move from competition to collaboration will play a key role.

Drawing from lessons that range from social movements to those of fungus, ants, and the natural world, we conclude that creating collaborative approaches to overcome barriers to scale is one of the most promising areas for future strategic action and investment.

Note

1. This work was conducted in partnership and with the strategic support of the Tällberg Foundation in Sweden, as part of their Rework the World initiative: www. tallbergfoundation.org.

6

Moving from Loose Global Associations to Linked Geographic Networks

Jon Huggett

Over the past decade a number of loose global associations of NGOs have become more deliberately linked geographic networks: "integrators." In the process, these organizations have been able to grow dramatically. This chapter takes stock of the "integrator" approach—demonstrating how it works, exploring the reasons for its emergence, and discussing the pros and cons of becoming an integrator. (Box 6.1 provides definitions of the terms associated with "integrating" that are used in this chapter.)

Box 6.1 Definitions

NGO: "Non-Governmental Organization" (NGO), "Nonprofit," "Non-Profit Organization" (NPO), "Not-for-Profit," and "Third-Sector Organization" (TSO) are terms used around the world interchangeably. They describe organizations that are neither part of a government, nor are businesses run for profit. This chapter reflects common parlance.

"Social enterprise" could also be used to describe the NGO networks discussed in this chapter: few are supported entirely by donations; some run sizeable businesses. While reasonable people disagree on the exact definition of social enterprise, most include organizations ranging from NGOs that charge fees through to businesses with both a social mission and a profit goal.

Linked Geographic Network: This chapter is about international networks of legally independent NGOs in different geographies. Most are global networks of country organizations, such as Save the Children or Médecins Sans Frontières (MSF). Each constituent NGO is a separate legal entity responsible to its own national board. The law on charities in many countries requires that a nonprofit be established independently in that jurisdiction. Legal frameworks vary from country to country and often rule against control from abroad.

The network does not "own" the constituent NGOs in the way that a for-profit multinational might own its subsidiaries. It may describe itself as a "confederation" (e.g., Oxfam), or "a federation" (e.g., World Vision). Constituent NGOs may share legal agreements, for example, over the use of the brand name.

Links among NGOs within a network can include: a branding; a consistent mission, goals, strategy, and point of view; shared services; transfers of money and resources from rich countries to the developing world; sharing of practices; and personal relationships.

Loose Association: Some of the oldest NGO networks in the world remain loose associations, and are not the focus of this chapter. They are often described as "movements" rather than networks.

Scaling: "Scaling" has come to have several distinct, albeit complementary, definitions in common parlance. Sometimes it means improved results or impact; sometimes it means organizational growth; sometimes scaling implies growing to the point where "economies of scale" are possible, or enhanced.

In this chapter we focus on linked geographic networks that have grown substantially over an extended period. Scaling in this chapter, then, refers to organizational scaling. However, as the chapter notes, in many cases scaling of impact has been both the reason for and the result of organizational scaling.

The integrator approach seeks to eliminate the traditional tradeoffs between centralization and decentralization. Integrators globalize while remaining highly localized, although at considerable cost of money and time. They justify the extra cost with the benefits of coherence (or avoiding the costs of incoherence). The integrator approach has parallels in the private sector, where in recent years a new pattern of "globalized" firms has emerged, distinct from the traditional spectrum of centralized and decentralized multinationals.

The integrator approach is possible because of falling costs of communication and cooperation. The cost of coherence, while significant, is no longer prohibitive. NGO networks can now enjoy the economies of scale previously only available to businesses or centralized NGOs. Conversely, the cost of incoherence is rising as NGOs operate in an increasingly globalized world where programs, advocacy, and fund-raising no longer exist in national compartments.

Integrating global NGO networks appear to use three strategies to varying degrees: moving beyond "entrepreneurial" leadership to "managerial" leadership, beyond mission to impact, and beyond organizational structure to complementary relationships or "complementarity."

Managerial leadership characterizes each of the integrating global NGO networks surveyed. This model of leadership contrasts with the approach of many "social entrepreneurs" (now receiving much attention), or "heroic leadership" (often seen in businesses of comparable size). Managerial leaders provide an effective decision-making service to the heroes in the field, drawing on the "wisdom of crowds," rather than taking on the role of a more traditional, hierarchical leader and "setting direction."

While a shared mission is sufficient to hold together a loose association, an integrating network also needs a *shared goal for impact*. This shared goal sets direction, enables decisions, and motivates donors and employees alike. Without shared goals, an NGO network risks evolving into an archipelago of activities around a cause.

Integrating networks surveyed are well characterized by many internal webs of *complementarity* among member organizations and individuals. Different members specialize to serve the network at scale. The resulting interdependent relationships tie the networks together.

A variety of different structural and legal paths to integration exist, with no one model yet predominating. The integrator pattern is still "work-in-progress" for each of the NGO networks surveyed. None report that that they have "arrived," or that progress is easy. The next ten years will be as instructive as the last.

The Emergence of the Integrator Approach

Traditionally, NGO networks have grown geographically by a range of approaches. Lindenberg and Bryant (2001) described a continuum including: (1) separate independent organizations; (2) weak umbrella organizations; (3) confederations; (4) federations; and (5) unitary corporate organizations. At one end of the continuum, the unitary corporate organizations "radiated" out from their center, retaining the benefits of ease of control. At the other end "replication" created many local organizations. Between the two, a range of options traded off the relative benefits of decentralization or centralization.

Huggett et al. (2009) identified an emerging approach—integration—that does not fit on this continuum. The integrator approach combines many of the benefits of replication and "radiation" but adds considerable costs. Integrating allows NGO networks to globalize without centralizing. Figure 6.1 provides a summary chart of the continuum, including integrators. Table 6.1 captures the pros and cons of the various growth trajectories.

The following sections explore the more traditional radiation and replication paths to growth.

Radiation

Americares, Feed the Children, Human Rights Watch, and The Nature Conservancy have each radiated out from a dominant NGO. Each of these four organizations has an American hub. This suggests the importance of fund-raising in the "home" country—it can get harder to raise money, advocate, and create programs beyond the home country. Absolute Return

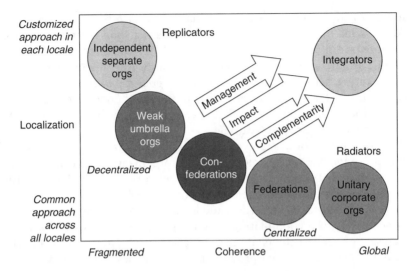

Figure 6.1 Breaking the tradeoff between coherence and localization.

Table 6.1 Pros and cons of various approaches to growth (Bridgespan)

Pattern	Centrally controlled NGOs *with sites in different countries* "Radiation"	Associations or partnerships around a founding NGO "Replication"	Networks of NGOs sharing strategy, brand and resources "Integration"
Pros	+ Coherence + Ease of control	+ "Multi-local": easier to raise funds, create programs, advocate in each country	+ Coherence + "Multi-local"
Cons	Can be harder to raise money, advocate, and create programs beyond home country	Can become incoherent beyond replication	Hard to implement: investment of time and resources may not pay back
Examples	• Americares • Feed the Children • Nature Conservancy	• Red Cross/Red Crescent • Scouts • YMCA	• Habitat for Humanity • Save the Children • WorldVision

for Kids (ARK) has radiated out from a London base of fund-raising to operations in Africa.

Radiating NGOs can experience tension between local supporters and the "head office." The Nature Conservancy is the largest radiator in the world with over one billion dollars of revenue (Annual Report, 2008). John Sawhill, the CEO of The Nature Conservancy from 1989 to 2000, had maintained a policy of "One Conservancy" with tight control over strategy. At the same time he allowed some local autonomy, for example, on fund-raising. His successor, Steve McCormick, experienced "backlash" when he tried to centralize further (Grossman and Wei-Skillern, 2003).

Some radiating NGOs have explored giving local NGOs more independence to help them raise more money and to ease program development. Sesame Workshop, for example, established an entity in India to support local development.

Replication

The YMCA is a prime example of a replicator. It is the oldest global NGO movement. It was founded in 1844 in London, and in 1851 opened locations in Boston and Montreal. Now, there are YMCAs in 124 countries. However, the central association is small and reports no shared results.

Founded in 1863, the Red Cross and Red Crescent is another example of replication. The Red Cross and Red Crescent can claim to be the largest NGO movement in the world with combined revenue estimated to be over eight billion dollars. There is a Red Cross or Red Crescent in 186 countries of the world. In some countries, such as the United States of America, a series of local Red Cross organizations exist, each set up as a separate legal entity. Worldwide, there is both the International Federation of Red Cross and Red Crescent Societies, and the International Committee of the Red Cross.

The century-old scouting movement—Boy Scouts, Girl Guides, Girl Scouts, and so on—provides another classic example of the replication approach.

Each of these broad organizations is "multi-local" (few in the United States would know the American Red Cross was a replicant from Europe.). However, as Lindenberg and Bryant (2001) commented on the global NGOs that they studied, "it is not yet clear that they have become more flexible and adaptable as opposed to simply big.

Integration

Described by one of its leaders as "more of a 'movement' a decade ago," Save the Children has been integrating worldwide. This NGO is now purposefully building what its leaders call a "Unified Presence." Before 2004, more than twenty member countries ran operations, fund-raising, and advocacy programs. As a result, there were often numerous (sometimes duplicative) offices in beneficiary countries. Half of beneficiary country programs are now unified. The "Unified Presence" program has driven harmonization across the network in finance, budgeting, reporting, and planning.

A diverse group of other NGO networks, ranging widely in size, have also been trying to integrate. The African Medical and Research Fund (AMREF), an over-seventy-million-dollar, nine-hundred-person NGO network across Africa, Europe, and America is working to turn "franchise AMREF" into "One AMREF."

Scaling from Integration

Over the last decade, Save the Children has more than tripled its revenue from $350M to over $1.2B. Founded in 1951, WorldVision is now the largest of the integrators with over $2B in revenue worldwide, having grown from less than $900M in 2000. Other integrators have also scaled significantly. Oxfam, since 1997, has almost tripled worldwide revenues from just over $350M to nearly $1B. Habitat for Humanity International grew from $454M in 1999 to $1,481 in 2007. Opportunity International has grown at 22 percent compound annual growth rate for a decade.

Each of these networks has grown partly because it has been able to become both globally more coherent without pulling out its local "grass roots." Traditionally the choice was centralize or decentralize, as reflected in the continuum laid out by Lindenberg and Bryant. Integrating networks have scaled by globalizing and localizing together.

Private Sector Parallels

Roberts (2003) categorized multinational firms in three models that roughly parallel radiators, replicators, and integrators:

- international (very centralized headquarters with a focus on efficiency);
- multi-local (units in different countries have a lot of autonomy with a focus on serving the local market); and
- global or transnational (a mix of multi-local and international).

The tradeoffs among the three mirror the tradeoffs among the three NGO network models. In particular he noted: "global models require intensive communication and can be expensive to run."

The next section looks at the benefits of integration, and how they have led to scaling. The key drawback to the integrated approach is that it is both expensive and hard.

Why Do Global NGO Networks Integrate?

Global NGO networks often begin to integrate to improve the delivery and content of programs (activities and services), strengthen their advocacy efforts, and to be more effective in fund-raising. Economics can also motivate an NGO to integrate.

Impact in Program Areas

The embarrassment of poor coordination of humanitarian relief has motivated some global NGOs to begin to integrate. Different members of the same network would each arrive in a disaster area separately with uncoordinated and duplicated efforts (Huggett et al., 2009). Humanitarian NGO networks that are integrating increasingly coordinate their member organizations in response to disasters.

Humanitarian aid has more than doubled in the past two decades; this trend reflects the results of better coordination, as noted by Webster and Walker (2009).

Individual NGOs have separate claims for how their impact has grown over this period. For example, according to World Vision, in 2008, "Over 3.6 million children benefited from sponsorship" versus 1.2 million in 2000 (www.wvi.org).

Programmatic impact also stands to improve when NGO networks more effectively share best practices and innovation (as well as lessons learned) among members. NGOs workers too often do not benefit from learning or experience of peers working on similar programs elsewhere within the network—even within the same country. Global incoherence does not allow local experts scattered throughout the world to share difficulties, and successes, and learn from one another.

Impact in Advocacy

Integrators aspire to globally coherent advocacy, which can make a thousand local voices heard as one. For example, grassroots experience gives an organization credibility that experts from the developed world can lack in policy debates. Yet if the organization does not tap local members for expertise, the value is lost. An organization that can speak confidently and knowledgeably for communities around the world can get heard at the UN or on CNN.

Oxfam provides an example. Before Oxfam began to integrate, the organization had traditionally focused on field work, and had not purposefully coordinated its brand messages across the network. Then, in the late 1990s, Oxfam's leaders determined that they needed to engage powerfully in the emerging worldwide debate on debt relief for the poorest countries.

Ray Offenheiser, the ED of Oxfam, USA, explained how Oxfam met the challenge:

> The collective of EDs of Oxfam organizations—for example, from the UK, the US, Holland, and Australia—decided to take a stand that debt relief was critical to education in developing countries…We turned the "child out of school" into a poster child. This was not about giving poor countries a free pass, but rather about illustrating the links between onerous policies of debt and structural adjustment and the collapse of social sector expenditure budgets in developing countries, and its impact on several generations of young people. With this as our first campaign, we opened our first small advocacy office in Washington DC. Our substantial report and positioning on this issue enable us to launch conversations with Kofi Annan [then UN Secretary General], Jim Wolfensohn [then head of the World Bank], the White House and a variety of governments. (Huggett et al., 2009)

Impact in Fund-Raising and Other Forms of Support

Consider a microfinance bank in Zambia supported by an American member of a global network. The local office of the British government's Department for International Development considered support. Should the Zambian head of the bank talk to DFID's people on the ground in Southern

Africa or first check with the American sponsors, who might want to bring in the British affiliate, possibly with contacts at DFID in London?

Funders think globally, too. The three largest philanthropic foundations have both global strategies and people who work around the world. The Bill and Melinda Gates Foundation works on six continents. The Ford Foundation has offices in Beijing, Cairo, Jakarta, Lagos, Mexico City, Nairobi, New Delhi, Rio de Janeiro, Santiago de Chile, as well as New York. The Rockefeller Foundation has as a focus on "smart globalization."

DFID, the UK Department for International Development, declined support for microfinance initiatives run by network affiliates after one of its members failed after receiving DFID investment. DFID felt that the network was not supporting the failing entity adequately. Future investments with the same network therefore looked less attractive.

Small funders now have a global perspective as well, as news is streamed live via TV from cell phone cameras. News also arrives from small, remote places that might not have received media attention just a few years ago, such as Samoa. People are willing to give money and volunteer time.

Public attention has put a premium on a network's ability to funnel the funds appropriately—another activity benefiting from the coordination of an integrator. Some NGOs, such as Médecins Sans Frontières, have, on occasions, even turned down donations when they have received enough for a specific appeal. Public concerns have erupted when an NGO receives funds for one purpose and uses them for another. The Red Cross in both the United States and Australia has had to answer concerns on this in the past decade.

Encouragingly, twenty-four-hour news has also created opportunities to gather resources beyond the immediate cause. Supporters recruited to help with a disaster can be approached later for support for different issues. Greg Baldwin, the CEO of VolunteerMatch, has also noted that interest in volunteering in assorted causes rose, for example, after Hurricane Katrina. Prepared nonprofits were able to engage the goodwill, even if they could not alleviate the distress in New Orleans.

Economic Advantages

Integrating is itself expensive. So any benefits need to be weighed against the cost of coherence. Nonetheless, economic benefits come from "network effects" and economies of scale.

Integrating global NGO networks enhances "network effects"
As networks of NGOs become more coherent, many internal networks develop, both formal and informal. Formal networks include the ability to respond to disasters, deliver programs, advocate and raise funds, as outlined earlier. Informal networks among individuals ease decision-making and help transfer innovations and best practice.

They can also capture economies of scale

NGO networks can create "virtual scale" by acting as one organization and therefore lowering average costs. A variety of program costs decline with scale, such as capabilities for humanitarian response and staff development. Advocacy can be much more effective if the NGO can take advantage of efficient forms of paid media or critical mass to attract notice for earned media. Fund-raising efforts are often more effective "at scale." Raising a mass appeal for funds requires a brand and media engagement. Dealing with large funders often requires the ability to develop and manage the relationships and to deal with the procurement requirements of accounting and reporting results. Administrative and back office costs can be shared across a network.

Integrators work to develop critical mass in specific areas

Some program expertise is expensive for any one affiliate, but affordable if the cost is shared across the network. Action Contre La Faim, for example, concentrates some expertise in the United Kingdom where it can form local alliances with universities and provide a depth of expertise that is valuable to the network.

Sometimes a lack of critical mass can inhibit productive investment. Ed Granger-Happ, CIO of Save the Children USA and chairman of Net Hope in a report by Accenture Development Partners (ADP), commented that:

> The private sector has been seeing huge leaps in productivity for decades because of advances in communications and information technology; its time to ensure we're all working together to deliver the same types of productivity benefits to the nongovernmental organization community and the hundreds of millions of people they serve.

The same report noted that while for-profit companies spent on average 3.9 percent of their revenue on information technology (IT), spending was at most 2.5 percent as low as 0.3 percent at members of Net Hope (the network of CIOs from the largest humanitarian and development organizations in the world) (Bulloch, 2009).

The cost of communication decreases

While global NGOs invest little in IT compared to the private sector, they have been early adopters of some technologies to great effect. Greenpeace was using email in the 1980s. The Clinton HIV and AIDS Initiative uses Skype to coordinate across three dimensions of its organizational matrix: geographic, access, and programs. Inspire Foundation developed consistent ReachOut! websites across three continents by coordinating with Skype and email. Such coordination would have been prohibitively expensive for an NGO a decade ago.

A variety of other global trends now make it less expensive for NGOs to coordinate and integrate. Consider: English is now a *lingua franca* outside the business world; some have estimated that English is spoken by more people than Mandarin, if second-language speakers are included. I attended a meeting of Médecins Sans Frontières, an NGO founded in France, conducted in English in Paris.

The ubiquity of cheap air travel brings together staff, volunteers, and supporters. In 2008 I was a judge in "Pitch for Change," a competition among students at Harvard Business School for new social enterprises. Of the twenty-three entries, 80 percent were for overseas ventures from students with first-hand experience of the issues.

Last but not least, the spread of mobile phones is making coordination possible with the most remote reaches of the world. According to UNICEF, there are now more cell phones in Africa than in the United States and Canada. While the population in Africa is roughly triple that in North America, incomes are but a fraction of North American levels.

How Do NGO Networks Integrate?

But no NGO finds the integrator approach easy. No integrator claims to be satisfied with the status quo. For all NGO networks, the cost of integrating—coordination and change—is expensive. Some patterns, though, are emerging among the more successful first-movers.

Common themes are management, impact, and complementary relationships. (A more traditional approach would say leadership, mission, and structure.) These are necessary, but not sufficient, conditions for success in a network that needs: a focus on *management, beyond leadership; impact, beyond mission*; and *complementary relationships, beyond structure*.

Beyond Entrepreneurial Leadership to Managerial Leadership

Entrepreneurial leadership often frames discussions of leadership in the nonprofit sector. Social entrepreneurs now receive much due attention. The spotlight shines on heroes that innovate and start organizations to meet social needs. The Skoll Centre at the Said Business School at Oxford University annually honors social entrepreneurs. The School for Social Entrepreneurs is now being brought from the United Kingdom to Australia. Ashoka nurtures its network of entrepreneurial fellows.

However, some leaders in the sector note that their organizations are "strongly-led and under-managed." Leadership meaning to "articulate an organization's vision and ensure that all of its stakeholders will support that vision." And management meaning: "the set of activities required to ensure that an organization will reliably produce results, especially as it grows larger and/or becomes more complex" (Stid and Bradach, 2009).

Managerial leadership appears to be the critical element of successful integration and scaling of global networks. The heroic entrepreneurial style may be dysfunctional in holding together a global network. A better definition might be that effective management is a "decision-making service" for the heroes in the field. Managerial leaders turn the hierarchy upside down: senior executives serve the people on the front line.

Management as a decision-making service

Defining management as a decision-making service suggests that the "service" can be judged like any other service: whether it is effective, efficient, and responsive. And, there are well-worn ways to make decision-making processes better, cheaper, and quicker. CEO John Heine advocated the concept of a decision-making service in his corporate work; the lesson is transferable.[1]

Wisdom of crowds

While effective entrepreneurial leadership needs people that will go against the crowd (Elkington and Hartigan, 2008), effective decision-making in network NGOs requires drawing on "the wisdom of crowds." Network management needs bring together organizations that are legally independent. Member organizations usually have boards that need to be involved in major decisions. Leaders are sometimes "elected" rather then "selected" or even "self-selected."

Collaborative decision-making is often less prone to mistakes (Campbell et al., 2009). Effective management in nonprofits engages people in decision-making (Wells et al., 2009).

Symphony versus Jazz

John Clarkeson, chief executive of The Boston Consulting Group, contrasted the conductor of a symphony with the leader of a jazz band (Clarkeson, 1990). He commented that while the role of the leader is often seen like that of a conductor—picking the score and setting the pace—effective leaders in growing organizations are often more akin to the leaders of a jazz band: assembling a great team, and helping them work together to make great music.

Teams lead many successful global NGO networks instead of a single leader. Médecins Sans Frontières, Save the Children, Oxfam, Action Contre La Faim each have no single global CEO. An expanding team of chief executives from fourteen country offices leads Oxfam: the team grows as each new affiliate joins, and each member has a vote. The article, "Increasing Effectiveness in Global NGO Networks" (Huggett et al., 2009) provides additional examples.

Jim Collins (2005) has remarked on unique challenges of leading NGOs: "Most social sector leaders...must rely on people underpaid relative to the private sector, or, in the case of volunteers, paid not at all." Volunteers arrive with a mission in mind. Members of NGO networks also join networks for a purpose of their own. Effective network management delivers global decisions that meet common purpose.

Management teams are well distributed in many global NGO networks. Terry Winters, the chair of Opportunity International, lives in Australia, while Adrian Merryman, the global CEO, lives in the United States.

Most NGO network leaders travel widely. One commented, "As president, I travel about 50 percent of the time because it's important to help teams feel a part of what we're doing and also for me to get a textural sense of what's going on." Most also seek to bring people into the team who will round out team members' collective global experience, sometimes because they've worked in a particular country, and sometimes because they have lived there (Huggett, et al., 2009).

Managers in MSF often have experience outside their own country. Marc Dubois, the head of MSF in the United Kingdom, is American, while Nicolas de Torrente, the head of MSF in the United States, is Swiss. Kris Torgeson, general secretary of the International office in Geneva, is American. Adrio Bacchetta, a Welshman, headed MSF in Germany.

Role of "global"

Independent networks of global NGOs usually work to the principle of "subsidiarity": decisions are made locally unless there is an overriding reason for it to be made globally. In this they reflect the wording of the U.S. constitution, which reserved powers to the states that had not been invested in the federal government.

The role of global in NGO networks can include a shared view of what matters most in terms of field impact; agreement around the use of the brand, particularly for fund-raising and advocacy (and the consequences for network members that do not adhere to that agreement); and common systems for administrative functions and reporting.

Global decision-making is most effective in the NGO networks studied when it is well defined. Some networks may have well-defined processes for some decisions and ill-defined ones for others. Various tools exist to map decision-making in nonprofits (Huggett and Moran, 2008).

Nicolas de Torrente, the US executive director of Médecins Sans Frontières, described three distinct processes for making decisions within the network. First, he commented, "we have a deliberative decision-making process for broader issues like strategy." The MSF leadership team makes decisions about the organization's long-term strategy carefully, listening to a wide range of voices from around the network, and respecting the rights of each of the legally separate founding-member organizations. Second, MSF appoints a single global leader on a rotating basis to respond quickly to emergencies (and lead the organization's response), no matter where they are. Third, operational decisions are made in the field. And in the field, MSF has clearly defined processes so that decisions can be made swiftly, especially for issues of safety. As de Torrente explained, the process is

kind of like a fire brigade... We learned [the importance of this approach] the hard way. We lost some people in the past. When it comes to the well-being of our people in the field, there is one person for each field mission that can make decisions on the spot. And it does not matter if there are people from the different parts of MSF in that operation. (Huggett et al., 2009)

The impact of an improved decision-making process on organizational culture has been noted in a U.S. nonprofit network (Huggett and Kramer, 2008).

Decentralized

Most global networks have tiny headquarters, or may not have a physical "center" at all, even if there is one organization that was the original founder. People doing global work and filling global functions can be based in different places around the world. The role of global is a set of decisions (made in any number of places) that affects the organization globally.

Distributed overhead in the form of global roles keeps capabilities close to the field and easier to fund. Raising money for "central overhead" is notoriously difficult, either from donors or member organizations.

Even organizations with relatively strong chief executives can have only a small number of staff at "headquarters."

Wikimedia is highly globalized and highly decentralized. As of 2009, it is one of the top ten sites on the web, yet has fewer than thirty people in its headquarters in San Francisco. The bulk of its work is done by volunteers distributed around the world.

Donors often say that they want to fund "programs" not "overhead." NGOs claim that donations support programs not overhead. Save the Children claims that 92 percent of donations go to program expenses, with only 4 percent on "management and general" (www.savethechildren.org). A recent study of nonprofits in the United States found that while reported overhead ranged from 13 to 22 percent, actual overhead in the same nonprofits ranged from 17 to 35 percent, which was lower than comparable for-profit businesses (Gregory and Howard, 2009).

Member organizations usually resist "tithes" for overhead or headquarters, and can threaten to resign. In 2008 a global NGO network of over fifteen organizations with over five hundred million dollars in revenue faced the loss of its largest member over a contribution to the headquarters that was less than 5 percent of revenue.

Even small, new networks scrutinize payments for overhead to headquarters. "One Inspire" is a global network spawned by Inspire Foundation of Australia. It now includes Inspire USA and Inspire Ireland. Together the three nonprofits run ReachOut (www.reachout. com) on three continents. Jack Heath, the founder, commented that "we cannot afford each country duplicating costs, yet donors in the USA and Ireland scrutinize carefully any money contributed for shared work done in another country."

Standardizing systems may not seem compelling. However, in practice, it is critical to success. A number of networks in our research found that their member organizations had, over time, customized administrative systems to the point where it was difficult to compare financials, program outcomes, personnel reviews, and a host of other items that, while mundane, are the arteries of communication through any network.

One key benefit of standardized systems is consistent, comparable data to inform global decisions. This is an iterative process, as standardizing systems usually requires global decisions.

Leadership by phase of growth in nonprofits may mirror patterns in the for-profit sector. A Silicon Valley executive search consultant once told me that he divided business leaders into three categories: "starters," "builders," and "runners." He had sought leaders for firms from tiny to huge. The starters he saw as entrepreneurs: great at bucking the status quo to get things off the ground, but dysfunctional once the organization gets critical mass. "Founder syndrome" is a term used in both for-profit and nonprofit sectors to describe this problem. Builders are more analytical and scale organizations, but get bored when growth slows. Runners manage the host of relationships required to keep large organizations on the road. Because they listen to lots of different people, they are good at managing risk. Each kind of leadership is different, yet appropriate for different kinds of organization.

If social entrepreneurs have skills in common with business entrepreneurs, then runners of large NGO networks would need to be strong at relationship management. Evidence from integrating NGO networks supports this hypothesis.

Management teams cultivate relationships in most of the NGO networks I have studied. Many of the managers we interviewed told us of the importance of getting the team together face to face, despite the logistical complexity and cost. Jean-Michel Grand, the U.K. CEO of Action Contre La Faim commented: "We do a conference call every month and a meeting every quarter. The physical meeting is a key in building relationships. We could cut the cost of a trip, but at the end of the day there is so much more by meeting in person" (Huggett et al., 2009).

Similarly, Paul Gilding, former global CEO of Greenpeace, observed: "When I first arrived I thought the organization was incredibly bloated—people flying around all the time, half of our meetings devoted to informal or social time. But then I realized that this was the glue that really held the organization together" (ibid.).

To further these collaborative relationships by bolstering mutual understanding, some networks transfer people proactively. Charlie MacCormack, the CEO of Save the Children USA commented: "We have 'job swaps' where, for instance, the CEO of Save UK and Save USA switch places for a week." Gilding shared that, "From a quarter to a third of our CEOs were on a rotation assignment at any given time. The purpose is not just about turning around members that might be struggling, but also internationalizing the organization" (ibid.).

Beyond Mission to Impact

Mission

Most networks, global or national, share a mission. Good missions motivate, but are not sufficient for decision-making, which usually requires a more specific definition of "intended impact" (Colby et al., 2003). A definition of intended impact enables a nonprofit to focus (Huggett and Saxton, 2006). Without this a nonprofit or NGO network can become an archipelago of programs that share a common cause but little else.

Impact

Global NGO networks use definitions of impact to drive decision-making, innovation, and even fund-raising. For example, Habitat for Humanity International has, at different times, counted "houses built" and "families served." This has helped it focus resources, share ideas, and recruit supporters.

Houses built reflected the American dream of a detached house owned by the family. With this measure Habitat for Humanity International housed over a million people in thousands of communities around the world. However, as Mark Andrews, SVP Operations, explained "We came to realize that in places like Bombay, India, the idea of building 36 houses a year was foolish, and that the best approach was to partner with other NGOs and find solutions to housing other than the North American single family home." The shift in thinking "came from our recognition that our real metric should be 'families served.'"

"Families served" has allowed country programs to collaborate with complementary NGOS, such as those providing clean water or microfinance (Huggett et al., 2009). It has also raised questions about the value of renovating versus building homes in countries with a large supply of housing, such as the United States.

Measures of impact remain a vexed issue for many scaling social enterprises, requiring investment but not always delivering useful information. NGOs are investing in improving measures (e.g., Oxfam), while foundations invest in measuring their outcomes (e.g., Childrens' Investment Fund Foundation). New intermediaries are springing up to interpret results (e.g., New Philanthropy Capital) or create "markets" (e.g., GEXSI). Various tools are offered to measure impact (e.g., Social Return on Investment). Nevertheless, considerable frustration is expressed one-on-one and at conferences (e.g., Valuing Impact, 2009).

Simple measures of impact, which have been the holy grail of social accounting, are not likely to emerge soon. Mulgan (2008) argues that trying to develop a single measure of net benefit often destroys relevant information in its conglomeration of variables. Social value is not one-dimensional. Even the business world lives with multiple measures of investment success: for example, net present value and internal rate of return.

The best measures can also be the enemy of good measures. Attempts to measure outcome by robust studies to an academic level of proof can lead to readings so infrequent that they are not useful for innovation. For example, serious longitudinal research has shown the value of mentoring, helping Big Brothers Big Sisters International, or preschool learning, helping Sesame Workshop. But these studies are expensive and hence infrequent.

In contrast innovation often requires frequent experimentation with quick feedback on what works and what does not.

Focusing innovation
A shared definition of impact allows front-line workers to share successes, good practices, and new ideas. The definition of impact allows people to say what works, and what does not. With a mission but no definition of impact front-line leaders often struggle to reconcile many local experiences. Individual leaders give long explanations that start "In our country..." but the sessions do not end with many leaders picking up ideas that they can use at home.

Stopping innovation
Scaling a social program or organization requires that some kinds of innovation need to stop. An organization or program worth scaling is doing something right. A clear definition of impact can help "program codification" (Bridgespan, 2005).

Motivating people
NGO leaders also point out that explicit goals motivate employees as well as mission. People know when they are working inside a mission, but want to know as well whether they are making a difference that counts, and that someone else can acknowledge. Without the feedback of results, employees are likely to look for other signs that they are having impact, such as involvement in decision-making (Wells et al., 2009).

Impact "fix"
Charlie McCormack, U.S. president and CEO of Save the Children, commented "The overwhelming performance incentive is to see your vision enacted, so rewarding people by giving them control over impact is a critical motivator" (Huggett et al., 2009). Others commented that an impact fix is a better motivator than money. NGO networks rarely compete on pay, but attract people who share the mission. Offering monetary incentives to deliver social impact could insult a volunteer forgoing a salary, for example, and therefore be counterproductive.

Including small member organizations
A clear definition of impact can help a small unit make a big contribution to a network, and receive much in return. Consider the Juvenile Diabetes Research Fund, a $150M global network. It not only has a shared mission "dedicated to finding a cure" but also a sharp focus on impact—funding the highest quality research published in the most respected scientific journals. While the Australian organization represents only 10 percent of the network's revenue and 6 percent of its staff, it is highly effective with the network. It has funded over 95 percent of research in the field in Australia, assessed as top quality by peers outside Australia. The Australian

organization is effective within the global network because each part of the network shares the same definition of impact.

Peer review

Clear definitions of impact can also enable peer review, which can provide robust feedback on the quality of programs to field practitioners. Dave Young, COO of World Vision, commented: "We have a system of peer review processes and assessments for all entities in the partnership. These have a range of functions from enhancing alignment to global priorities and strategy, to internal audit, to risk assessment, to program quality enhancement, to sharing best practices, and improving stewardship and accountability" (Huggett et al. 2009).

Peer reviews can also build personal relationships and trust across a network. They therefore contribute directly to complementarity discussed in the next section.

Beyond Structure to Complementarity

Complementarity

Instead of centralizing resources into a powerful headquarters, integrating networks use the principle of complementarity—a web of complementary roles, responsibilities, and relationships (Huggett et al., 2009). A key ingredient is differentiated roles within the network for "virtual scale" and to strengthen interdependency.

Action Contre La Faim, for example, shares global roles among its members. UK CEO Jean-Michel Grand noted:

> there is complementarity among our network members. France, Spain, and the US manage country operations, while Canada provides us with access to additional French-speaking expatriates and funding and the UK does program evaluation, leads on advocacy and partnerships with local NGOs and provides funding to the network's programs. (Ibid.)

Structure, however, does not seem to define integration. Webster and Walker (2009) noted, "Our work does not point to any one operational arrangement being better than any other." Different NGOs have different structures of boards and management, developed over time. There does not appear to be an "ideal" structure, although a common thread heard from many NGOs is that it makes sense to be clear about how decisions are made.

Different organizations have tried different global governance, ranging from one vote for each member organization (Oxfam) through a board with membership reflecting relative size of member organization (Child Fund International).

Similarly, in the private sector Bartlett and Ghoshal (1990) noted of multinationals that matrix management has proven disappointing except when it follows the "physiology" and "psychology" of effective working relationships.

Specialized roles allow the network to benefit from economies of scale in specific functions that can be delivered more effectively and efficiently for the whole network than by each member. They also embed global capabilities closer to the field.

Opportunity International was formed from a merger of two organizations, recognized and built on the respective strengths of each. As Chairman Terry Winters noted,

> Our founding reflected the desire to put together the best of what each member had to offer. Our U.S. founder was funding enterprises in Latin America for improved employment, but it wasn't a successful model. Our Australian founder was running a promising microfinance organization in Bali but was having trouble raising capital. By joining forces, we had a great model and a way to fund it. (Huggett et al., 2009)

Complementary Relationships

Distributing global capabilities around the network develops a set of interdependencies that tie a network together. These relationships between member organizations force collaboration. Clear role definition can help build trust among members. Each of the integrating global networks has a web of personal relationships that tie the organization together, ease decision-making, and nurture innovation.

Webster and Walker (2009) noted,

> Investing in people is one of the most critical ways to improve response. Particularly in federated structures, the range of multicultural, complex and diverse affiliates must actively work to create common standards and shared approaches. Regardless of the details of an organization's structure or processes, building relationships and trust across the entire organization is essential...Federations work on trust and relationships, not rules. Federation affiliates need to do significant work to make their federation function, and need to continuously do this work. It is not just a matter of putting a system into place.

Macquarie Group Foundation shows how an organization can use complementary relationship for great impact when a centralized approach might be less effective, or even just impractical from a headquarters location as remote as Sydney. For example, Macquarie Group Foundation supports One Inspire globally with local relationships in each market. Colin Hunt heads Macquaries' operations in Dublin and is board chair of Inspire Ireland. Paul Daitz, an executive director of Macquarie in New York, serves on the board of Inspire USA. Julie White, head of Macquarie Group Foundation in Sydney, supports Inspire Foundation in Australia and facilitates communication among the three supporters of Inspire. The relationships enable Macquarie Bank to make philanthropic investments coherently and globally in One Inspire. They also help tie the different parts of One Inspire together.

Members acting with other members within global NGO networks reflect the behavior of successful nonprofits working with allies: they empower others to be "forces for good" (Crutchfield and Grant, 2007).

Legal Arrangements

While many complementary relationships can be seen in integrating global networks, the value of legal agreements and structure seems to be limited.

"Franchises" can prove hard to enforce in the social sector, with many agreements relying on the "nuclear option" of withdrawing a franchise, or ejecting a member from a network. This is invariably a painful process, and results only long after collaboration has broken down. Moreover, national courts may invalidate "disenfranchisement" of a long-established local organization by a foreign body.

Interlocking Boards

Rather than relying purely on legal agreements, some NGOs try to tie members together with interlocking directorships of country boards. Some people serve on more than one board, such that a country board may have one or two members who also serve on other boards.

Mobile Management

Many NGO networks actively transfer management to share skills and build relationships around the network. Opportunity International has a network of mobile CEOs, so it can place people in hotspots where their skills are needed.

Informal Relationships

Integrators encourage informal relationships among people of different network organizations. These relationships transfer best practices and innovation, and ease decision-making. The World Wildlife Federation (WWF) provides a good example. WWF employees, working on marine ecosystems in distinct parts of the Pacific, took the initiative to form a Marine Advisory Group that met annually to share lessons learned pertaining to coral reefs. The team was global, consisting of staff from Indonesia, Malaysia, Fiji, Papua New Guinea, Europe, and Washington. One evening, while working together on various projects, the team hatched an idea for a strategy for conserving marine life in a fragile region of the Pacific known as the Coral Triangle.

After a series of iterations, progressively improving and elevating the plan, senior WWF leadership adopted this strategy as the Coral Triangle Initiative and approached donors. The strategy caught the eye of multilateral donors such as the World Bank and the Asian Development Bank, the president of Indonesia, and a bilateral donor that awarded a multimillion dollar grant for the project.

It did not stop there. The governments of the region are now exploring the potential for a new multilateral partnership: a Coral Triangle Initiative on Coral Reefs, Fisheries, and Food Security. This followed from the endorsement of twenty-one world leaders at the 2007 Asia Pacific Economic Cooperation (APEC) Summit of a Coral Triangle Initiative. Huge impact has come from relationships across the WWF network (Huggett et al., 2009).

Small Countries Contribute

A network of complementary relationships can make it easier for small countries to make special contributions to the global network. The U.K. organizations of Médecins Sans Frontières have specialized skills in PR that serve the whole network, even thought the United Kingdom is not one of the five "operating centers" of MSF.

The globalization can reinvigorate the localization. A simple choice between centralization and decentralization looks bleak for a small, under-resourced member of a global NGO network. Centralization raises the specter of power shifting offshore to somewhere that neither knows nor cares about. Decentralization suggests isolation with little help from overseas in the form of knowledge, people, or money.

Development: Where Can Global NGO Networks Go?

Impact

The integrators described in this chapter each claim that they are achieving more impact as they scale. The complexity of the tasks they undertake suggests that an organization of some size is needed to scale the impact.

Humanitarian relief, for example, requires moving large amounts of resources around the world at short notice. A coherent network or organization can accomplish this. Movements of independent social entrepreneurs have not done so at scale. The large NGO networks have increased the volume of aid they deliver substantially over the past decade.

Many global NGOs are seeking greater coherence for more effective, efficient, and responsive programs. Coherence also enables advocacy with a single clear voice, and coordinated fund-raising to global philanthropists. By acting as coherent networks, NGOs can start to reap economies of scale, and harness innovations and best practices from all over the world. They provide more attractive career paths for their people, and hence for the network a stronger supply of future leaders.

Global NGOs can therefore scale to have more impact globally.

Effort

Senior managers at each integrator say that it is difficult to build coherence. Integrating demands large investments of time, talent, and treasure. For all it is hard work, marked by frustration and failure as well as success and progress.

Going beyond entrepreneurial leadership to managerial leadership requires the expensive attention of senior people. Going beyond mission to impact requires the effort to bring agreement on impact goals, and the pain of rejecting opportunities that might be within the mission, but do not contribute as much to goals as alternatives. Going beyond structure to complementary relationships requires investment in time and communications up, down, and across the network.

All remark that it takes time: both lots of hours of people's times to coordinate, collaborate, and congregate; and many years to develop the web or relationships, experience, and trust needed to make networks truly coherent. The scale of the investment shows how they see the value of coherence in achieving impact. Still, integration is not the single "correct" path. No group should undertake an effort of this magnitude unless it believes that achieving more coherence globally will enable it to have much more impact.

Journey

Each nonprofit leader that has seen this research has commented on how much their journey shares in common with other integrators. On seeing quotes from leaders of a variety of other organizations, one remarked how many of them could have been made by people in his own network. While the scaling journey of each NGO network is unique, they share patterns.

The challenge for the future will be to understand the patterns more thoroughly, and to spot new patterns as they emerge. Three key questions merit watching:

What are the best models of managerial leadership beyond entrepreneurial leadership? Effective managerial leadership in global NGOs deserves attention, as recent years have shed light on entrepreneurial or heroic leadership. Its ability to scale and motivate volunteers and staff alike may have lessons for smaller social enterprises, or other sectors, too.

How do the best global NGOs define impact beyond missions? Measurement of impact has vexed NGO networks and the whole social sector in recent years. Many still hunt for satisfactory metrics despite an array of tools, studies, conferences, and experts. The measures of the measures may be critical: which are useful; which ones are accurate. NGO networks that develop robust measures of impact can lead the way for other social enterprises, businesses, and governments looking to understand their social impact.

How will integrating NGO networks build complementarity beyond structure? Most NGOs networks struggle with structure, and will continue to do so. They need structure to be legal and legitimate. But structure may remain a "hygiene" factor": necessary but not sufficient. If the glue that binds NGO networks together is the web of complementary relationships, the best integrators will develop winning ways to build complementarity, systematically if not formally. In particular, their networks of relationship can drive useful innovation. NGO networks may provide useful models for innovation without either centralized R&D or "heroic misfits" innovating outside an organization.

Vision for 2020

The NGO networks that can address these questions will be able to integrate more effectively and efficiently. As they do, they may continue to scale. And we hope that as they scale their organizations, they scale their impact commensurately. We will know more in a decade.

Note

1. John Heine was an Australian for-profit CEO who took SOLA from its Adelaide roots to a global company operating on five continents listed on the New York Stock Exchange. Running a multinational from Australia was different from running one from the United States or Europe, and had some similarities with leading a global NGO network. His company was spread thinly over continents and time zones. Most of action was far from Adelaide. With a small domestic market, he could not assume that what worked for Australia would be alright for the rest of the world, too. His managers in different countries had independent minds. He could not always depend on their loyalty. Coming from a small country, he was always the outsider. John believed that to be effective, he had to provide a "decision-making service" that was accountable to its users in the same way that any services provided by his company was accountable to its customers.

Appendix

The following is a list of the NGOs interviewed for writing this chapter:

Absolute Return for Kids
ACCION
Action Contre La Faim (Action Against Hunger)
African Medical and Research Foundation
Americares
Asia Society
Big Brothers Big Sisters International
CARE
Child Fund International

Children's Investment Fund Foundation
Clinton HIV/AIDS Initiative
Covenant House International
Earthwatch
Engender Health
Girl Guides
Greenpeace
Habitat for Humanity International
Human Rights Watch
Inspire Foundation
International Planned Parenthood Federation
International Reading Association
Juvenile Diabetes Research Fund
Leaders' Quest
Khulisa
Médecins Sans Frontières (Doctors Without Borders)
Mercy Corps
National Geographic
Open Society Institute (including Soros Economic Development Fund and
    European Council on Foreign Relations)
Opportunity International
Oxfam
PACT
PATH
Plan International
Population Council
Save the Children
Sesame Workshop
Teach for All
The Hunger Project
UN Foundation
United Religions International
United Way
World Vision
World Wildlife Fund

7

Whose Change are We Talking About? When Multiple Parties and Multiple Agendas Collide

Scott L. Newbert and Ronald Paul Hill

While the field of entrepreneurship is relatively young compared to most other social sciences, the area of social entrepreneurship is even younger. In fact, it was not until 1991 that the term "social entrepreneur" was first used in the academic literature (Waddock and Post, 1991). Since that time, scholarly interest in social entrepreneurship has increased, but "with minimal progress in theory development" (Short et al., 2009: 168). In response, Short et al. address ten areas in which scholars can advance theoretical and empirical research on social entrepreneurship. While the areas these authors identify and the related research questions they propose are certainly both relevant and important to increasing the rigor and validity of what we know about social entrepreneurship, their focus on the firm and individual levels of analysis ignores what we believe to be an equally significant issue at the dyad level of analysis—conflict.

Before engaging in an exploration of the manner in which conflict might complicate social entrepreneurship, we first seek to define this phenomenon. Unfortunately, little consensus exists in the literature on what social entrepreneurship is or even what it means to be a social entrepreneur. Amid this lack of agreement, we define social entrepreneurship as a "process involving the innovative use and combination of resources to pursue opportunities to catalyze social change and/or address social needs" (Mair and Marti, 2006: 37), which is in turn carried out by social entrepreneurs, defined as those "who play critical roles in bringing about 'catalytic changes' in the public sector agenda and the perception of certain social issues" (Waddock and Post, 1991: 393).

These contributions suggest the unifying element of social entrepreneurship is positive societal change. In contrast with traditional definitions of entrepreneurship that include "the scholarly examination of how, by whom, and with what effects opportunities to create future goods and services are discovered, evaluated, and exploited" (Shane and Venkatraman, 2000: 218), a process carried out by individuals working independently or as a part of existing organizations (Guth and Ginsberg, 1990), significance of distinction between entrepreneurship in general and social entrepreneurship in particular becomes clear. While entrepreneurship focuses on the processes by which all opportunities to create and/or fulfill needs are exploited, social entrepreneurship focuses on the subsector of opportunities that, by way of their exploitation, may bring about some increase in the collective welfare.

Based on this nuance, Dees (1998a) contends "social entrepreneurs are one species in the genus entrepreneur" (p. 2). While we agree with Dees that social entrepreneurs may play a unique and developmental role in their communities, we also contend that effective social entrepreneurship need not and should not necessarily emanate from a specific individual type or organizational form. The global economy manifests a variety of complex organizations that cannot easily be labeled as either socially or commercially oriented since many pursue both sets of goals. Gone are the days when social change was enacted solely by philanthropic individuals, activists, community organizations, government agencies, and nonprofit organizations. Today it has become quite apparent that self-interested individuals and for-profit organizations are highly alert to the social and economic value that can be appropriated from the exploitation of social opportunities.

If we are correct that successful social entrepreneurs are no different than their profit-seeking counterparts (i.e., both seek to create economic value), then why do most social entrepreneurs fail to deliver social value on a scale commensurate with the problems they seek to solve? As anecdotal evidence of the premise, consider that entrepreneurs such as Henry Ford, Ray Kroc, Sam Walton, Bill Gates, and Steve Jobs, to name but a few, have exploited opportunities at levels that have impacted the lives (for better or worse) of hundreds of millions of people. Yet, there are few, if any, similar champions in the social sector. Indeed, of those entrepreneurs that have succeeded in creating social value, arguably none has scaled his/her impact to an appreciable level.

We contend that at least one contributing factor to the failure by social entrepreneurs to scale impact is their inability to develop an efficient business model. Scaling impact requires, at a minimum, sizable financial resources; thus, to the extent that social entrepreneurs pursue the creation of social value without regard for the creation of economic value, they are hindering their ability to generate the type of resources necessary to implement social innovation on a large scale. These types of smaller, ineffective efforts to improve social conditions suggest a flaw in the business model that can be broadly construed to reflect an inefficient use of resources. Such a condition is particularly problematic for social entrepreneurs as these operational inefficiencies are largely agreed upon to reflect high opportunity costs, suggesting that the manner in which the resources in question are used is actually bad for society at large. Additionally, if these resources are directed toward other ends, they likely could be put to more efficient use, which would have the ironic effect of actually increasing social welfare.

Unfortunately, adoption of profit-seeking goals is not a panacea for social entrepreneurs. In fact, by assuming profit-seeking motives, social entrepreneurs establish misalignment between their interests and those of the parties with whom they will likely ally in exploiting a particular social opportunity. As suggested earlier, social entrepreneurs do not necessarily pursue purely altruistic goals; rather, many pursue them in combination with economic goals. Therefore, it is important for social entrepreneurs to not merely do good, but also to do well in the process. Yet the institutional challenges they tend to face in markets in which they operate may lead social entrepreneurs to find themselves entering into alliances with partners from the public sector, including community organizers, nonprofit organizations, governmental agencies, and activist collectives. Although these partnerships can provide many benefits to social entrepreneurs, such as acquisition of knowledge about and expertise in navigating local institutional environments, provision of social capital and legitimacy within the local community, and links to important community players (Kanter, 1999), they also engender important challenges for social entrepreneurs. For instance, partners operating in the public sector are unlikely to be governed by typical profit-seeking motives. Thus, they seek only to do good, even at the expense of doing well. To use Maddy's (2001) terminology, whereas most social entrepreneurs tend to be, at least in part, "do-wellers," their partners tend to be solely "do-gooders."

This disparity in agendas between social entrepreneurs and their partners is likely to manifest in some level of disagreement regarding what successful social change looks like. It seems then that in remedying one problem, social entrepreneurs may unwittingly create another. Given this potential for conflict, we contend that social entrepreneurs must carefully weigh the costs and benefits of joining with potential public-sector organizations so as to minimize the propensity for conflicting agendas. Fortunately for social entrepreneurs, there is a rich literature that has emerged from the management field that can inform social entrepreneurs on how to both preempt the potential conflicts prior to partnerships and establish mechanisms for resolving such conflicts. Thus, we believe that by applying good business practices to the alliance selection and management processes, social entrepreneurs may improve their ability to scale social impact.

Throughout the remainder of this chapter we endeavor to articulate why reducing conflict is critical to scaling impact in the social sector. In so doing, we begin by articulating the benefits and costs ascribed to social entrepreneurs when engaging in partnerships with public sector individuals and organizations. We then demonstrate how the application of well-established best practices in alliance management benefit social entrepreneurs by reducing the conflict inherent in these partnerships, with a particular attention to scaling. Finally, we illustrate our prescriptions with a case that includes effective and ineffective efforts by public-private partnerships to scale social impact.

Social Entrepreneurs are Entrepreneurs

Given the lack of consensus regarding what social entrepreneurship is and who the entrepreneurs are that seek to enact social change, the following definitions are advanced. We define social entrepreneurship as a "process involving the innovative use and combination of resources to pursue opportunities to catalyze social change and/or address social needs" (Mair and Marti, 2006: 37). This process is carried out by social entrepreneurs, who we define as those individuals, working alone or within organizations, "who play critical roles in bringing about 'catalytic changes' in the public sector agenda and the perception of certain social issues" (Waddock and Post, 1991: 393).

These definitions both align and distinguish social entrepreneurship from more traditional conceptions of entrepreneurship. To begin, the aforementioned conceptualization is easily subsumed into a typical definition of entrepreneurship: "the scholarly examination of how, by whom, and with what effects opportunities to create future goods and services are discovered, evaluated, and exploited" (Shane and Venkatraman, 2000: 218), and entrepreneurs, those individuals who carry out new combinations of resources that engender radical economic change by the introduction of new goods and/or methods of production in the pursuit of economic rents (Schumpeter, 1934). Although both share a common theme of discovery and exploitation, there are two important distinctions. The first is the context; namely that definitions of entrepreneurship focus on the process by which all opportunities to create and/or fulfill needs are exploited, whereas definitions of social entrepreneurship tend to focus on the subset of opportunities that relate to challenges facing society at large. The second is the objective; namely definitions of entrepreneurship focus on innovating as a means for earning profits, whereas definitions of social entrepreneurship tend to focus on innovating as a means solely for improving the welfare of the larger community, thereby ignoring profit as a goal. It is with this last issue that we disagree.

The fact that social entrepreneurship is but a subset of the larger discipline does not mean that social entrepreneurs do not, or should not, seek to profit from commercializing a new idea. In support of this notion, in a recent survey of the field, Short et al. (2009) acknowledge the dual focus social entrepreneurship places on the creation of social and economic value. In fact, the perception by some scholars that social entrepreneurs ought not to be concerned with profit-seeking motives (c.f. Austin et al., 2006) is problematic since it inhibits their ability to scale impact. Scaling impact to a meaningful level requires disposable financial resources. While social entrepreneurs often rely on philanthropy to provide these resources, expending effort toward attracting them in this way is an exorbitantly time-consuming process that diverts attention from operations (i.e., seeking solutions to social problems) to fundraising (Maddy, 2001). Thus, to the extent that social entrepreneurs pursue the creation of social value without regard to the creation of economic value, they are hindering their ability to generate the type of resources necessary to implement their social innovations on a grander scale.

As an additional consequence of a lack of attention to fiscal concerns, the deployment of resources in ineffective ways and on a small-scale suggests operational inefficiencies. Although some degree of inefficiency may be offset by philanthropic donations to the social entrepreneur, the mere existence of inefficiency signifies that this business model is plagued by opportunity costs (Stiglitz, 1997), which in turn suggests that resources deployed by the social entrepreneur would better serve society if deployed toward alternative ends.

In light of the necessary and instrumental roles secure revenue streams play serving the greater good, social organizations have begun more for-profit activities to subsidize their scaling efforts (Alvord et al., 2004; Wallace, 1999). Yet, some scholars maintain social entrepreneurs are different from traditional entrepreneurs; that although both may seek to profit, the former have a relatively greater focus on producing social value (Austin et al., 2006; Leadebeater, 1997; Mair and Morti, 2006). We believe that this premise is problematic. Consider that for any organization to be sustainable, it must generate continuously the economic resources necessary to survive and grow. Such a fundamental maxim does not discriminate by context. Rather, even the most mission-driven social entrepreneurs must, as private-sector entities, garner revenues necessary to subsidize and scale impact in proportion to the social ills for which they were created (Alvord et al., 2004; Wallace, 1999).

Thus, while social entrepreneurs are no doubt motivated by their vision to serve society, they ought to avoid the observed tendency to feel constrained by it (Weerawardena and Sullivan-Mort, 2006). Social entrepreneurs must allow themselves the freedom to explore and exploit the profit-seeking opportunities that emerge along with their efforts to improve social conditions. We agree with Dees (1998b) that for entrepreneurship to be "social," some social value must be created; we also agree with Peredo and McLean (2006) that for social entrepreneurs to succeed in creating this end, they must, for the good of society, seek to increase both social *and* economic value concurrently. In other words, social entrepreneurs ought not to seek good at the expense of doing well; rather, they ought to seek to do well so that they can do good. In this sense, they are simultaneously do-wellers and do-gooders.

Partnerships: A Necessary Evil

Unfortunately for social entrepreneurs, despite the important benefits to be gleaned from positioning their organizations as profit-seeking businesses, this action is likely to engender an additional, and unintended, obstacle to the scaling process that ultimately stems from the institutional voids that characterize the contexts in which social entrepreneurs tend to operate, such as inner cities and emerging economies. According to Khanna et al. (2005), the quality of an institutional environment is a function of the stability of political and social systems, the degree of openness to foreign investments, the makeup of the product markets, the availability of qualified labor, and the sophistication of capital markets. Khanna et al. argue that because these institutions are more mature in advanced economies, organizations need to rethink how they do business when entering less developed markets in order to navigate underdeveloped institutional infrastructures. While Khanna et al.'s discussion is focused squarely on international markets, Kanter (1999) suggests that the types of institutional voids that plague emerging economies are characteristic of those found throughout all social sector markets, including poor, urban areas in developed countries. Thus, while Khanna et al. (2005) implicitly assume that the institutions of developed nations are of consistently high quality, Kanter (1999) notes there is considerable variability across industries and geographic locations. As support, Kanter cites inner cities as an exceptionally daunting and complex place to conduct business even in the United States, one of the most highly developed markets in the world.

Institutional environments are relevant to a discussion of social entrepreneurs because the institutions supporting social sector markets (whether at home or abroad) tend to be of extremely low quality and exceedingly ambiguous. These conditions render such markets more complex than those in developed areas, leading to uncertainty on the part of social entrepreneurs regarding how to navigate them effectively (Townsend and Hart, 2008). For most such markets, traditional Western business models are ineffective as they tend to assume an absence of institutional voids. As a result, social entrepreneurs often find it necessary to adapt their business models in an effort to navigate this diverse environment.

Unfortunately, given the lack of knowledge and experience with these immature markets, it may not be immediately apparent how to adapt. Thus, one key to knowing which organizational assumptions and business models are valid involves an understanding of the differences in institutional quality between traditional and social sector markets. Kanter (1999) contends one of the best ways to gain the institutional knowledge necessary to overcome potential institutional voids in the social sector is by co-opting partners from local communities. These partnerships typically are found in the public sector and include community organizers, nonprofit organizations, governmental agencies, and activist collectives. Their input may be essential to the success of social entrepreneurs as they provide knowledge about and expertise in navigating local institutional environments, credibility to social entrepreneurs as organizations invested in making change, and links to other community players (Kanter, 1999). Not surprisingly, these types of alliances are argued to be one of seven essential components to successful scaling efforts (Bloom and Chatterji, 2009). In short, public-private partnerships (PPPs) expand the menu of opportunities available to social entrepreneurs by facilitating engagement with and legitimizing their presence in public domains, thereby facilitating their ability to engender catalytic social change.

Despite their intended benefits, much of the research on PPPs has focused on their presence or absence in scaling efforts. However, little attention has been given to the process by which partners can manage them. This is particularly important in a discussion of partnerships between do-wellers and do-gooders as they are typically plagued by an underlying source of conflict regarding what a successful outcome of the partnership will be. Because do-gooder partners operate in the public sector, they are not governed by profit-seeking objectives. Yet, as noted earlier, the most effective social entrepreneurs will be those that are, at least in part, do-wellers (Peredo and McLean, 2006). This scenario can be problematic for social entrepreneurs given evidence that the alignment of goals is a significant determinant of the success of inter-firm relationships and that collaboration is impeded when partners hold different strategic interests (Stephen and Coote, 2007). In other words, social entrepreneurs should only pursue scaling activities to the extent that they are lucrative, whereas their public-sector partners will likely engage in scaling activities regardless of their pecuniary outcomes.

Thus, the inherent disparity in agendas between social entrepreneurs and their partners is likely to manifest in some level of disagreement regarding what successful social change will look like. It seems then that social entrepreneurs may find themselves in a paradoxical situation: to create the most social value, they must seek also to create economic value; yet, by seeking to create economic value, they are adopting an agenda that is distinct from that of their most likely partners, thereby creating conflict that will likely undermine their ability to advance social value.

Mitigating Conflict through Alliance Management

In response to this paradox, we review the literature emanating from the management field that addresses how interorganizational conflict can be preempted prior to and resolved during a partnership. To begin, we acknowledge that the majority of what has been written about interorganizational partnerships involves the context of alliances between for-profit entities. Therefore, while advice to do-weller organizations to simply align their interests with those of do-weller partners (Bamford et al., 2004; Stephen and Coote, 2007) is no doubt useful toward establishing a shared set of goals and objectives, such as defining which financial targets best reflect that the alliance is indeed "doing well," it is less useful for "do-weller/do-gooder" social entrepreneurs who are unlikely to arrive at common ground with do-gooder public-sector partners on specific performance metrics. Notwithstanding this apparent challenge, we seek herein to demonstrate how alliance management theory can be applied to PPPs in an effort to give prescriptive advice to social entrepreneurs regarding how they might effectively manage their interorganizational relationships toward the goal of scaling social impact to a meaningful level.

It is widely agreed that there are three main threats to any interorganizational alliance: misrepresentation, opportunism, and hostage. Of these risks, it is opportunism and hostage that are most germane in a discussion of partnerships in which organizations possess misaligned interests such as PPPs. Opportunism occurs when an organization seeks to acquire resources and/or capabilities from a partner without consent and/or that were not agreed to prior to the alliance, whereas hostage occurs when an organization refuses to make available to its partner the resources and/or capabilities it promised. The reason these risks are particularly relevant to PPPs is that they are likely to arise as a direct result of the conflict regarding the misaligned goals of the parties involved in the alliance.

According to Khanna et al. (1998), when partners do not agree on the objectives of an alliance, there are few objectives that can be achieved that will satisfy both parties. As a result, partners are likely to view the alliance as a means to attaining their own ends, and thus focus their efforts on obtaining advantages that will benefit themselves, often at the expense of their partners. In other words, in the presence of conflicting agendas, the ratio of "common benefits" to "private benefits" is likely to be quite low. In such contexts, partners are less likely to engage in the cooperative application of learning so as to increase the prospects for alliance success, and more likely to engage in the competitive poaching of skills and assets from their partners (while withholding their own) and apply them in ways that are unrelated to the success of the alliance.

This type of anti-cooperative behavior undermines social entrepreneurs' chances for scaling impact to meaningful levels in two related ways. First, by holding hostage their own resources, possibilities for synergies by fully integrating their resource bases with those of their partners are all but eliminated. Second, by opportunistically appropriating partners' resources, the power relationships among partners are drastically altered, resulting in a state of resource dependence (Inkpen and Beamish, 1997). Although social entrepreneurs, partly driven by do-weller motives, may believe that this type of competitive behavior is in their self-interest, the absence of the synergies and sense of mutual dependence upon which alliances were established in the first place will only serve to exacerbate the level of conflict among parties, thereby accelerating the premature dissolution of the PPPs and any chances of long-term, large-scale efforts along with them.

In order to encourage cooperative behavior, social entrepreneurs can take a variety of steps. To begin, all partners in the alliance must agree on the resources to which they will provide access (Bamford et al., 2004). By pledging to invest specific resources in the partnership, parties build mutuality and demonstrate a commitment not only to arriving at local solutions to social problems, but also to sustaining and replicating those efforts on a larger scale (Kanter, 1999). While this advice seems straightforward, it is difficult to operationalize in practice due to the mechanisms by which these agreements are governed as well as the contexts in which they are governed.

Most scholars agree that alliance terms can be governed by some combination of trust and contracts. According to Das and Teng (1999), both mechanisms are effective at reducing the threat of anti-cooperative behavior but in different ways; trust being an intrinsic source of risk reduction and contracts being an explicit source. Unfortunately, reliance on either mechanism is often problematic for social entrepreneurs for contextual reasons. As noted earlier, the majority of social problems are argued to exist in developing countries (Prahalad and Hammond, 2002). Given that such environments are also characterized by far lower levels of entrepreneurship than developed countries (Doh et al., 2009), a substantial proportion of social entrepreneurs are likely to be engaged in cross-border PPPs.

Due to the nature of these relationships, reliance on trust or contracts is problematic for the following reasons. With regard to contracts, it is important to begin by noting that because social entrepreneurs, like most entrepreneurs, are small (Kirchhoff, 1994), they lack the financial resources necessary to obtain the legal services that could detail terms of alliances. Yet, even in cases where social entrepreneurs do possess the means to write contracts, the markets in which they tend to operate are plagued by a host of institutional voids that will likely render contracts unenforceable. Due to the weak rule of law, inefficient court systems, prevalence of political corruption, and the like, legal documents are often unenforceable in less affluent areas (Khanna et al., 2005). For these reasons, trust seems an important and valuable alternative for social entrepreneurs, given low monitoring and control costs compared to contracts (Carson et al., 2003; Hansen, 1994). However, because cross-border PPPs result in partnerships among organizations from different cultures, partners in these alliances have divergent understandings of trustworthy behavior (Lane et al., 2001). It is important to note that although cultural differences tend to be most dramatic the farther they are from their own borders, such differences are not merely relegated to partnerships between parties from different countries. As Kanter (1999) observes, much social entrepreneurship occurs in the poor, urban centers of developed economies, and in cases where domestic social entrepreneurs from outside those regions form PPPs, they are often confronted with substantial cultural differences.

In light of these challenges, scholars advocate allying only with potential partners who have managed alliances well in the past (Ahuja, 2000; Gulati, 1998). To identify such organizations, social entrepreneurs should seek those with a history of trustworthy behavior (Gulati, 1998). Thus, social entrepreneurs ought to gather information from prior direct experiences with potential partners or from organizations that share common ties (ibid.). In so doing, social entrepreneurs may focus on behavioral characteristics, such as upholding of agreements and reciprocal sharing of resources (Inkpen and

Beamish, 1997). Of course, social entrepreneurs seeking to establish PPPs, particularly in cross-border situations, may find that neither they nor other members of their networks have aligned with any of the potential partners in the past (Child and Yan, 2003). Thus, social entrepreneurs should also consider the degree and nature of strategic interdependence between themselves and potential partners (Gulati, 1998), and they must identify not only which organizations possess the resources that they require, such as information about the local market and the provision of connections to other local players, but also which organizations could benefit from the resources the social entrepreneurs bring to bear. It is only through provision of these inducements that the potential for resource dependence can be mitigated, thereby allowing for open sharing of resources and the synergies that may result from their integration (Ahuja, 2000). In sum, while the partner selection process is complicated in cross-cultural PPPs, it is essential as it is only by engaging in this level of due diligence that social entrepreneurs may identify those organizations that not only *can* provide access to the necessary resources, but more importantly, those organizations that *will* (Stuart, 2000).

Public-Private Partnerships: An Illustrative Case

In this section, we examine a particular PPP that demonstrates many of the concerns and resolutions of those concerns articulated previously. The context is contained and reveals how even local problems with discernable boundaries face serious obstacles in their resolution (see Hill, 2001, for more details). The partners are from the public, nonprofit, and for-profit sectors, and their alliances are fraught with the goal incongruence, resource constraints, and lack of trust that limits potential social changes on a scale consistent with perceived needs. Their struggle shows that resolution of some, but not all, of the underlying conflicts can only take the partners so far toward reaching their goals, leaving the collective more cohesive and realistic about what they can accomplish. Yet to reach this point also involves a giving-up on the scale of impact originally sought and giving-in to external pressures for compromise.

Creation and Operation of a Public-Private Partnership

The creation and operation of any PPP passes through a number of interrelated stages that move from one to the next according to how the alliance develops. In this particular case the five that emerge include *community uprising* by downtown business and civic leaders as the presence of homeless youths became increasingly obvious and intrusive. The next category chronicles a *negotiated peace* that manifested because of proactive efforts by the local government to moderate the increasing conflict between the downtown business community, nonprofit service providers, and the new social enterprise. From this point forward, *a service-delivery system emerges* that meets the explicit approval of all three partners. However, *serious dissension occurs* in the implementation of the resulting service-delivery model, and nonprofit providers experience grave concerns about their working relationships with for-profit entities. A *coming together* ultimately demonstrates the desire of all partners to see the system survive when it meets with unprecedented public scrutiny after an initial eighteen months of operation.

Community uprising

With the coming of the important summer tourist season, the situation of homeless youths living in downtown Portland, OR, became untenable. The nearly fifteen hundred teenagers were congregating, panhandling, and using drugs and alcohol in a defined area of the city, almost triple the number from ten years earlier and taxing the woefully underfunded local social-service network. Although only limited data existed at the time, informed observers believed that this subpopulation was composed mostly of runaway adolescents escaping physical and sexual abuse, throwaways discarded by parents or guardians, teens that abandoned the foster care system, and children who grew up on the streets. Unfortunately, from federal government to state and county, focus had been on more traditional homeless groups that included veterans, single-parent families, and mentally ill/substance-abusing adults.

The rise in their numbers and increased visibility led to media reports of expanded drug use, property crimes, and citizen intimidation, causing some proprietors to fear possible declines in downtown shopping and dining like other urban centers such as Detroit. Negative experiences of civic leaders who worked on the boards of the few nonprofits serving this population provided an additional call-to-arms. As a consequence two organizations formed a committee led by well-known corporate executives to examine the situation. A shared concern involved the contrast in philosophical approaches of the two primary service providers. The dominant nonprofit agency adopted a social welfare model believed to be inappropriately grounded in the provision of relief-based services for youths without regard for willingness to enter treatment or to seek permanent solutions to their homelessness. The social enterprise sponsored by members of these committees was viewed as superior, and it employed an outcomes-based business model with the goal of removing youths from the streets and into independent living through family reunification or transitional housing and education. The remaining agencies used some combination of the two philosophies, holding youths to a greater or lesser degree of accountability for their actions.

Nonetheless, even if resource levels were adequate and the focus of providers reoriented to good business practices, members of the committee believed that the current delivery system lacked effective governmental oversight to ensure that publicly funded services were meeting any reasonable and measurable standards. According to the most vocal members, this problem was due, in part, to the dearth of clear systemic goals and objectives for service delivery by the nonprofit providers. Of course, given the differences in orientations just noted, there was little agreement on what might constitute successful service provision. The do-gooder agency discussed was satisfied with getting them off the streets, even if this situation was temporary, while the do-weller/do-gooder social entrepreneur espoused success occurred after youths moved to permanent housing. This fundamental conflict was made more visible because the latter relied mostly on anecdotal evidence of effectiveness in lieu of more rigorous evaluation when reporting to funding sources.

Negotiated peace
To deal with identified problems as well as to improve the service delivery system, the committee drafted the following recommendations: (1) Responsibility for oversight of the provider network should be vested in the local government; (2) a systemic plan of action should be developed that forms a PPP among concerned parties and organizations; (3) this alliance should adopt one clear philosophical approach that supports movement of these youths from the streets to safe and secure housing; (4) clear and measurable objectives should emanate from this overarching goal, and data on the resulting outcomes-based parameters should be amassed and disseminated to various constituencies.

The report was reviewed by the county commissioners, and they ultimately approved a resolution that adopted most, if not all, of these recommendations. As a show of support, the county's Department of Community and Family Services was mandated to take the lead in the coordination of the current service delivery system. Further, the county chair empowered an ad hoc committee composed of a diverse mix of nonprofit, business, and governmental leaders to evaluate the current service delivery system, outline components of an ideal system, develop outcomes for that system, make recommendations for the use of available funding, and identify additional issues to be addressed.

The committee's deliberations and analysis blended the principal goals of the various providers by calling for a responsive, market-driven approach to serving these youths. The guiding belief was that it is unacceptable for any teenager to live on the streets, and it is the community's responsibility, through a PPP, to ensure that their basic shelter, health care, and nutritional needs are met. Nonetheless, there must be a balance between short-term relief and long-term programs that help youths move to permanent accommodations. To ensure that the model was implemented properly, an oversight committee was established that contained members from the major constituencies represented on the committee as well as the executive directors of the four agencies that provided services to homeless youths. This group met monthly to discuss activities of the providers, new opportunities for and threats to service provision, and public and private funding sources.

A service delivery system emerges

With this new charge, employees of the Department of Community and Family Services went about the task of assembling the diverse membership of the new oversight committee. To ensure that all relevant constituencies were included, persons from the mayor's staff, the county commissioners' offices, the Joint Homeless Youth Assessment Committee who issued the original report, the juvenile justice system, the police department, the public school district, the academic community, and the social-service network (but not from the current providers) were asked to serve. The multidisciplinary nature and disparate perspectives of this group led many participants to question their ability to come to agreement on the current service delivery system or the makeup of an ideal system. The first few meetings were designed to ensure that they shared the same baseline information about the youths themselves, the current provider network, and regional and national best practices for service delivery, often challenging their knowledge of children suffering from abuse, neglect, poverty, mental illness, and addiction.

The committee was also provided with first-hand accounts of the current service delivery system from the perspectives of these youths as well as the providers. Approximately sixty young men and women offered written recommendations for change that they felt would support movement from the streets to permanent shelter. Their needs involved improvement and availability of basic services, increase in relevant and accurate information about services within the homeless population, and expansion of their ability to make informed choices. Additionally, the current providers were allowed to describe their service delivery philosophies along with operational details. Two subsequent field trips by committee members helped make these approaches and their resulting challenges more tangible. Finally, national, regional, and local experts exposed the committee to best practices for serving homeless youths. They described the discontinuity, disruption, and trauma of the early lives of these teens and the need to establish a development model that was appropriate to their level of maturity and receptivity.

One outcome from deliberations was a warming to one another and real movement away from adversarial and rigid positions toward a consensus mentality. Consequently, a merging of their primary interests into a single unified approach occurred. The ideal service delivery system ultimately articulated contained a single overarching goal that homeless youths be able to leave street life to become productive members of the community. This system was anchored by two guiding principles: (1) Homeless youths would have access to basic resources; and (2) community laws and regulations would be enforced for such youths. Thus, these young men and women were to be provided with an unconditional access to food, companionship, clothing, health care, shelter, and transportation as a demonstration of the community's compassion. Nonetheless, the enforcement of standards of licit behavior showed the community was willing to set boundaries to convey appropriate models of adulthood. These positions were codified in a set of basic and specific outcomes designed to lead to the achievement of the superordinate objective.

Dissension in the ranks

The service delivery system that eventually emerged from deliberations was met with high praise from all quarters. Unfortunately, resulting euphoria quickly evaporated when county executives explained that funding was expected to increase significantly but not rise to the level necessary to finance the total system. As a consequence, the committee was asked to prioritize the services contained within the model. A vocal contingent felt that this request was incompatible with a systems approach to service delivery because it failed to take into account the connections between the various components of the model that were essential for successful exit from the streets. After considerable debate, the committee finally agreed to establish a minimum package of services that they believed was critical to the safety of homeless youths. Nonetheless, they also made it clear that anything less was insufficient and strongly urged that the minimum package be funded, even if it exceeded currently available budgets, for the system to function and important outcomes to be achieved.

This decision to fund only essential portions of the ideal system had longer term negative consequences for its implementation. For instance, the minimum package only provided for basic services, needs assessment, and service coordination, without many of the transitional services necessary to move youths from initial crisis to permanent accommodations. Further, money for alcohol/drug treatment and mental illness services was cut in the hope that other public sources might materialize, ensuring that the most difficult cases could not be properly cared for within the system. The young people privy to the model felt substance abuse was a key problem that needed immediate attention within their homeless community. As a result of these deficits, several members of the committee questioned the ability of the new delivery system to meet the overarching goal of helping homeless youths successfully exit street life.

After agreement was reached, a request for proposals was distributed to the current set of four providers, asking that they create a unified continuum of services based on each agency's experience and expertise. Together, they were required to divide the key elements of the service delivery system, assign responsibilities to each according to its abilities, and develop a plan for implementation. However, the providers recognized immediately that they would not be able to accomplish their assigned tasks without additional revenue sources. Thus, each agency sought private and/or other public funding to supplement the county's allocation. Not surprisingly, the providers expected to cooperate for service delivery, but they were in competition for the money necessary to meet their obligations. The oversight committee charged with supervision never addressed the balance between cooperation and competition, and the manager selected by the county to play a leadership role struggled with this issue during her entire tenure.

Also, when providers successfully raised funds, organizations or persons providing financial support often had agendas associated with their philanthropy that conflicted with the espoused goals of the service delivery system. This situation led to philosophical conflict reminiscent of other days, causing a serious strain on provider relationships.

Coming together

A year and a half after initial implementation, the oversight committee was asked to evaluate its early effectiveness and present findings at a public meeting of the county commissioners. A private consultant who was an ex officio member of the committee was asked to provide a preliminary evaluation of the system based on data gathered during the first twelve months of operation. His findings revealed a mostly upbeat but decidedly mixed assessment of success by the current providers. On the positive side, a large majority of the homeless youths living in the downtown area entered the system at the designated point of entry, and most were screened to determine their immediate needs for services. Of those served, almost half met the criteria for hardcore homeless, a group of particular interest to county officials and the business community. Finally, most homeless youths who moved from screening to assessment to service coordination to exit successfully obtained safe and secure housing.

On the negative side, several troublesome issues were revealed. First, a bottleneck was uncovered at the point of entry to the system. Of the homeless youths initially screened, only about one-third received any formal assessment of long-term needs, limiting the likelihood of appropriate referral to other providers within the network. News of this finding spread among committee membership, resulting in defensive remarks from managers of the organization that operated as gatekeeper and angry reactions by the other providers, especially the social venture of the business community. Another troublesome issue involved the number of homeless youths accessing the service delivery system with criminal backgrounds, especially an increase in drug convictions due to a proliferation of black-tar heroin. Concern developed among representatives from the business community and the police force that providers may have been harboring fugitives. Taken together, the two problems further exacerbated expressed conflict surrounding perceived philosophical differences.

Given initial negative reactions to these data by the providers as well as some committee members, the presentation to the county commissioners was postponed. In its place, meetings were held by the Oversight Committee to seek resolution to these conflicts. They eventually arrived at a consensus on the following points: (1) The new service delivery system was a significant improvement over the old system despite its current shortcomings; (2) the point of entry bottleneck was resolvable without dramatic changes to the organizational philosophies of the providers; (3) the manner in which the providers dealt with criminal warrants among youths required a unified policy; and (4) the resources necessary to cope with the drug problem among homeless youths must come from private or noncounty sources of public funding through joint efforts by providers. With this settlement, the committee membership developed a presentation that would highlight the positive outcomes of the new system yet demonstrate that the providers were proactively resolving trouble spots.

A Different Case

While this situation shows the ups and downs associated with PPPs, many successful outcomes ultimately were achieved. However, such alliances do not always meet their objectives despite good intentions, the importance of goals, and an initial enthusiasm. Consider as an alternative the situation of "Old City," a fictitious name for an African American town located in the south (see Hill, 2010). This community was where people of color lived and shopped prior to desegregation and remaining citizens typically faced job loss and poverty rates two–three times that of the nearby "white Downtown." The contrast of available work and retail establishments was stark, with the former lacking such basic purveyors as post offices, banks, and supermarkets, while the latter was characterized by high-rise condominiums, many local and national financial institutions, and a large variety of restaurants and museums.

The *community uprising* occurred as a result of two events that demonstrated the divide along racial lines. In the first, local NAACP leaders came to a Downtown Chamber meeting to discuss use of Old City contractors. They were told the Chamber maintained a list of available firms but no specifics about who was receiving business or any future commitments were given. The second event concerned disruption at the only movie theatre complex, which was located in the heart of Downtown. The African American community had a custom of meeting there on the first Friday of the month, and on this occasion a fight broke out among some teenagers and their parents. A forum to discuss this disturbance was called by local political and civic leaders on both sides, and most of the conversation was directed at the African American community and centered on a dearth of Old City recreation options that allowed residents to stay near home.

Unfortunately, the *negotiated peace* never occurred. Local business leaders (the do-wellers in this case) believed that continued patronage from Old City African American consumers was not worth cultivating since their average purchases were significantly below that of more affluent white consumers living in or near Downtown, and the presence of Old City residents, particularly teenagers, tended to drive away this more lucrative clientele. On the other hand, Old City advocacy groups (the do-gooders) with a history of extreme tactics were unwilling to compromise, viewing any decision from the predominantly white Downtown community as another example of racial discrimination. In other words, the do-wellers viewed the problem as an economic one, the solution to which involved the patronage of their existing businesses by affluent (i.e., white) patrons, while the do-gooders viewed it as a social one, the solution to which involved equal access and opportunity for both whites and African Americans. Not surprisingly, no proffered solution was able to muster the necessary support to galvanize the do-wellers and do-gooders to work together to solve these dilemmas. As a consequence, the divide between blacks and whites that plagued their lives throughout their long history of coexistence seemed to continue unabated.

Given this divisive state of affairs, the *emergent plans* lacked the systemic understanding required of long-term solutions that incorporated the goals of the do-wellers and do-gooders. African American leadership in the neighborhood became increasingly fractured, and no single set of voices was available to chart their course. In its place was a group of well-meaning businesspeople from Downtown, who established a loose consortium of executives, government officials, and nonprofit organizations to bring forth a new shopping center in the heart of Old City containing many of the retailers previously unavailable. This social venture had the political power to persuade a large grocery chain and regional bank to locate stores within its perimeters, filling out the remainder of the city-long block with Old City entrepreneurs. On the surface, this collection of establishments seemed to meet many needs of the community including a greater variety of goods and service as well as lower-cost providers.

However, because the do-wellers representing the people most significantly impacted by the social entrepreneurs' activities were not consulted, their goals and objectives were not considered, resulting in a continued *dissension in the ranks* for several reasons. First, the venture's African American partners were more akin to the Downtown community in backgrounds and ideologies rather than to their Old City counterparts. Second, decisions concerning selection of retailers attempted to replicate what was available across the racial divide without consideration given to the detrimental impact on current purveyors. Third, while stores did fill a valuable need within Old City, it did not have much influence over the original issues associated with historical discrimination. The end result was a beautiful new shopping center that was touted by the local politicians as an answer to restrictions faced by African American consumers, yet it ultimately failed to result in a *coming together* since this "solution" reflected only the do-gooders' goals. As such, the intended social impact was never fully realized.

Important Lessons for Alliances with Social Entrepreneurs

Our previous discussion emphasizes several important points regarding the success or failure of social entrepreneurs. First, the issues, concerns, and conflicts experienced by social entrepreneurs in their attempts to meet the primary societal goals are similar to other forms of entrepreneurs and require the same good business practices. Second, the alliances sought and consummated will inevitably lead to disagreements that have the potential to reduce effectiveness and scale of impact unless public and private partners can come together and support the overarching goals of the collective.

Third, even a cohesive and proactive alliance may face several significant obstacles that limit long-term impact, suggesting serious threats to accomplishment remain regardless of the quality of interorganizational relationships. A few important lessons follow that may help social entrepreneurs navigate this difficult terrain.

Impetus for involvement by social entrepreneurs may come from outside the current system of provision, requiring a special sensitivity to but not necessarily support of existing organizational forms, interfirm alliances, and goal structures. The rationale for establishment of social ventures springs to life because some set of actors believes that a healthy market exists for essential goods and/or services. In the case first described, the business community conspired to present the existing public-nonprofit network with an alternative social venture built upon the philosophical tenets advocated here. Nonetheless, their early aspirations to reconfigure the entire network in their image and likeness met with stiff resistance, requiring their leadership to coop the overarching goal structure of the system in order to develop workable relationships across partners. In the end, compromise led eventually to a decrease in expected scale of impact.

Leadership of the development, implementation, and evaluation of a public-private alliance optimally is located in a single entity with the authority to mandate change. As our discussion clearly indicates, social ventures originating outside the existing system based on dissatisfaction with current delivery may lead to conflict and dissention that is likely to make social entrepreneurs poor candidates for leadership, despite belief in the superiority of their perspectives. As a consequence, governmental or other entities that control resources and enforce guiding regulations may be the best option for true systemic change and coordination. Within our cases, local business communities were able to exert the necessary influence over city and county governmental leadership, creating impetus for reevaluation of product delivery with a directive to modify the roles, responsibilities, and expectations of providers.

Major decisions concerning the delivery system are more effective if they involve all partners and parties with direct or indirect interest in the outcomes. This simple management practice often is violated when the collective holds competing visions and tactics. The cases presented reveal how fundamental differences between the provider community and the social venture may cause a hunkering-down mentality, isolating social entrepreneurs and the business people from the other players. Clearly, this "us-versus-them" mindset became unworkable when the levels of conflict rose to the point requiring interventions by local governments. In the end, forward movement necessitates sitting together and trying to iron out differences so cooperation across operations might occur. Without such a coming-together, little real progress is possible.

Establishing common ground and trust among the partners and other interested parties may help in the development of superordinate goals to guide the alliance. Conflict rarely is resolved if the various constituents lack some negotiated and agreed-upon frame of reference. In the first case, the county executive was instrumental in establishing a common ground by waiting to discuss any outstanding issues or complaints until after the committee's exposure to a variety of expert opinions, local and national statistics, meetings with some homeless teenagers, and site visits to several providers. As time passed and interpersonal barriers were lowered, some level of trust was established, and individuals representing different perspectives began interacting with one another and came to appreciate many possible problem-solving methods. Thus, once roadblocks to cooperation are reduced, interfirm goals can be developed to support advancement of PPPs.

Lack of the resources necessary to adequately resolve the problem and a diverse pool of funds with limited access may disrupt the system and lead to conflicts among alliance partners. After the working committees in the first case came to agreement on goals and tactics, the lack of appropriate funding led to internal squabbling over which providers should receive the limited resources from public and private sources. Resulting programmatic failures were a direct result of this mismatch between objectives and finances, causing some finger-pointing that jeopardized working relationships due to the concomitant rise in old conflicts. Thus, agreements involving goals and responsibilities become invalid, constraining cooperation and leading to dysfunctional competition. For alliances to meet their scaling aspirations, it is important that necessary funding exist prior to implementation of their strategic plans.

Once established, the ultimate survival of the delivery system becomes a superordinate goal in and of itself, potentially limiting the scale of operations and effectiveness. The same processes that allow disparate parties to come together in order to tackle difficult social issues may plant the seeds of their undoing. For example, disagreements by the partners in the first case led to serious consideration of drawbacks associated with the current delivery system as well as innovative solutions based upon the model provided by the business-oriented social venture. Yet, as the individuals representing various constituencies on the committees met and developed some semblance of trust, they began to invest more in obtaining common rather than private benefits. Unfortunately, when the system was under fire for a lack of impact, they selected to close ranks rather than seek new solutions, ignoring a second opportunity to innovate.

Conclusion

Despite the fact that much has been written on social entrepreneurship over the past two decades, our knowledge of the phenomenon is limited. And, while Short et al. (2009) lay out a robust agenda designed to advance what we know about social entrepreneurship, their focus on firm- and individual-level issues ignores an important dyad-level issue, namely interorganizational conflict. In today's global economy, organizations no longer (if they ever truly did) operate in isolation. Rather, they seek to achieve their goals in cooperation with other organizations and individuals. Unfortunately, despite the potential benefits partners might offer social entrepreneurs (such as access to resources, legitimacy, access to markets, etc.), their inconsistent agenda is often an insurmountable source of conflict. As a result of this unintended tension, social entrepreneurs may find themselves unable to scale impact to the desired level.

In light of this issue, this chapter has sought to examine the trials and tribulations of social entrepreneurs as they seek and operate within a variety of strategic alliances such as PPPs to enact catalytic change in the social sector. When entering into PPPs, social entrepreneurs would be wise to recognize that the benefits these do-gooder partners can and often do provide may be offset by the conflict that results from their own do-weller goals. This conflict, in turn, may shift the various partners' focus from promoting common benefits for all parties to securing private benefits.

Notwithstanding these challenges, we contend that social entrepreneurs may effectively manage their alliances by adhering to the same management practices traditional entrepreneurs do. By agreeing on outputs of and inputs to the alliance, as well as by allying with trustworthy partners, social entrepreneurs may mitigate (if not eliminate) conflict such that the PPP can effect large-scale social change. To illustrate this position, a case example of a local PPP made up of business executives, a social venture, nonprofit organizations, and two layers of government was used to demonstrate how multiple agendas may inhibit innovation until a more trusting working environment is established. Yet, as was also described, even after goals are aligned, a lack of resources may potentially limit the scale of the partners' combined impact by shifting the focus from cooperative to competitive behavior. In our second case, even less was accomplished.

Social entrepreneurship has become an important phenomenon in recent years. Indeed, Ban Ki-moon, current UN secretary general, recently launched the UN Global Compact, an initiative designed to establish a worldwide system of PPPs between governments, nonprofit organizations, and for-profit organizations in order to seek innovative solutions for its Millennium Development Goals (eradicate poverty and hunger, improve global educational opportunities, promote gender equity, reduce child mortality, improve maternal health, fight diseases such as HIV/AIDS and malaria, and inspire environmental sustainability) by 2015 (Biscoux, 2008). The nature and form of these partnerships are important, and they reflect Ki-moon's understanding of the complexity of real-world social problems/opportunities that exist, which only can be resolved/exploited when financial resources and innovative leaders from for-profit firms are linked with intellectual resources of nonprofit organizations along with logistical resources of government agencies. However, as we have endeavored to demonstrate in this chapter, while many organizations seek to effect social change, doing so on a measurable scale is extremely challenging. Thus, we hope the advice and lessons drawn from the cases presented in this chapter can provide social entrepreneurs with a roadmap by which they may effectively navigating this difficult terrain in the future.

8

Scaling Social Innovations: The Case of Gram Vikas

Imran Chowdhury and Filipe Santos

There are hundreds of innovations brought to the market every year by socially oriented entrepreneurs (Dees et al., 2004; Phills et al., 2008). While many of these innovations fail, some prove successful in their local context, addressing a pressing social problem and improving the economic and social conditions of populations. Successful social entrepreneurs then face a choice: Do they want to continue working in their current region, and fulfill predominantly local needs, or do they want to increase their impact by replicating their innovations in other geographies? Entrepreneurs who choose to scale social impact are faced with limits to organizational growth such as scarce resources or decreasing returns to scale. They often confront this challenge by transferring their innovations to other socially oriented organizations.

The purpose of this study is to better understand the process of innovation transfer between social sector organizations, an area that is at the nexus of research on social entrepreneurship, scaling, and knowledge transfer. While there is prior work on "social alliances" that involve at least one nonprofit organizational partner and serve noneconomic objectives such as increasing social welfare (e.g., Berger et al., 2004), for the most part there is very limited research analyzing how social entrepreneurs use *knowledge transfer as a strategy to achieve increased impact*. We aim to fill this gap with the present study. By taking the perspective of a successful social innovation and following the process through which the organization transfers the innovation to a partner, we hope to shed light on the various theoretical and practical concerns that arise in social innovation transfer.

In particular, we look at how social entrepreneurs work to maintain the fidelity of their innovation across a replication attempt; fidelity relates to whether the innovation being transferred resembles or deviates from the original innovation as it is transmitted (Ansari et al., 2010). Knowing where variation is likely to emerge during the transfer process may be useful in aiding social entrepreneurs to minimize deviation from a preferred model, or at least from the "core" elements of that model (Winter and Szulanski, 2001). Social entrepreneurs who fail to limit the extent of variation in their innovation as it is adopted by outside organizations may end up losing the meaning and goals of the original innovation during the transfer process, thereby impacting the reputation and acceptance of the original innovation (Malkin, 2008).

We are guided by a primary research question: *How are social innovations transferred to other organizations to increase their impact?* We address this issue by focusing on Gram Vikas, an Indian rural development organization. Founded in 1979 in the state of Orissa, Gram Vikas delivers comprehensive water and sanitation systems by working together with beneficiaries in villages that have limited access to such infrastructure. Our goal is twofold. First, we explain Gram Vikas's unique approach to rural development issues, in particular through its flagship Movement and Transformation Network for Transformation of Rural Areas (MANTRA) program. This is the successful *social innovation* the chapter focuses on. Second, we elaborate upon the strategies used by Gram Vikas to scale the MANTRA program beyond Orissa to other parts of India. Drawing on field observations, interviews, and archival data, we describe an ongoing attempt by Gram Vikas to transfer MANTRA to an organization outside Orissa. We show that the scaling process is fraught with challenges but can nevertheless be managed by focusing on the "Arrow core" of elements (Winter and Szulanski, 2001) that enable the social innovation's success. Although a focus on replicating the Arrow core during transfer attempts may result in less widespread implementation of the social innovation, such focus maximizes social impact by identifying the contexts in which transfer is most likely to succeed. The chapter concludes with some observations for future field-based research on scaling social innovations.

Theoretical Background

The literature on transfer of innovations offers contrasting views on how successful transfer happens. Work in the area of knowledge transfer emphasizes the use of templates as a strategy for achieving successful transfers (Szulanski and Jensen, 2006; Winter and Szulanski, 2001). These studies follow a classical engineering-based approach to knowledge transfer, which sees knowledge bundles as interlinked routines and processes that interact in specific ways to produce specific results. Tampering with these elements and their associated interconnections can lead to the breakdown of the whole system. This view contrasts with findings from the institutional perspective in organizational theory, which stress the importance of adapting innovations to the local context (e.g., Boxenbaum and Battilana, 2005; Djelic, 1998; Kostova and Roth, 2002).

Winter and Szulanski (2001) established the theoretical foundations of a strategic view of replication by developing the concept of the Arrow core, which refers to an understanding of the knowledge attributes that are replicable and worth replicating, together with knowledge of how these attributes are created and the characteristics of environments in which they are worth replicating. This information set can be thought of as the complete answer to the question: "What, how, and where should the replicator be trying to replicate?" With respect to the practice transfer and innovation diffusion literature, Winter and Szulanski note that replicating a template often involves transfers not only of varying scope (narrow versus broad), but also transfers of knowledge or elements that may be nonessential. As an example, the Intel Corporation utilizes a "copy exactly" strategy in the construction of new manufacturing plants based on the design and operation of successful existing facilities, down to the color of walls in new plants (McDonald, 1998). This is because of the complexity and precision of microprocessor fabrication and an inability to pinpoint the essential elements of the process. By zeroing in on an Arrow core over various replication attempts, organizations can come to a better understanding of the essential elements necessary for replication to succeed, and of the elements that can be left out without jeopardizing this success.

Some empirical research supports the Arrow core hypothesis. These studies provide evidence that presumptive adaptation of knowledge assets from one national setting to another may be detrimental to performance (Szulanski and Jensen, 2006), that adhering to a template during the knowledge transfer process leads to more effective knowledge transfer (Jensen and Szulanski, 2007), and that firms replicate more when organizational knowledge is ambiguous, but prefer adaptation when knowledge is context-dependent (Williams, 2007).

On the other hand, there is evidence to the contrary. Djelic's history (1998) of postwar reconstruction in mid-twentieth-century Europe demonstrates how France and Germany, to differing degrees, adapted American business models to "fit" their particular national contexts, resulting in hybrid industrial models that fueled substantial economic growth. Similarly, Boxenbaum and Battilana (2005) show how the "transposition" of human resources practices across national boundaries required adaptation to the institutional context of the target organization in order for successful implementation to occur.

For the most part, however, research in this area remains limited to transfer of knowledge within and between for-profit enterprises. It has yet to be applied in settings where transfers of knowledge take place between firms that have a primarily social mission such as innovations developed by social entrepreneurs (Dees, 2001). Social entrepreneurship involves "entrepreneurial activity with an embedded social purpose" (Austin et al., 2006), and is often characterized by the allocation of resources (financial, human, political) to neglected social problems (Mair and Marti, 2006; Santos, 2009). Social entrepreneurs are the source of numerous innovations in both the developed and developing world, from the provision of low-cost preventive cataract surgeries to the distribution of low-cost loans to poor women to the revitalization of neglected urban and rural school systems (Bornstein, 2004; Elkington and Hartigan, 2008; Phills et al., 2008). Because social entrepreneurs are often more interested in sharing their innovation to maximize impact rather than "owning" it to maximize profits, the knowledge transfer process may be qualitatively different from what is observed in transfers between purely for-profit enterprises. For instance, a profit-motivated transfer attempt implicitly represents a speculative judgment about what is profitable to replicate: it is important to replicate features that add value commensurate to their costs, value that can then be appropriated for the firm's stakeholders (Winter and Szulanski, 2001; Desa and Kotha, 2006; Bloom and Chatterji, 2009). Social entrepreneurs also seek to add value, but do so with the primary intent of delivering solutions that address neglected positive externalities rather than to capture value: social entrepreneurs work to ensure that the value they create spills over to the whole of society rather than a small part. Thus, profit may be a concern, but only to the extent that it helps to sustain their solutions (Santos, 2009).

This then begs the question: What is the most effective way for social entrepreneurs to deliver these solutions and add value? While social entrepreneurs are often successful in establishing effective business models to address problems in their local areas of operation, they face enormous challenges in scaling their operations and also to achieve greater "social" returns for constituents such as funding agencies (Bloom and Chatterji, 2009). Transferring knowledge to partners represents a relatively low-cost way for social entrepreneurs to scale a successful innovation, but it is a phenomenon that remains understudied as a method for scaling. It can be achieved by: (1) disseminating information through the use of "best practice" blueprints or intermediaries such as multilateral organizations and consulting firms; or (2) forming alliances with one or more partners for the purpose of knowledge sharing and replication (Dees et al., 2004).

The former strategy results in broad dissemination of the innovation, but suffers from a lack of control over the solution by the source firm. Organizations that choose to adopt the innovation can do so without any formal collaboration with source firm, and there is a greater possibility that the innovation may be utilized less effectively, or in a way for which it was not intended. On the other hand, the latter strategy—forming alliances with partners—leads to the dissemination of information over a much smaller sample of firms, but with greater control over the knowledge transfer process by the source firm (Powell et al., 2005). While this is certainly a slow-growth method for spreading the innovation, the source firm has greater room for flexibility with respect to the elements of its model it wishes to share and emphasize in its interaction with partners. The source firm can also more easily capture lessons on best practices and potential hold-ups to transfer when a strategy of direct partnership, rather than indiscriminate dissemination, is chosen. It is thus most appropriate at the earlier stages of scaling up a social innovation. For these reasons, we choose to concentrate on this second form of transfer in this chapter. In doing so we address a problem at the nexus of research on social entrepreneurship, scaling, and knowledge transfer that deserves academic attention.

Research Context and Methods

In this study we focus on a single case: a dyadic alliance between two social entrepreneurs, a source organization and a target organization, with the goal of knowledge transfer. The partners had engaged in reciprocal staff visits to share ideas and best practices in the two years prior to signing a transfer agreement, though no formal mechanism for innovation transfer was established before the agreement was signed. There is a clear source of knowledge and receiver of knowledge in this setting, so the outcome of the relationship is more straightforward than in other relationships where transfer can be noncooperative and in both directions.

Case Selection and Data Sources

We chose Gram Vikas, the source social entrepreneur for our study, for its pioneering role as a social innovator. The organization, along with its founder and executive director Joe Madiath, has received numerous social venture awards, including the Ashoka Changemakers Innovation Award, the 2007 Skoll Award for Social Entrepreneurship, and the 2006 India NGO of the Year Award. The partnership between Gram Vikas and the Comprehensive Rural Health Project (CRHP), the target organization in the study, is one of the best-documented ongoing partnerships in the organization's portfolio. Both of these organizations operate in the rural public health sector in India, albeit using different approaches to address the root problems of access to better sanitation and health in village areas. We were granted access to virtually all the paper and electronic records related to the partnership, which originated several years before the current transfer attempt, and were additionally able to interview key players involved in the partnership at both organizations, including beneficiaries at the village level.

In Yin's (2009) terminology, our method choice is an "in-depth case study" of the transfer attempt from Gram Vikas to CRHP. This approach is particularly suited to the study of social entrepreneurship: while being context and story "rich," social entrepreneurship suffers from a paucity of theoretical development (Austin et al., 2006; Dees et al., 2004; Eisenhardt, 1989). Thus, our primary goal in choosing the in-depth case study research method was not to develop theoretical propositions or test specific hypotheses, but rather to generate insights that can guide future theory development research in social entrepreneurship by looking at a situation that previously has not received significant research scrutiny.

We relied on multiple data sources to develop the case study, including: field observations, interviews, organizational records, emails, meeting notes, annual reports, project reports and updates, briefs and monographs,

Table 8.1   Case study data collection sources

Interviews	Archival sources	Observation	Preliminary survey
On-site at project locations	Annual reports	Participation in meetings and direct observation at both source and target organizations	Data on innovations developed by source social entrepreneur
Multiple levels— managerial and operational— within the organization	Reports to foundations and other stakeholders	Visits to project sites, at both source and target social entrepreneur	Information on past, ongoing, and future innovation transfer attempts
With beneficiaries	Internal memos	Direct observation at points of interaction between beneficiaries and operational staff	Data on geographic scope of innovation transfer attempts
Follow-up via telephone	Email exchanges	Public presentations	
	Official correspondence	Other interactions between social entrepreneur staff and local population, government officials, donors, and other stakeholders	
	Draft documents Websites Consulting evaluations Books		

books written about Gram Vikas and CRHP, consulting evaluations, and survey data. Table 8.1 provides an exhaustive list of sources of information used in the course of this project.

Data Gathering and Analysis

Data gathering and analysis proceeded in four phases as summarized in table 8.2. In the first phase, a preliminary survey was sent out to Gram Vikas and several other social entrepreneurs in July and August 2008 to gather information on the innovations developed by these organizations and to gain a greater understanding of past, present, and future attempts to transfer these innovations. Data gathered from this survey and archival material were used to identify the CRHP partnership as most worthy of study, as it was ongoing and a potentially large volume of data would be available for analysis.

During the second phase, the first author undertook a one-month-long visit to India in January and February 2009, approximately six months after the preliminary survey was administered. During this visit he visited both these organizations and conducted twenty-eight interviews with senior

Table 8.2   Data gathering and analysis stages

Stage	Name	Time period	Description
1	Preliminary survey	July–August 2008	Short survey was sent out to Gram Vikas to gather data on its social innovation, MANTRA. Information on past, present, and future attempts to transfer MANTRA was also gathered.
2	Field visit	January–February 2009	Field data gathered during a one-month-long visit to India in January and February 2009. A total of twenty-eight interviews were conducted, including eighteen at the source entrepreneur site and ten at the target organization site. Most of the interviews (twenty-four out of twenty-eight) were taped and transcribed.. Additionally, important organizational documents available only on-site in India were collected.
3	Intensive analysis	March–September 2009	A thick description of MANTRA was developed along with a chronological event trace for the period 2005–2011 outlining the various transfer steps to MANTRA to CRHP. An integrated narrative of the transfer steps was created.
4	Follow-up	November 2009	Follow-up by telephone and email with both Gram Vikas and CRHP to obtain further information and views on the transfer attempt.

executives, mid- and field-level project managers, and program beneficiaries. The conversations ranged from thirty to ninety minutes in length, and a total of eighteen interviews were conducted at the source entrepreneur site. Additionally, ten interviews were conducted at the target organization site. As several interviews at both the source entrepreneur and target organization were undertaken in a group setting, a total of thirty-nine individuals were interviewed across the sites. Most of the interviews (twenty-four out of twenty-eight) were taped and transcribed.

In the third phase data from the field visit, including archival materials gathered on-site, were intensively analyzed. In addition to the interview transcripts, we were able to obtain access to periodic reports to a funding agency detailing aspects of the Gram Vikas-CRHP transfer process, as well as a proposal for funding related to the transfer attempt. Additionally, the first author was were able to gather copies of numerous email exchanges related to the transfer attempt on-site in India, as well as legal documents and agreements related to the transfer attempt. First, we developed a thick description of MANTRA, Gram Vikas's social innovation, presented in the next section of this chapter. Subsequently, we constructed a chronological event trace for the period 2005–2011 outlining the various transfer steps to MANTRA to Gram Vikas (Lincoln and Guba, 1985; Miles and Huberman, 1994). Finally, we "added flesh" to the chronology, including relevant quotes and creating an integrated narrative of the transfer steps. The summary of this chronology is presented as table 8.3.

Table 8.3   The stages of transferring of MANTRA to CRHP

Stage	Time period	Duration (months)	Description
Informal collaboration	2005–2007	24	Senior-level staff members and field coordinators engage in exposure visits; sharing of best practices, but no formal implementation of practices.
Transfer formalization	2007–2008	12	Needs assessment conducted; meetings held in six CRHP villages to gauge interest in the program; one village selected as model village for implementation of MANTRA; villagers and CRHP staff travel to Gram Vikas for exposure visit; transfer agreement signed; technical staff from Gram Vikas will come to CRHP to help identify good water sources and confirm the appropriateness of model village for the project; a group of villagers from model village as well as a CHRP field coordinator travel to Orissa for a four-week training program.
MANTRA implementation	2008–2009	18	Trained villagers share their knowledge and implement MANTRA in model village with the help of CRHP staff members; gathering building materials; forming a Management Committee for the corpus fund; construction of soak pits for toilet facilities; constructing the actual bathing and toilet rooms as well as a communal well and water tank.
Maintenance	2010–2011	Up to 24	MANTRA up and running in model village; regular village-driven meetings held to discuss problems with use or maintenance of the new facilities; villagers and CRHP staff work to maintain 100 percent community participation, to ensure proper upkeep, and to prevent abuse or overuse of the water supply; proper functioning of MANTRA in model village is expected to facilitate the spread of the program.

In the fourth and final phase of the study we followed up in November 2009, nine months after our initial visit, by telephone and email with both Gram Vikas and CRHP to obtain further information and views on the transfer attempt. One phone call was made to each organization and several emails were exchanged. The data collected during this stage provided a fuller picture of the end of the "MANTRA Implementation" stage (described in table 8.3 and in the following paragraphs) we had observed in mid-operation in January and February 2009.

The Social Innovation

Gram Vikas has its roots in the Indian voluntary movements of the 1960s and 1970s. During this period many university students became social volunteers. One of them, Joe Madiath, led a group that came to the state of Orissa (traditionally one of India's poorest and least developed) from its southern neighbor Tamil Nadu in 1971. Setting out in the wake of a devastating cyclone that hit the eastern part of the Bay of Bengal, the group was highly motivated by the idea of social equity and wanted to do something for the countryside. After the crisis was over, Madiath and several other volunteers stayed on to continue with rural development activities in the state. For the next few years they experimented with various activities to help the poor, mostly in irrigation technology and agriculture. This group formed the core for what would become an officially registered organization, Gram Vikas, in January 1979, with Madiath as its executive director.[1]

Gram Vikas, which means "village development" in both Hindi (India's official language) and Oriya, the local language in Orissa, was originally formed to address the needs of the so-called *adivasi*, or tribal minorities, of the state. After an initial period of success addressing the intertwined problems of alcoholism and debt within these communities, Gram Vikas began to get involved in other areas of rural development, including education, health care and sanitation, income generation, and small-scale energy production through the development of biogas generators. Table 8.4 summarizes Gram Vikas's main areas of activity. The driving logic behind all of these activities was to develop a comprehensive approach to addressing the underlying social conditions that kept the people poor. In particular the company's biogas program became very successful in the 1980s when the government of Orissa approached Gram Vikas to expand what was a nascent effort to bring energy to rural areas; between 1983 and 1993 Gram Vikas built over 80 percent of the biogas generators in the state, representing fifty-five thousand individual units, while using only 15 percent of all the public funds allocated by the government in support of biogas projects (Gram Vikas, 2009).

While Gram Vikas's biogas program was very successful, senior managers within the organization felt that it did not adequately address the fundamental problem of inequality in Orissa, and, further, it did not allow the organization to work with the really exploited section of the rural

Table 8.4 Gram Vikas's focus areas for activity

Focus area	Description
Self-governing people's institutions	By reinforcing the concept of community using universally important needs of drinking water and sanitation, a common ground is made for villagers to sow the seeds of a "village republic."
Health	Water and sanitation are the first activities undertaken by any new village under MANTRA. This is the first step toward better health. The program brings safe piped drinking water and a toilet and bathing room for each family. This project coalesces the community, releases women and girls from the drudgery of fetching water, and gives them privacy with dignity.
Education	Village-based preschools, primary schools, residential schools for tribal (*adivasi*) children and resource centers
Livelihoods and food security	Supporting communities to manage their natural resources such as land, water, and forest in a sustainable way is an integral part of Gram Vikas's programs. Such support actively promotes conservation of water resources, crop diversification and rotation, which leads to improved food production and food security at the household level.
Livelihood-enabling infrastructure	Community-based renewable and energy-efficient technologies are promoted by Gram Vikas to provide energy for cooking, lighting, and provision of water in villages without electricity.
Human and institutional development	Gram Vikas works to enable people, both staff and community members, to widen their horizons and upgrade and expand their skills. This increases motivation and maintains momentum in addition to the direct benefits of newly learnt skills.
Outreach and networking	Dissemination of information relating to the work of Gram Vikas happens through participation in various state- and national-level workshops and consultations organized by the Indian government, as well as by various national and international organizations. Links forged in these meetings, as well as with visitors and volunteers, result in great rewards in the long term.

population—the extreme poor. In the course of a period of reflection and experimentation in the early 1990s, the biogas program was "spun off" into numerous smaller companies and the organization shrunk in size from one thousand staff members to less than five hundred. During this period, Gram Vikas developed a study of rural development problems and found that 80 percent of the morbidity and mortality in rural Orissa could be traced to the poor quality of drinking water. A direct cause of poor water quality was the unsanitary habits around human waste disposal. The organization thus began an initiative covering 337 families in five pilot villages to bring water and sanitation services to rural villages (Gram Vikas, 2002). This program, known as the Movement and Action Network for Transformation of Rural Areas or MANTRA, is now the foundation of Gram Vikas's activities and its most powerful social innovation.

MANTRA begins with the starting assumption that water and sanitation services are not privileges exclusively reserved for the most prosperous, highest-ranking, elements of urban society; rather, they are a right and resource to be equally shared among all members of a community, regardless of social position or geographic location. Nevertheless, the prosaic reality of life in rural Orissa belies this aspirational ideal: even to this day—after seventeen years of work on the problem by Gram Vikas and other NGOs as well as continuing work on the problem by the state government for decades—less than 20 percent of the rural population in Orissa has access to protected water, less than 1 percent to piped water supply, and less than 5 percent to sanitation facilities (Gram Vikas, 2008). For Gram Vikas this seemingly intractable problem presented an opportunity. By working to address the problem of poor (or nonexistent) water and sanitation facilities, the organization could simultaneously address the deep-seated problems of poverty and social exclusion in rural Orissa. MANTRA was therefore developed as a program that goes well beyond simple infrastructure development for water and sanitation: "MANTRA unites communities to overcome barriers of social exclusion. Water and sanitation, as an entry point activity in new settlements, is not only a vehicle for improved health, but also a way of transforming hierarchical chaste and gender based exclusion into **equitable inclusion**" (ibid.; emphasis theirs).

At the surface level, MANTRA delivers concrete water and sanitation infrastructure to villages. Gram Vikas ensures that all the families in a MANTRA village will have access to the same minimum level of products and services, including: (1) toilets and bathing rooms in every house; (2) twenty-four-hour piped water supply to the toilet, bathing room, and kitchen of every family; and (3) the construction of a water tank as a community asset (Gram Vikas, 2008; Keirns, 2007). Beyond this, MANTRA is guided by five core values—inclusion, social equity, gender equity, sustainability, and cost sharing—which link in fundamental ways to the broader social mission of "equitable inclusion" that Gram Vikas espouses. Table 8.5 provides a full description of Gram Vikas's core values.

To achieve "equitable inclusion" in MANTRA villages, Gram Vikas lays out two primary conditions, each of which encompasses different core values. First, villages join MANTRA only through an "all or none" scheme. Either 100 percent of the families in a village join the program, or none does. There is no in-between. In this way, Gram Vikas emphasizes the value of "inclusion" as a core value. This requirement is highly related to the values of "social equity" and "gender equity" as well, and these are manifested in villages by representation of all sections of the community in village decision-making processes and equal participation of men and women in community level decision-making and control.

Second, to ensure the financial and operational stability of the water supply and sanitation installed, all families must participate in the scheme by contributing, on average, one thousand rupees toward a "corpus fund" that goes toward maintenance costs and expansion of the water supply and sanitation system once it has been installed. This condition is most closely tied to the two core values of "cost sharing" and "sustainability," and is based

Table 8.5   The core values of MANTRA

Core value	Description
Inclusion	All households must be involved in the development process and must benefit equitably. Participation of all households of a habitation is a non-negotiable condition of the program.
Social equity	Representation of all sections of the community in decision-making processes across caste, economic status, and other barriers to ensure that a level playing field is created.
Gender equity	Equal representation and participation of men and women in community level decision-making and control.
Sustainability	Development processes have built-in institutional and financial mechanisms for sustainability, and are necessarily based on sound environmental issues.
Cost sharing	Poor people *can* and *will* pay for beneficial development services but there are some *social costs* that society at large must meet.

on the principle that the poor can and will pay for development services, and that the beneficiaries of MANTRA themselves are reliable sources of revenue for maintaining the water and sanitation systems.

The Transfer Attempt

While MANTRA started small, initially in five villages covering 337 families, the program has grown since 1992 to become Gram Vikas's central program around which the vast majority of the organization's extant activities are organized. As of March 2009, MANTRA was operational in approximately seven hundred villages covering nearly 45,000 families and a population of over 240,000 people. Most of this population was within Orissa but a few scattered projects have reached neighboring states as well; Gram Vikas's goal is to cover 100,000 families by the end of 2010 (Gram Vikas, 2009). With the maturity of MANTRA, Gram Vikas's leaders sought to increase its impact beyond the general area of Orissa. Joe Madiath, the executive director, in particular, saw the organization's mandate as being much broader:

> [after] the spin off [of Gram Vikas's biogas program] as the leader I had realized that we were not doing something for activities, we were trying to fill a gap. So if the government could not do it and there was no mechanism to do something then we would do it, and that also not forever. Only till it became mainstream, till it got assigned within the government programs, and so it was in my philosophy to never do an activity forever—do an activity, demonstrate it over a period and mainstream it.[2]

Part of this mainstreaming effort at Gram Vikas involves developing partnerships with other organizations that might be able to leverage the MANTRA model and Gram Vikas's unique approach to rural development.

Such networking and outreach activities constitute a "core strategy for expansion" of MANTRA for the years to come (Gram Vikas, 2008). Indeed, in mid-2008 the organization hired a full-time, senior-level "expansion manager" charged with growing MANTRA outside Orissa by partnering with other organizations, both within India and internationally.

One of the most prominent of these out-of-state partnerships, with the Comprehensive Rural Health Project (CRHP) in Jamkhed, Maharashtra, began as an informal collaboration with Gram Vikas a few years before the arrival of the expansion manager. CRHP has developed its own successful model of the Village Health Worker (VHW) as the basis for the overall health of a particular village over the past four decades. The VHW model is well-known as a primary health care model for rural areas in the developing world (Arole and Arole, 1994). By partnering with Gram Vikas, CRHP—which operates on a much smaller scale, covering approximately seventy villages—sought to bring comprehensive water supply and sanitation services to the rural areas around Jamkhed. Indeed, although CRHP's work has greatly decreased the incidence of infant mortality and numerous preventable diseases in project villages, while concomitantly increasing the life expectancy relative to surrounding populations, the availability of good water and sanitation facilities remains limited for the vast majority of families served by CRHP.

Planned Transfer of MANTRA to CRHP

The transfer of MANTRA to CRHP from Gram Vikas is proceeding over a number of years. We identified four distinct phases of in the course of our analysis, and these are presented along with a timeline in table 8.3. First, in the period before implementation and prior to signing a transfer agreement, several senior-level staff members traveled to Gram Vikas to observe project villages and to better understand the underlying principles of MANTRA (as outlined in table 8.2). Exchange also occurred in the other direction, with several Gram Vikas staff members traveling to Maharashtra to gain an overview of CRHP's village health worker program. This *informal collaboration* period lasted approximately two years, from 2005 to 2007.

In the second stage of transfer, a needs assessment was conducted and it was determined that the transfer of MANTRA to CRHP was desired by both parties. Meetings were held in six CRHP villages to gauge interest in the program, and one village, Sharadwadi, was selected as the model village for implementation of MANTRA. Two villagers from Sharadwadi, along with two CRHP staff, traveled to Gram Vikas for a short exposure visit, including on-site demonstration of water and sanitation facilities construction and discussions with communities that had benefited from MANTRA. Thereafter, a written agreement that outlined the steps for the transfer of MANTRA was signed; this created a formal mechanism for innovation transfer from Gram Vikas to CRHP. Following this, a group of four villagers from Sharadwadi, as well as a CHRP field coordinator, traveled to Orissa for a four-week program to study sites that had successfully implemented MANTRA, and also to receive training in the construction of bathing rooms and toilet areas as part of the program. This period of *transfer formalization* lasted approximately one year, from 2007 to early 2008.

In the third phase of transfer, actual implementation of MANTRA began in Sharadwadi. Upon returning from Gram Vikas the villagers sought to share their knowledge and implement the MANTRA model in Sharadwadi with the help of CRHP staff members. This implementation took the form of: gathering building materials such as bricks and stone chips; forming a management committee for the corpus fund; construction of soak pits for toilet facilities; readying every household in the village to receive materials for necessary items that are unavailable locally (e.g., toilet pan, door, cement, steel, etc.); and, finally, constructing the actual bathing and toilet rooms as well as a communal well and water tank. This *MANTRA implementation* period has just recently been completed, and lasted for approximately one-and-a-half years, from early 2008 to the end of 2009.

In the fourth and final phase of transfer, MANTRA will be up and running in the model village. Staff from the target organization, CRHP, will work with Gram Vikas to facilitate regular village-driven meetings to discuss and solve any problems with use or maintenance of the new facilities, while working to maintain 100 percent community participation, to ensure proper upkeep, and to prevent abuse or overuse of the water supply. The functioning of MANTRA in this village will facilitate the spread of the program to other CRHP villages. This *maintenance* period began in January 2010 when implementation at the model village was completed, and continues for at least one–two years until the model village becomes independent in maintaining the newly constructed water and sanitation facilities.

Actual Transfer of MANTRA

Despite the extensive collaboration between Gram Vikas and CRHP both before and during the *MANTRA implementation* phase, transfer of the program did not proceed as planned. Sharadwadi, the model village chosen by CRHP, failed to follow through on the actual implementation of the program. While at first weather conditions, including a particularly dry few months during the traditionally rainy monsoon season, were seen as a cause of inaction on the part of villages, it was soon evident that this was not the real cause. Out of the eighty families in the village only fifty-four had contributed to the corpus fund by April 2009. A much smaller number of families (twelve in total) had contributed brick, sand, and other construction materials necessary for the project. Additionally, since many of the villagers who had not contributed were involved in seasonal work at sugar processing factories in another part of Maharashtra, and would not return home for several months, getting 100 percent contribution was at best going to be delayed till mid-2009. CRHP wanted to go ahead with construction nevertheless, with the assumption that the families who had not given building materials or money toward the corpus fund would eventually offer their contributions once they returned from the factories and saw the benefits received by participating village members.

This turned out, however, to be a serious point of tension between the leadership of Gram Vikas and CRHP. Whereas CRHP's leaders saw fifty-four out of eighty families (approximately 68 percent) contributing as a relatively impressive feat, for Gram Vikas this did not meet one of the fundamental elements of the MANTRA program, namely, 100 percent participation of families in project villages in the construction of a bathing area and toilet facilities for each household and also in the creation of a self-sustaining corpus fund for maintenance costs and subsequent installations. Gram Vikas's leaders see these conditions as being a non-negotiable part of MANTRA. There are two justifications for this. In the first instance, there is a public health imperative:

> water is a common need for all, whether rich or poor, and clean water, that too is a common need for all...So there is a logic [in MANTRA] for [100 percent] inclusion...if you do sanitation only for a certain section of the people, those who can afford to do it and the rest you just leave out, you are not going to get clean water in the area.[3]

The second justification goes to the deeper meaning of MANTRA. Because the program uses water and sanitation as an "entry point" into project villages where developing greater social equity is the overarching goal, compromising on this condition would jeopardize one of the fundamental reasons for creating MANTRA in the first place. Leaving aside the impracticality of getting clean water in a village where even a small percentage of the population persists in unsanitary hygiene practices, the 100 percent requirement ensures that all villagers, regardless of caste or class or income, are equal on at least one dimension: access to clean water and good sanitation facilities. While this meaning was clear to Gram Vikas, which had purposely adopted a slow-growth strategy to ensure that this requirement be met in all project villages, for CRHP, which was less concerned with equality than ensuring the good health of villagers in its project areas, it was secondary to the goal of putting in water and sanitation facilities where they were not available before (an accomplishment unto itself!).

After much back-and-forth between the leaders of both companies, Gram Vikas and CRHP came to develop a temporary solution to the problem of less-than-100-percent inclusion at Sharadwadi. Instead of continuing to directly motivate Sharadwadi's villagers to get to 100 percent contributions, CRHP created a "contest" between Sharadwadi and another nearby village in its project area, Mandwa. Mandwa, which is a much smaller village of forty-nine families consisting mostly of tribal peoples and nomads, was selected on the basis of the motivation and enthusiasm displayed by villagers to implement MANTRA (including the 100 percent requirement of contributions) dating back to the original attempts by CRHP to gauge interest in the program. In the end, it turned out that Sharadwadi was unable to implement MANTRA as originally intended, but Mandwa, with its smaller, more-motivated population, was able to complete implementation of the project in December 2009 and provide the successful demonstration project that CRHP needed to expand the program further.

Key Findings and Discussion

This study addresses the following research question: *How are social innovations transferred to other organizations to increase their impact?* Our in-depth case study of Gram Vikas's transfer of MANTRA to CRHP validates earlier work in the area of knowledge transfer. At the same time, we suggest some interesting applications of this work to the areas of social entrepreneurship and scaling social enterprises, where knowledge transfer may proceed with particular nuances and differences when compared to other settings.

Our first finding relates to the transfer of core elements of an innovation. They are essential. As noted by Winter and Szulanski (2001), by zeroing in on an arrow core of elements over various replication attempts, organizations can come to a better understanding of how innovation replication succeeds, and which elements can be left out without jeopardizing this success. Gram Vikas's work in rural Orissa since 1992 allowed many such replication attempts to take place, the vast majority of them under the organization's control and administered through project suboffices. As the organization starts to expand by partnering with other organizations outside the state, this level of control is inevitably lost. Differences among partners make the loss of control more problematic by leading top differences in implementation. Aside from differences in organizational size, structure, mission and culture—Gram Vikas is a registered social organization with roots in social movements whereas CRHP is a social organization that was founded on the religious conviction of its founders, who are devout Christians—regional differences between various states in India may also play a role in the acceptance and implantation of MANTRA. For instance, states differ significantly in their legislation and arrangements for water and sanitation, and they also differ in terms of what may or may not be culturally acceptable to the rural populations (Gram Vikas, 2009; Keirns, 2007).

With this understanding, Gram Vikas's attempt to transfer MANTRA has been characterized by a focus on the two key elements it feels are necessary to ensure the program's success: (1) 100 percent participation of families in project villages through the construction of a bathing area and toilet facilities for each household; and (2) creation of a self-sustaining corpus fund—for maintenance costs and new installations—belonging to the village into which every family contributes an average of one thousand rupees (approximately twenty-one dollars at current exchange rates in January 2010). These are the elements the organizations insists that partners, such as CRHP, replicate as part of the MANTRA transfer. Changing these elements would change the nature of the innovation such that the expected outcome (100 percent availability of water and sanitation services in a village) would be compromised. Yet, we also observed that Gram Vikas was quite open to adaptation of MANTRA "around the edges" of the innovation, away from the core. For instance, in Orissa the sourcing of specialized materials for construction other than those contributed by villagers is done with the help of the state government, and subsidies are paid to villagers to aid in the MANTRA-related construction costs once the initial corpus fund contributions have been made. This ensures that villagers continue to feel an ownership in the project beyond their initial contributions. Gram Vikas was willing to relax these conditions, however, and fit them to the needs of CRHP, which relies less on government funding and more on charitable donations as a supplementary source of funding for its operations, and where the concept of direct subsidies to families in project villages is less established. This is in line with prior research on replication of innovations, which associates effective knowledge transfer with adhering to a template (in this case, the two broad "core" elements of MANTRA) while acknowledging the role of necessary adaptation when knowledge is context-dependent (Williams, 2007) as with the case of varied sourcing procedures for procurement of MANTRA-related construction materials arising from differences in resource availability between Orissa and Maharashtra.

Importantly, this finding is also related to the nature of social entrepreneurs and the organizations they lead. Freed from the need to answer questions such as "who wins?" or "who competes more effectively?" during an innovation transfer, social entrepreneurs can focus on the long term value created for society from spreading a particular technology or practice (Austin et al., 2006; Santos, 2009). Gram Vikas is able to pay greater attention to ensuring the impact of MANTRA on helping to break down caste and class barriers, even though such attention results in less widespread implementation of the program. Thus, by focusing on the arrow core—the 100 percent involvement requirement and creation of the corpus found—Gram Vikas increases the likelihood that MANTRA's deeper intent will be realized, but it comes at the cost of slower growth for the organization. This is a cost Gram Vikas is willing to bear as such focus maximizes social impact by identifying the contexts in which future transfer attempts are most likely to succeed.

Our second finding relates to the process of scaling innovations for social entrepreneurs. For Gram Vikas, which has worked for almost two decades to develop and refine MANTRA, its particular model of water and sanitation for rural areas is "patent free." This means that the innovation can be freely shared with partners without consideration of concerns related to competition and losing "market share" to organizations that perform similar activities (Rothaermel and Boeker, 2008). In this respect Gram Vikas is similar to other social entrepreneurs, who have a predominant focus on value creation for the society rather than value appropriation for shareholders and management (Santos, 2009). However, this does not mean that the innovation is freely implementable. For Gram Vikas creating value means creating value for all the members of a community, from the richest to the poorest in the village. As such the organization engages in a very controlled version of knowledge transfer with respect to MANTRA, a process that is governed by four distinct periods of engagement with the implementing partner, including: (1) an intensive period of "courtship" where Gram Vikas and the target partner learn about each other's work (the *informal collaboration* period); (2) intensive training for both staff and villagers at the tartget partner's project sites and the signing of a formal transfer agreement that governs the implementation of MANTRA at these sites (during the *transfer formalization* phase); (3) an extensively monitored implementation of MANTRA at the transfer partner's pilot project village (the *MANTRA implementation* phase); and (4) institutionalization of the MANTRA program through regular village meetings at the pilot site and collaboration with neighboring villages (the *maintainence* phase). By having a high degree of control over the transfer process, as is the case when firms enter into dyadic partnerships with well-defined milestones, social entrepreneurs can thus scale their innovations while keeping the original version of it relatively intact.

This leads to our third broad finding: the scaling process for social entrepreneurs is fraught with challenges, including those that arise with respect to the meaning of innovations as they flow from one organization to another. Social entrepreneurs are often interested in assuring consistent and faithful implementation of their innovation, but they are also aware that contextual adaptation of certain elements of the innovation may nevertheless be inevitable (Ansari et al., 2010). As noted by Powell et al. (2005), the temporal and experiential nature of contact between the source and target organization in an innovation transfer process can shape adoption at the target site. Thus, in the case of Gram Vikas and CRHP, the regular and faithful interaction of each organization's leaders during the various phases of the innovation transfer helped Gram Vikas limit deviation from the MANTRA model's core elements as it traveled from Orissa to Maharashtra. Gram Vikas was able, in this sense, to control the core and the "meaning" of the innovation, which is to increase the level of social equity in rural villages by means of comprehensive (i.e., 100 percent) water and sanitation coverage. To the extent that the philosophy of Gram Vikas's work is present at CRHP it may not be because of the two organizations' shared ideologies, but rather because the organization used various strategies to maintain core elements of the innovation and ensure fidelity to it (Ansari et al., 2010). Though Gram Vikas doesn't have formal power over CRHP, there is considerable influence as a result of the formalized partnership (Bradach, 1997).

Our fourth and final finding relates to the nature of partnerships that social entrepreneurs enter into, not only to scale their innovations, but also for the more general purpose of sharing knowledge and best practices.

One of the notable characteristics of alliances and partnerships generally, in both the social and purely commercial realms, is the increasing diversity of partners, motives, and goals in entering alliances (Austin, 2000; Rothaermel and Boeker, 2008). This diversity is also manifested in the variety of governance structures or the formal contractual structures used to organize the partnerships. The variety of organizing structures implies that firms face an array of choices in organizing their alliances (Powell et al., 2005). For Gram Vikas, this structure was formalized in the form of a *transfer agreement* that laid out the conditions and specifications related to implementing MANTRA. In the early stages of interorganizational transfer of a successful social innovation, we believe that this agreement may serve a function that is analogous to a *franchise agreement* for commercial firms—including fast-food chains such as McDonald's and services companies such as MailBoxes, Inc.—which expand through outlets run by non-company management (Bradach, 1997; Szulanski and Jensen, 2006).

Conclusion

The purpose of this study was to gain a better understanding of the process through which social innovations transferred to other organizations to increase their impact. We highlighted the importance of several key factors that influence these partnerships, including a focus on the core features of the innovation being transferred, the perils of not paying attention to potential variations in the meaning of the innovation at the source and target site, and strategies used by Gram Vikas to ensure that its "patent-free" innovation was not freely implementable, but rather followed a relatively precise sequence of steps as it was implemented by a partner organization. We believe that this study provides a foundation upon which future field-based research on scaling social innovations can build. In particular, we believe that the in-depth, single-case-study design utilized can be expanded to including multiple cases that can then be compared (Eisenhardt, 1989) to determine patterns related to the innovation transfer process for social entrepreneurs. This kind of study would go a long way toward advancing research in the fields of scaling, social entrepreneurship, and knowledge transfer.

Notes

The field research supporting this chapter was also used to develop a teaching case in two parts: "Gram Vikas (A): Social Entrepreneurship in Rural India" (2010, No. 810–002-1) and its companion piece "Gram Vikas (B): Scaling Up Social Innovations" (2010, No. 810–003-1). The case and an accompanying Teaching Note (2010, No. 810–002-8) are available from the European Case Clearing House.

We are thankful for funding provided by the INSEAD R&D Committee, the APAX Partners Social Entrepreneurship Fund, and the ESSEC Business School PhD Program.

The research project underlying this case is being developed in partnership with the Schwab Foundation for Social Entrepreneurship and the Lemelson Foundation.

1. Personal Interview with the executive director, Gram Vikas, February 2009.
2. Ibid.
3. Personal interview with the program manager, Natural and Human Resources, Gram Vikas, February 2009.

IV

Communicating and Branding

9

Communications Strategies for Scaling Health-Focused Social Entrepreneurial Organizations

Lauren Trabold, Paul N. Bloom, and Lauren Block

Poor health and inadequate health care have become enormously difficult issues to address in the twenty-first century. The need for innovation in health issues is being addressed by many new, health-focused, social entrepreneurial organizations, yet scaling their efforts to produce broad social impact has proven to be challenging. This chapter reviews the types of social entrepreneurial initiatives that have been tried in the health care area and then presents a set of heath-communication propositions about how these initiatives might be scaled up to have greater impact. We offer case examples of organizations that have had success with the recommended communications strategies.

The term "social entrepreneur" is typically used to describe *individuals who start up and lead new organizations or programs that are dedicated to mitigating or eliminating a social problem, deploying change strategies that differ from those that have been used to address the problem in the past.* Notable social entrepreneurs include (a) Wendy Kopp, founder of Teach for America, which places recent college graduates as teachers in inner-city schools for a two-year stint, and (b) Paul Farmer, founder of Partners In Health, which has provided low-cost treatment for AIDS, TB, and other diseases throughout the developing world. These innovators—and their social entrepreneurial organizations—pursue scaling because they want to have as big an impact as possible on social problems and because their donors and supporters are hungry to achieve high "social" returns on their investments.

The social entrepreneurial organizations that focus on health problems tend to emphasize *Prevention, Treatment,* or *Advocacy,* or some combination of the three. Figure 9.1 presents a way of categorizing these organizations, based primarily on their "change strategy," or on what some would

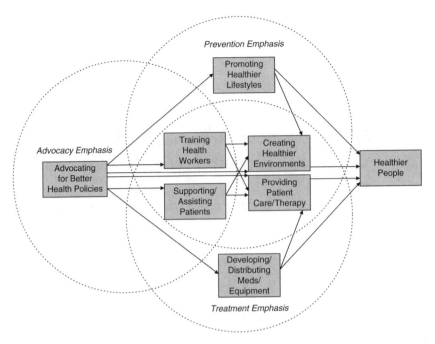

Figure 9.1 Theories of change employed by health-focused social entrepreneurial organizations.

call their "Theories of Change." They have a causal model in mind that links their programs or interventions to a series of outcomes that eventually will help resolve a social problem (Colby et al., 2004). We suggest that the "Theories of Change" of health-focused social entrepreneurial organizations tend to fall in one of seven different categories:

1. "Promoting Healthier Lifestyles" (a purely prevention approach)—for example, programs such as Girls on the Run that promote self-esteem and health for preteen girls.
2. "Developing/Distributing Medications/Equipment" (a purely treatment approach)—for example, programs supported by the Bill and Melinda Gates Foundation.
3. "Creating Healthier Environments" (a combination prevention and treatment approach)—for example, innovative programs promoting sanitation and natural resource conservation.
4. "Providing Patient Care/Therapy" (a combination prevention and treatment approach)— for example, innovative programs providing drug rehabilitation therapy, medical treatment, and so on.
5. "Training Health Workers" (a combination prevention, treatment, and advocacy approach)—for example, programs promoted by several major pharmaceutical companies.
6. "Supporting/Assisting Patients" (a combination prevention, treatment, and advocacy approach)—for example, programs focused on "cancer control" (as opposed to on finding a cure).

7. "Advocating for Better Health Policies" (a purely advocacy approach)—for example, the Campaign for Tobacco Free Kids.

Bloom and Chatterji (2009) propose that successful scaling of social impact by a social entrepreneurial organization will require the possession of some combination of seven organizational capabilities, identified using the acronym SCALERS. This stands for: *staffing, communicating, alliance-building, lobbying, earnings-generation, replicating,* and *stimulating market forces.* They also propose that the extent to which an individual SCALER (i.e., driver or capability) will influence scaling success will depend on certain situational contingencies. Each social entrepreneurial organization may find itself facing rather unique situational contingencies, indicating that the most important capabilities for effective scaling of better health outcomes will vary across organizations. For example, organizations with weak public support for what they are trying to accomplish will likely need to become more effective at communicating to be successful at scaling social impact.

It is extremely common for health-focused social entrepreneurial organizations to face a situational contingency of having weak public acceptance or support for the behaviors they would like their beneficiaries to engage in. They often have had only limited success in persuading individuals to (a) take preventive actions such as wearing sunscreens, using condoms, eating healthier or obtaining inoculations, (b) obtain screening tests for HIV/AIDS, cancer, or other diseases where early detection can save lives, or (c) comply with therapy and drug regimens. Communicating persuasively about the value of engaging in healthier behaviors has become a critical scaling challenge for many organizations, especially those involved with "Promoting Healthier Lifestyles," "Creating Healthier Environments," "Providing Patient Care/Therapy," and "Supporting/Assisting Patients."

In this chapter, we offer propositions about communications strategies that have a higher likelihood of changing the behavior of beneficiaries. Based on the literature in consumer behavior, social marketing, and health communications, we identify several communication strategies that can help guide a health-focused social entrepreneurial organization to scale its impact. We provide additional support to the propositions by citing several case studies of organizations that seem to have had scaling success, in part, by using some of the identified communications strategies.

Potentially Effective Communication Approaches

Given the growing importance of creating effective health communications that allow companies to scale their resources and successfully elicit desirable health behaviors, we have developed a variety of propositions that are illustrative of different message tactics. Overall, we believe our propositions can aid the construction of effective health communications to nearly any audience. Examples of social entrepreneurial organizations that appear to have adopted the advice from the first eight propositions are presented in the appendix. The propositions are followed by "Media Touchpoints" that illustrate the importance of the avenue through which the message reaches its audience in addition to message characteristics.

Scaling Up: Type of Health Behavior

Commencement versus cessation behaviors

Health messages can both encourage and discourage recipients from engaging in different types of behaviors. These behaviors may be categorized broadly as commencement (*start* a new behavior, e.g., mammograms, exercise) or cessation messages (*stop* a person from engaging in an old behavior, e.g., drug use, smoking). Commencement behaviors may be further categorized into detection, prevention, and enforcement behaviors. Detection behaviors are those, such as getting a mammogram, that can be adopted in order to determine whether or not an individual is at risk for negative health consequences; prevention behaviors, such as using birth control, can be encouraged as a preventative measure against detrimental health consequences; and enforcement behaviors are suggestive of actions that are enforced by law (e.g., wearing a seatbelt).

Two meta-analytic review papers present somewhat inconsistent evidence of the best type of behaviors to communicate in a health message (Keller and Lehmann, 2008; Snyder et al., 2004). While the meta-analytic results are difficult to reconcile, it is notable that theory and single studies overwhelmingly support the greater effectiveness of commencement versus cessation messages (Floyd et al., 2000, and Taylor et al., 2007, as cited in Keller and Lehmann, 2008). Thus, we propose the following and strongly encourage additional public health research on this issue.

> **P1:** Health communications that encourage the commencement of a new behavior (e.g., screening behaviors) are more effective than messages that try to prevent the adoption of a new behavior (e.g., reduce smoking trial), and both are more effective than those that aim to stop an old behavior (e.g., increase smoking cessation).

Because new behaviors are not yet habitual, it is easier to prevent nonusers from adopting a behavior than it is to prevent users from ceasing a behavior. For example, antismoking messages have been found to be more effective for adolescent recipients who have not yet begun smoking (Wakefield et al., 2003). Likewise, Block and colleagues (2002) found that antidrug advertising is effective at discouraging drug trial for nonusers, but less effective at decreasing usage for those already using drugs. Thus, health communications are more effective for an audience that had not previously engaged in the unhealthy behaviors than for those who had previously instituted unhealthy habits. However, since it is still important to use mass communication and media to encourage current users to cease the unhealthy behavior (e.g., drug abusers), we suggest that the messages must be targeted appropriately for each group.

> **P1a:** Communications need to distinguish between encouraging non-commencement of an unhealthy behavior and encouraging cessation or diminished engagement of an unhealthy behavior. Two separate approaches specifically targeting nonusers versus users must be employed.

The effectiveness of cessation communications will vary depending upon the strength of the person's preexisting attitudes toward and commitment to the behavior, such as when behaviors are addictive. Overall, health communications that encourage the cessation of addictive behaviors will be least effective (Snyder et al., 2004). Addictive behaviors present a unique challenge because there are physiological barriers to change that must be dealt with, such as withdrawal symptoms and the physical distress of terminating an addictive behavior, which make the recipient of the health communications more likely to dismiss the messages (ibid.).

Given the increased difficulty of terminating a behavior, communications promoting the cessation of old behaviors should focus on increasing the self-efficacy of the recipients and on their ability to make a behavioral change. This will encourage the recipients to feel more confident in their abilities to change and more likely to become determined to achieve the desired outcome (Schwarzer and Renner, 2000). Measures of self-efficacy are very good predictors of behavioral intentions, and behavioral intentions are the best indicators of actual behavioral change (Block and Keller, 1997; Jordan et al., 2007; Schwarzer and Renner, 2000). Self-efficacy is important at all stages of change. In the early stages increased self-efficacy will encourage the message recipients to set goals and motivate them to engage in behavioral change; later on, when the message recipients already have intentions to change their behavior, increased self-efficacy will make them more confident in overcoming the obstacles that are presented during the change process.

> **P1b:** Communications encouraging the cessation of a non-addictive behavior are more effective than communications encouraging the cessation of an addictive behavior.
>
> **P1c:** Communications encouraging the cessation of a behavior should focus on increasing the self-efficacy of the recipient by illustrating the person's ability to make a behavior change.

Scaling Up: Message Variables

Message customization

The degree to which health communications are customized to the attributes of their recipients is an important component of their success (Noar et al., 2007). Such customization generally takes one of two forms: targeted or tailored. Targeted health communications are slightly more individualized than generic health communications; they are directed at a specific segment of the population, but they lack individual specificity. However, the most effective health communications contain tailored message content to suit each recipient based on individual assessments (ibid.); tailored messages enhance the relevance of health behaviors to the targeted individuals and increase the likelihood that they will benefit from the message content and adjust their behavior.

Increasing the number of individualized components, such as tailored demographics and personally relevant theoretical concepts, amplifies the personal relevance of the message that in turn increases the likelihood of critically examining the information contained in the health message, rather than relying on heuristics (Petty and Cacioppo, 1981, as cited in Noar et al., 2007). Encouraging more elaborate processing of the information will subsequently result in stronger attitudes toward the message content and an increased likelihood of both behavioral intentions and actual behavioral change.

In addition to the inclusion of as many individualized components as possible, theoretical concepts, such as self-efficacy, stages of change, social norms, behavioral intentions, attitudes, and social support, will help to strengthen tailored communications (Noar et al., 2007). Health messages that include *both* tailored demographics and tailored theoretical concepts have been shown to be more effective than messages containing either tailored demographics or theoretical concepts alone (Noar et al., 2007). Furthermore, Noar and colleagues suggest that, similar to individualized demographics, the number of theoretical concepts seems to impact the effectiveness of the message; tailoring on more (four–five) theoretical concepts is more effective than tailoring on fewer (zero–three) ones.

Interestingly and counter to common intuition and lay theory, the theoretical concept of perceived susceptibility does not positively impact message effectiveness (ibid.). Noar and colleagues (2007) conjecture that the ineffectiveness of perceived susceptibility may be a result of the inability to be individually tailored; perceived susceptibility to a health threat does not vary significantly on an individual level. An alternative explanation is that statements of susceptibility in a message may lead to message denial, counterarguments, or less elaboration on the consequences (Block and Williams, 2002).

A very important theoretical concept that should be tailored in health communications is the stage of attitudinal and behavioral change the recipient is in (e.g., contemplating making the change, initiating the change, maintaining behaviors). Individuals may move at different rates through the cycle of change than their peers, and they often backtrack and then move forward again before behavior change is permanent, thus tailoring based on stage of change provides feedback that is relevant to the message recipient's present position in the cycle of change (Noar et al., 2007). Moreover, people in different stages of behavioral change require different types of reinforcement (Bull et al., 2001). Those in the earlier stages of change may be more receptive to communications that underscore the need for change, such as self-evaluation, as well as enhance the recipient's expectancy of positively achieving the desired behavioral change; those in the later stages of change may be more receptive to messages communicating behavioral strategies and emphasize the recipients ability to change, or self-efficacy (ibid.; Schwarzer and Renner, 2000).

P2: Tailored health communications are more effective than generic or targeted health communications.

P2a: The greater the number of individualized components there are in the message, the more effective the message will be.

P2b: Health communications that tailor on both theoretical concepts (e.g., self-efficacy, stages of change) and demographics are more effective than health communications that only tailor on either alone.

P2c: Health communications that tailor on the theoretical concepts of attitudes, self-efficacy, or stage of change are more effective than messages that tailor on the theoretical concept of perceived susceptibility.

Message framing

Health communications often use gain/loss framing to either instill the benefits of adopting healthy behaviors (gain-framed messages) or the detriments of not adopting healthy behaviors (loss-framed messages). Interestingly, while there has been research supporting both the superiority of gain-framed and of loss-framed messages under different conditions, a meta-analysis of gain and loss framed health communications found them to be equally effective (O'Keefe and Jensen, 2007). Though the overall average effectiveness of gain and loss-framed health communications is quite similar, research suggests that the regulatory focus of the message recipient may moderate the persuasiveness of each type of framing (Keller and Lehmann, 2008; O'Keefe and Jensen, 2007). In general, gain-framed health communications are more effective for prevention focused individuals. Such individuals aim to ensure a secure future and a gain-framed message will illustrate the secure, positive future that can be established by adopting desirable health behaviors. Loss-framed messages are more effective for targeting promotion focused individuals because such individuals aspire toward accomplishments and will be deterred from unhealthy behaviors. As the loss-framing illustrates an especially undesirable outcome for promotion focused individuals, they will adopt healthy behaviors in order to achieve a desirable outcome (Keller and Lehmann, 2008).

P3: Health communications that frame the outcome as a gain to the current status quo versus the threat of a loss are equally effective.

P3a: The effectiveness of gain and loss framing may be moderated by regulatory focus; gain-framed messages are more influential for prevention focused individuals and loss-framed messages are more influential for promotion focused individuals.

Scaling Up: Individual Difference Variables

Conscientiousness

Research suggests that particular traits may increase the likelihood of adopting healthy behaviors; traits such as conscientiousness may increase message effectiveness if they are made salient in the communications (Bogg and Roberts, 2004). Conscientiousness encompasses an individual's propensity to ascribe to social norms, exhibit self-control, responsibility, industriousness, traditionalism, order, and virtue (ibid.). It is not surprising that these facets of conscientiousness positively correspond to healthy behaviors; health communications that make these characteristics salient will be more effective in encouraging the message recipient to stifle unhealthy impulses and strive to meet societal norms, such as maintaining good health, in an orderly, organized fashion.

Additionally, research suggests that individuals possessing personality traits such as conventionality or traditionalism are more likely to adopt healthy behaviors; those who are highly responsible are likely to exhibit self-control, avoid trouble, and adhere more strongly to health recommendations (ibid.). Studies show that people with conscientiousness related traits versus those without are more likely to avoid consumption of alcohol and tobacco and risky sexual behavior and behaviors that do not abide by societal norms and may be seen as troublesome (ibid.). Therefore, health communications that encourage conscientiousness are more successful because they promote traits that will subsequently increase the likelihood of adherence to traditional social norms and regulations; unhealthy behaviors will lose their attractiveness.

> P4: Health communications should make conscientiousness-related personality traits (e.g., self-control, responsibility, industriousness, order, traditionalism, and virtue) salient.

Age

As previously mentioned, health communications that target the prevention of a new behavior are more effective than those that target the cessation of an old habitual behavior (Snyder et al., 2004). For this reason, it is understandable that health communications would be more effective when they target younger audiences, in hopes of intervening before they adopt unhealthy behaviors. Therefore, it is important to know the best persuasive tools for a younger audience. For such an audience, health communications that evoke strong negative emotional reactions elicit greater intentions to behave healthily than messages that do not incite negative arousal (Biener et al., 2004; Kees et al., 2006; Wakefield et al., 2003).

It has been suggested that the effectiveness of health communications eliciting strong negative affect may be attributable to the higher rate of recall of such ads over humorous ads (Biener et al., 2004). The emotions experienced after viewing the health message may reinforce the recipient's susceptibility to the negative consequences and mitigate the perceived social benefits of engaging in the behavior. Interestingly, a message that elicits an affective response, rather than a cognitive response, may be more effective in encouraging cessation of a behavior (versus the prevention of a behavior) (Andrews et al. 2004).

If a sequence of health communications is going to target a youthful audience, they should vary in the intensity of negative affect elicited in order to prevent "wear out." Constant extremely sad and frightening messages will eventually lose their effectiveness as recipients acclimate to seeing them repeatedly (Biener et al., 2004; Wakefield et al., 2003). Thus, while communications eliciting extreme negative affect will be more influential on youthful audiences, ability to elicit behavioral intentions in this way is limited; its effectiveness declines as exposure to the communications increases.

P5: Health communications targeting youth behavior change are more effective when they evoke strong negative emotions and are varied in intensity so as to avoid "wear out."

It is common for people to engage in unhealthy behaviors such as tanning and smoking in order to reap positive social benefits. Interestingly, people are often aware of the negative ramifications of such behaviors, but the harmful physical consequences are outweighed by the social benefits (Jones and Leary, 1994). Younger people seem particularly vulnerable, possibly due to a greater salience of social consequences and desire to conform to social norms (Goldstein et al., 2005; Pechmann et al., 2003). As confirmed by a recent meta-analysis, health communications that emphasize detrimental social consequences do correlate significantly with desirable behavioral intentions (Keller and Lehmann, 2008). When unhealthy activities are knowingly pursued for social reasons, health messages that reiterate the detrimental health consequences will be ineffective (Jones and Leary, 1994). Instead, health communications encouraging the cessation of unhealthy behaviors that provide social benefits should appeal to the mindset of the message recipient; since social consequences are very important to this population, messages should emphasize the social detriments of continuing the behavior, such as being seen by others in an unfavorable light (dirty, disheveled), being made fun of by peers, and negative effects on one's physical appearance (Greene and Brinn, 2003; Jones and Leary, 1994; Pechmann et al., 2003). Moreover, older recipients tend to respond more effectively to physical consequences than do younger recipients, supporting the fact that younger recipients are less concerned with physical ramifications that will occur later in life (Keller and Lehmann, 2008).

Finally, older message recipients will respond more favorably to new, novel information rather than to common knowledge (Jordan et al., 2007) and do not respond as strongly over time to repeated messages (Tangari et al., 2007). Adolescents, however, may have less exposure to certain health behaviors, such as smoking, and therefore have more malleable beliefs and will be influenced by a greater frequency of messages (ibid.).

> **P6:** Health communications aimed at younger audiences will be more effective if they focus on social consequences and are repeated frequently. Conversely, communications targeting older audiences are more effective if they focus on physical consequences and present novel information.

Scaling Up: Language and Culture-Specific Factors

It is imperative to account for the culture of the message recipient and create a message that will be appealing and easily understood. Cultural variables that should be addressed include language, family structure, cultural orientation, and methods of communication (Elder et al., 2009; Hinyard and Kreuter, 2007; Kreuter and McClure, 2004; Larkey and Gonzalez, 2007).

Methods of communication

Many cultures have strong narrative traditions; health messages targeting these populations are more effective when they include narratives in their messages versus statistical evidence and logical appeals (Hinyard and Kreuter, 2008). A narrative is a "cohesive and coherent story with an identifiable beginning, middle, and end that provides information about scene, characters, and conflict; raises unanswered questions or unresolved conflict; and provides resolution"; they are easily understood because basic human interaction involves the construction of stories (ibid.).

Traditional cultures, such as Latino populations, have a strong oral tradition. They pass down stories orally through the generations about the history of their culture and as a method of establishing cultural norms and values (Larkey and Gonzalez, 2007). Because these populations utilize narrative communications at the core of their culture, they will be more receptive to health communications that deliver messages in a way that they are used to; further, narrative messages are more likely to be interpreted as stories about societal norms by members of cultures that utilize storytelling to establish social values.

> **P7:** Health communications must account for culture specific processing styles of recipients.
>
> **P7a:** Health communications using narrative approaches are especially effective for members of cultures that have a strong oral tradition.

Cultural orientation

Successful health communications should also acknowledge cultural orientation (collectivist or individualist) and structure message content accordingly. Collectivist and individualist cultures possess distinctive values and

will be more receptive to health messages that emphasize health consequences that are relevant to their own orientation. Members of individualist
cultures view the individual as an autonomous being and focus on his/her
own health outcomes and abilities to make a change, without considering
family members in the process (Elder et al., 2009). Therefore behavioral
change will only involve the single message recipient and communications
should be focused on the individual's health (Keller and Lehmann 2008).

Conversely, for members of collective cultural groups, family connect-
edness is very important and members seldom are concerned about their
individual selves. For collectivists, change will take place in the context of
the family (Elder et al., 2009). They consider the family an extension of the
self, and thus worry about the detrimental impact of personal health risks
on the entire family, rather than just on themselves. There is an exagger-
ated importance of the wife/mother figure; she is seen as the leader of the
family and will have the central role in behavioral change for both herself
and the entire family (ibid.). Gearing health communications toward the
mother figure will increase effectiveness because it acknowledges her role in
the family and appeals to the singular person that will bring about change
for all family members. Mothers will be encouraged to consider behavioral
change if emphasis is put on how it will help their family members (Ford
et al., 2005).

P8: Health communications will be more effective if they are customized for
collectivist and individualist audiences.

P8a: Health communications targeting collective cultures should emphasize
group and family unity and potential harm to the entire family; communications targeting individualist cultures should emphasize individual health
needs and personal ramifications.

In addition to collectivist and individualist cultural orientation, differences between Western cultures and traditional cultures will effect how
each population is persuaded by health messages. Members of traditional
cultures weigh the impact of faith and religion on their lives much more
heavily than modernized Western cultures. They are also fatalistic and
view disease as an unavoidable punishment from God, over which they do
not have control; members are not very receptive to health communications
that utilize logical reasoning to encourage behavioral changes because this
suggests that control is in the hands of the individual (Hinyard and Kreuter,
2007). Narrative communications may be useful when targeting traditional
cultures because the message is embedded in a story that the recipient can
relate to. Narratives also allow information to be presented without the
use of statistical data and logical reasoning, which will be discounted by
fatalistic populations (ibid.). Successful narrative messages will absorb their
audience into this story, which will make the recipient less likely to counter-
argue the information contained in the message (Deighton et al., 1989).
Lastly, these stories can model skills by making the story's characters role

models to increase the reader's confidence in their own ability to make a behavioral change (Hinyard and Kreuter, 2007).

> **P8b:** Messages targeting traditional cultures need to be consistent with ideology of the audience, namely that illness and disease is fatalistic, and approach the audience through narrative communications that embed the health message in a way that diminishes counterarguments.

Language
When health communications are targeted at diverse cultural groups, it is prudent to translate the message into the primary language of the intended audience. This will ensure that the message is accessible to its target beneficiaries in a language in which they are proficient and comfortable. Translating a health communication is meant to enhance the audience's ability to relate to the message, but to do so it must be linguistically appropriate; translations must be done carefully to maintain the proper meaning and context of the original message (Kreuter and McClure, 2004); literal translation may not preserve the original meaning of the message;

In addition to preserving meaning and context, it is important that a message is translated at an appropriate reading level for its recipients. Minority populations within the United States generally exhibit lower literacy rates; messages that are translated directly from high-level English may not allow for readability by the general lower-level readers within other cultures (Elder et al., 2009). Thus, it is important not only to maintain the desired meaning of the message, but also to deliver it in such a way that its recipients can easily read and understand its content.

Lastly, while message recipients may be of diverse ethnic backgrounds, it is important not to simply infer the appropriate language by the recipient's ethnicity. As mentioned, minority populations within the United States tend to exhibit greater illiteracy than nonminorities; however, research has shown that members of the Latino population report greater readability for English, versus Spanish, communications (ibid.). English as a Second Language (ESL) classes sometimes teach pupils to proficiently read nutrition labels and prescription medicine instructions in English and, therefore, certain minority populations may be more familiar and more comfortable reading health related topics in English than in their native language (ibid.).

> **P9:** Communications targeting minority groups should be translated appropriately.
>
> **P9a:** Translated health messages should account for cultural and linguistic language structure; direct translation from English is often unsuitable.
>
> **P9b:** Translated health communications should be written at a literacy level that is comprehensible to the target population.
>
> **P9c:** Health communications should acknowledge the written language preference of the targeted minority populations.

Media Touchpoints

Health communications have surfaced in a myriad of new media, particularly when targeting youthful audiences about topics such as sexual education. The *New York Times* recently printed an article about a health initiative undertaken by the Adolescent Pregnancy Prevention Campaign in North Carolina, and similar programs in Washington, D.C., Chicago, Toronto, and San Francisco. These programs utilize the latest technologies to reach teenagers. Users can send text messages anonymously to the "Birds and Bees Text Line" and receive answers via text message to their questions. Supporters of these programs suggest that the success is due to the perceived privacy that a teenager has when sending a question via text message. Their cell phones are not monitored by their parents and there is a feeling of anonymity due to the impersonal nature of question and response that reduces "shame and embarrassment" (Hoffman, 2009).

There are also a variety of websites that offer teens a variety of health information and provide them with the opportunity to post questions and receive answers without disclosing personal information. The *New York Times* mentioned Go Ask Alice! (http://www.goaskalice.columbia.edu/) and Teen Health FX (http://teenhealthfx.com/), both of which provide honest, uncensored information about health risks, including smoking, drugs, alcohol, and risky sexual behavior.

Health messages are also being communicated on social networking websites, such as Twitter, Facebook, and Myspace. These websites provide a unique opportunity for the teens to "friend" or "follow" companies that provide information about health behavior risks. Even the U.S. government website (womenshealth.gov) sends "tweets" to its nearly six thousand followers on Twitter with information and links to various health resources for women. AIDS Roko is another social cause that aims to stop the spreading of AIDS in India and uses Twitter to get its message out there to today's youth. While its website (www.aidsroko.com) is youth oriented, featuring blog-style messages and bright colors, AIDS Roko has gone a step further and sends out messages to its eighty-five followers several times a day with the latest news about the AIDS epidemic in India, links to its website and other resources detailing how to stop the spreading of this disease. Health initiatives have also embraced other social networking sites, such as Facebook and Myspace, to reach "friends" and keep them up to date on today's health concerns. Within weeks of the swine flu epidemic circling the globe, more than five hundred groups, some containing upward of ten thousand members, can be found on Facebook spreading news and preventative tips about this particular illness. Similar groups can be found for nearly any health behaviors that one can think of.

Media Touchpoint 1: Each target group's favorite media and technologies must be used to promote health advocacy.

A growing trend in the promotion of healthy lifestyles is "message placement," or to embed a health message into a well-known television show, such as *ER*, *Law and Order: SVU*, and even *America's Next Top Model* in a way that is similar to product placement. The Bill and Melinda Gates Foundation, the Kaiser Family Foundation, and Common Sense Media are all foundations that promote healthy behaviors through existing media outlets (Arango and Brian, 2009). The Gates Foundation has established a deal with media conglomerate Viacom, which will allow them to access viewers of popular television channels MTV, VH1, BET, and Nickelodeon. These healthy lifestyle storylines will reach young audiences by simply being woven in the television shows that the recipients are already watching, and provide information about health issues that are relevant to this age group, such as risky sexual practices. Communications come across as realistic, informative, accurate, and importantly, they are entertaining to the audience.

Message placement may occur in television programming for any age group. *USA Today* recently featured an article about the show *Grey's Anatomy* and the message placement that has been worked into episode scripts about topics such as HIV prevention (Marcus, 2008). Kaiser Family Foundation worked with *Grey's Anatomy* writers to insert educational messages into the script and also tested whether or not the messages were successful in reaching their audience. They found that viewers were able to recall the messages up to six weeks after the show and a significant portion of viewers that were not previously aware of the topic were aware after viewing the show (ibid.).

In addition to targeting adults and young adults, message placement has also been used to target teenagers and even toddlers. ABC Family Channel's *Secret Life of the American Teenager* is a show about a fifteen-year-old average high school student that gets pregnant after her first unprotected sexual experience. The show chronicles her pregnancy, as well as the sexual behavior of her fellow students, which ranges from promiscuous to nonexistent. Further, the website for this television show allows viewers to seek advice regarding their own experiences and partners with stayteen.org, a website that encourages teens to "stay a teenager" by candidly discussing the realities of sexual behavior and referring them to other television shows and websites that can provide information. Younger children have been targeted by message placement in Sesame Street, "Healthy Habits for Life," in which Elmo exercises and Cookie Monster limits his cookie intake to encourage young viewers to adopt healthy eating and exercise habits. Similarly, a cartoon called "Lazy Town" on the kid's channel Noggin stars a superhero-like character that encourages kids to exercise, refers to fruits and vegetables as "sports candy," and is weakened when he consumes sugar. Message placement allows viewers of all ages to be reached with informative, relevant, and entertaining health messages.

Media Touchpoint 2: The rich multimedia environment can be used to achieve vicarious learning. Particularly, message placement in television shows can be utilized to spread awareness of health causes and illustrate healthy behaviors to audiences of all ages.

Interactive video games also provide a unique method for health communications and facts to be dispersed to the general population in a way that is interesting and fun. Online games such as "Sneeze" (http://www. miniclip.com/games/stop-swine-flu/en/), in which the main objective is to sneeze on a large group of others, to illustrate the subsequent spreading of germs that will infect a large percentage of the game population, Colgate's "Toothman" (http://www.colgate.com/app/Kids-World/US/ Game_Toothman.vsp) in which the player tries to fill in the letters of a word related to healthy teeth before the plaque monster gets them, and "Lunch Crunch" (http://www.playnormous.com/game_lunchcrunch.cfm) in which the player has to create a healthy combination of lunch foods are perfect examples. These games are both entertaining to play and inform users of the health risks that they are exposed to and healthy habits that they should adopt. Games creatively illustrate the effects of healthy behaviors and can also implant health facts and trivia that intermittently appear throughout the game that may encourage the player to be more conscientious when it comes to their own health behaviors.

Media Touchpoint 3: Interactive video games, available free online, can help promote healthy habits and behavior. Such interactive games may be particularly effective for youth, since they can appear to be "subversive" while in actuality they are educational.

Recipients of health communications often discount the relevance of the message and conclude that their personal risk is not very high. However, it has been suggested that a self-assessment of risk provides recipients with a more realistic estimate of their health risk and is not as easily discounted (Greene and Brinn, 2003; Jordan et al., 2007). Research has suggested that having recipients fill out a short survey about their personal behaviors (a risk self-assessment) and providing them with an objective assessment of their individual risk level resulted in much higher perceived susceptibility to negative health consequences (Greene and Brinn, 2003; Jordan et al., 2007). In turn, greater perceived susceptibility led to greater behavioral intentions and subsequent actual behavioral change (Greene and Brinn, 2003). Supporting findings were found by Jordan and colleagues (2007), in that behavioral intentions were partially dependent upon the feedback of a self-assessment of risk. Even when people were aware of certain health risks, they presumed that they were not an immediate threat and did not engage in preventative behaviors until their individual risk was affirmed objectively by self-assessment.

The difficulty of allowing for self-assessment in media messages may be overcome by utilizing Internet technology to create interactive media in which the user can answer questions and receive immediate, personalized risk-assessments based on the information that they entered. Additionally, this technology has more extensive reach than print communications (anyone worldwide with Internet access) and is quick and easy for recipient's to take part in.

Washington University School of Medicine (http://www.yourdiseaserisk. wustl.edu) has utilized the self-assessment technique to increase awareness of major health problems. They provide tools for the self-assessment of cancer, diabetes, heart disease, osteoporosis, and stroke, the "five most important diseases in the United States," as well as information about prevention and treatment.

Media Touchpoint 4: Interactive media can be used to encourage self-assessment of the recipients' own previous behaviors.

Bull and colleagues (2001) found that the perceived visual attractiveness of a health message is strongly correlated with the preliminary steps toward behavioral change; the more attractive the recipient finds the message, the greater their behavioral intentions. Tailoring attractiveness may be achieved more easily through interactive media outlets, such as the Internet, because user preferences can be obtained and applied to the health message quickly and at very low cost. Bull et al. (2001) suggest that minor details such as color and font preferences will enhance attractiveness and may subsequently increase the effectiveness of the message.

Further, shorter materials such as pamphlets and leaflets tend to be more effective than their longer counterparts, such as manuals and newsletters. In the meta-analysis by Noar et al. (2007), the authors find that this disparity in effectiveness of written communications may be due to attractiveness in addition to length. Pamphlets and leaflets are more likely to have pictures and graphics and a superior, more eye-catching layout than longer communications, and, therefore, may keep the attention and interest of readers and consequently be better understood; understanding of information is a precursor to being persuaded and altering behavior (ibid.).

Media Touchpoint 5: If using print communications, keep them short: Shorter print messagews (pamphlets/leaflets) are more effective than longer print messages (manuals/letters/newsletters).

Conclusions

Our propositions and the examples provided in the appendix, as well as our media touchpoints and the examples provided in describing them indicate that much can be drawn from previous research about how health-oriented social entrepreneurial organizations can become more effective at communicating to target audiences in order to help them scale their social impact. Further research is needed to determine whether organizations that seem to have followed these propositions and touchpoints have actually achieved desired outcomes with their communications approaches.

Appendix

We have repeated our first eight propositions here, accompanying each one with an example of how a social entrepreneurial organization seems to have adopted the given advice.

P1: *Health communications that encourage the commencement of a new behavior (e.g., screening behaviors) are more effective than messages that try to prevent the adoption of a new behavior (e.g., reduce smoking trial), and both are more effective than those that aim to stop an old behavior (e.g., increase smoking cessation).*

Example: Mothers Against Drunk Driving (MADD) encourages people to become designated drivers or to hand over their car keys to one. (See www.madd.org)

P2: *Tailored health communications are more effective than generic or targeted health ones.*

Example: Renascer, an organization in Brazil that helps poor children with serious illnesses obtain the health care services they need, initiates all relationships with lengthy interviews of mothers—conducted by volunteers following a standard protocol to make the process more efficient—so that a treatment plan and communications about that plan can be tailored to the specific needs of each child. This system has contributed to successful scaling (Bornstein, 2004).

P3: *Health communications that frame the outcome as a gain to the current status quo versus the threat of a loss are equally effective.*

P3a: *The effectiveness of gain and loss framing may be moderated by regulatory focus; gain-framed messages are more influential for the prevention focused; loss-framed messages are more influential for the promotion focused.*

Example: The Infant and Young Child Nutrition Project in Zambia, which is trying to communicate with pregnant women, many who are likely to be prevention focused, uses gain-framed messages that lead with "Pregnant? Congratulations" and then go on to say "Remember the health of your baby depends on your health." (See http://www.iycn.org/files/Pregnant_Congratulations_Poster_Zambia.JPG)

P4: *Health communications should make conscientiousness-related personality traits (e.g., self-control, responsibility, industriousness, order, traditionalism, and virtue) salient.*

Example: Mothers 2 Mothers is a program in Africa combating transmission of HIV from mothers to newborns. According to their website: "M2M trains and employs HIV-positive mothers who have themselves benefited from our services to become 'Mentor Mothers'. These Mentors comprise a team of caregivers and educators for other HIV-positive mothers and become an integral element of clinical prevention of mother-to-child transmission (PMTCT) care. Located in antenatal clinics, maternity wards, post-delivery clinics, and hospitals that offer medical treatment to women living with HIV, M2M works alongside established PMTCT treatment programs. We provide a comprehensive service to foster a supportive environment—one that promotes empowerment and companionship, assists women in combating stigma within their families and communities, supports a mother's adherence to medical treatment, and reduces the likelihood that her children will become AIDS orphans." (See http://www.m2m.org/programmes/how-we-work.html)

P5: *Health communications targeting youth behavior change are more effective when they evoke strong negative emotions and are varied in intensity so as to avoid "wear out."*

Example: The National Youth Anti-Drug Media Campaign has a varied array of messages that it uses, from anti-meth messages that say "No one thinks they'll try to tear off their own skin. Meth will change that" to anti-marijuana messages that show young marijuana smokers entering a cocoon and emerging as a un-cool middle-aged man.

P6: *Health communications aimed at younger audiences will be more effective if they focus on social consequences and are repeated frequently. Conversely, communications targeting older audiences are more effective if they focus on physical consequences and have novel information.*

Example: Girls on the Run is a self-esteem enhancement program for girls aged eight–twelve that teaches them different lessons about healthy living twice a week for twelve weeks in after-school sessions consisting of about ten girls. It uses games involving running to get messages across about the importance of accepting people for who they are, eating well, avoiding peer pressure, serving the community, and setting personal goals (e.g., completing a 5K run at the end of the program). Positive social consequences are emphasized throughout, and the girls get considerable social support from one another.

P7: *Health communications must account for culture specific processing styles of recipients.*

P7a: *Health communications using narrative approaches are especially effective for members of cultures that have a strong oral tradition.*

Example: VisionSpring is an organization that markets inexpensive reading glasses throughout the developing world. According to their website: "Before conducting a vision campaign in a new town, they approach the mayor or leader, who refers them to their first set of customers and often offers to co-host the campaign. Vision Entrepreneurs learn to employ innovative marketing techniques, such as hiring radio announcers, acting troupes, or drummers to announce campaigns." (See http://www.visionspring.org/how-we-work/business-in-a-bag.php)

P8: *Health communications will be more effective if they are customized for collectivist and individualist audiences.*

P8a: *Health communications targeting collective cultures should emphasize group and family unity and potential harm to the entire family;*

communications targeting individualist cultures should emphasize individual health needs and personal ramifications.

Example: MADD has a public service announcement on its website (www. madd.org) that is targeted toward Latinos, stating: "Take care of your family—don't drink and drive."

10

Scaling Social Impact through Branding Social Causes

Minette E. Drumwright and Mercedes Duchicela

What helps causes to scale? Before social impact can scale, commitment to the cause must scale. By scaling, we mean expanding those involved with the cause and expanding efforts on behalf of the cause with the ultimate goal of increasing social impact. The central thrust of our chapter is to report on the experiences of people on the ground who were intimately involved in trying to scale causes. They described what facilitated the scaling of their causes (and what did not). We also offer some insights from scholarship that lend credence to their observations. Notably, we access literatures that are not typically discussed in relation to cause marketing and scaling.

Much of what we learned about scaling causes blends well with the traditional understanding of marketing and branding. Marketing literature suggests that a cause must develop a meaningful identity or brand, and it must be communicated effectively (Aaker, 1991, 1996; Keller, 1993, 2003). A brand typically encompasses a cluster of associations that may be related to symbols, the sponsoring organization, emotional benefits, self-expressive benefits, and user imagery, among others (Aaker, 1996). These associations must be favorable, strong, and unique (Keller, 1993, 2003). Scholarship on marketing and branding is generally well known by those who study causes, and the reports of our respondents often confirm traditional understandings. There are, however, particular, and in some instances unique, challenges to scaling causes. At times, our findings run counter to traditional wisdom in marketing and branding.

Our research has also led us to realize that there are literatures outside of marketing that lend theoretical justification to what worked—most notably the literatures on agenda setting and diffusion of innovation. Because those literatures are less well known by those who study and practice marketing, we focus on them in a bit more detail.

The agenda setting literature deals primarily with the process by which issues get the attention of the public and the policymakers and how those issues proceed to make it onto the national decision agenda. It is remarkable how similar the challenges of scaling a cause are to those of elevating issues to the national agenda. Given the limitations of time, money, and other resources, getting onto the national agenda is a very difficult process, and many worthy issues never make it. We focus on a few key insights from this literature (e.g., Kingdon, 1984, Perry, 1991). In a seminal book on agenda setting, John Kingdon (1984) found that the availability of a solution vastly increases the likelihood that an issue will make in onto the agenda. When a problem seems intractable and unsolvable, it is difficult for people to justify investing time and attention in it. The agenda setting literature also focuses on a reality that is endemic to politics and public policy generally. To advance a policy, coalition building is crucial, and coalitions often must be built among unnatural allies. To get on the decision agenda, a grassroots movement often must be mobilized, and its efforts must be channeled toward promoting an issue. The manner in which an issue is framed is of surpassing importance. It matters for all sorts of reasons, but of particular importance is that it often dictates who will be willing to join the coalition and which types of solutions will be considered. Many players are important to the process of moving an issue to the national decision-making agenda. Policy entrepreneurs play a crucial role, but others can assist as well. For example, experts such as academics, researchers, and consultants can help put a problem on the agenda by documenting it and its effects through their studies. Media can play a powerful agenda setting role by repeatedly drawing attention to a problem. Indeed, much research argues that the importance of media is that it tells people what to think about rather than what to think. Timing matters because "policy windows" open, and they close. Openings may be predictable such as those associated with a new administration or a planning process, or they may be unpredictable such has those created by disasters or crises. The agenda setting literature deals with other issues, but those mentioned earlier are central; and again, there are many parallels with efforts to scale a cause.

The diffusion of innovation literature wrestles with the manner in which a new idea spreads from its originator or source to its users or adopters (Rogers, 1962). The diffusion of innovations is, in essence, "the process of human interaction in which one person communicates a new idea to another person" (p. 13). Diffusion requires targeting opinion leaders, prompting them to adopt early, and motivating them to influence others. Identifying active rejecters of the innovation and attempting to neutralize their negative impact on others is important as well. Key characteristics of an innovation influence its adoption in important ways: (1) its relative advantage over other competing ideas, (2) its compatibility with the existing culture and beliefs, (3) its complexity or the difficulty involved in understanding it, (4) its divisibility or the ability to try it on a limited basis, and (5) its communicability or how readily it can be observed and communicated.

The reports of our informants of what helped causes to scale frequently mapped onto the insights in the literatures of agenda setting and diffusion of innovation. We now turn to our methodology.

Methodology

A case history approach using elite interviews was employed because the research objective was to examine our informants' understandings of how causes scaled. The term "elite interviews" is commonly used to refer to long interviews of decision-makers as opposed to consumers, an electorate, or a mass population (Dexter, 1970). Unlike highly structured interviews, elite interviews are designed to ascertain the decision-makers' understanding of the phenomenon, its meaning to them, and what they consider relevant. Elite interviewing stresses the informant's definition of the situation, encourages the informant to structure the account of the situation, and allows the informant to reveal his or her notions of what is relevant. These are especially useful when one cannot be sure what interpretation, code, norm, affect, or rule is guiding the actors (Dexter, 1970; Miles and Huberman, 1994; Strauss, 1990).

We conducted interviews with twenty-four informants who were involved directly in attempting to scale twenty-one causes. Eighteen of the interviews were conducted in person, and six were conducted by telephone. Confidentiality and anonymity were promised to all informants and organizations to help mitigate biases and demand effects related to social desirability and posturing. Promises of confidentiality and anonymity enhance the willingness of informants to talk candidly about difficult issues. Absent these promises, some would refuse to participate, and others would screen out important information. Many of the causes had received media coverage, so we drew on public data as well.

We examined a varied set of causes. Most of the cause initiatives began during the past five–ten years. The most recent began three years ago, and a couple began considerably earlier. Fourteen of the causes were classified as successes in that they achieved scale, and seven were not considered successes because scale was not achieved. Six were related to disease prevention or treatment, and four to preventative health care behavior change. Three causes were related to public safety, and international development and education accounted for two causes each. One cause was related to each of the following categories: tolerance, financial security, civic engagement, antipornography, and environment.

Interviews were audio recorded, and the data were analyzed using standard qualitative data analytic methods. The themes that are reported were common to many of the causes. When a quotation is presented, it is representative of what multiple informants told us unless otherwise noted.

Findings

We found that several themes emerged across informants' accounts and causes. We identify the important themes and discuss the ways in which they enhanced or inhibited scaling.[1]

Theme 1: Collaboration

Scaling requires collaboration. Policymakers have long known that collaboration with diverse groups is key to electoral and legislative success as the agenda setting literature points out. Policymakers must join forces with friends and sometimes with foes to further their issues. So, too, for those who wish to scale. Organizations attempting to scale causes are not always quick to recognize this political reality, but those that scale successfully do.

Theme 1a: The organization views itself as part of a team

There is much fragmentation in the nonprofit marketplace. Often weak organizations work independently on their own initiatives, many of which sound and look similar. As one informant said: "There's a lot of fragmented work going on, and one of our main roles is just being able to bring people together." She went on to say that her organization viewed itself as a convener of organizations and a catalyst for a movement. Another informant said, "Early on, I said that I wanted to be known as the organization that plays well with others."

The reasons why collaboration is important are obvious. It takes resources—ideas, money, feet on the ground, to name a few—to accomplish goals related to diffusing an idea or behavior through society. As another informant said, "It could not have been done without partnerships and other organizations." Moreover, when organizations compete to further the same cause, not only do they dilute resources, but they can breed antagonism and confusion.

Perhaps less obvious are Kingdon's findings (1984) regarding the benefits of a closely knit community, which collaboration engenders. Such a community creates common outlooks, orientations, and ways of thinking that enhance integration and create agenda stability. When such a community develops, it can become a powerful force in itself. It can help an issue stay on the agenda, and it can propel an issue forward at opportune moments.

Theme 1b: Credit is shared

When organizations compete for donors, volunteers, and other resources, their natural inclination is to want to bolster their own reputations by taking credit for everything they possibly can. In contrast, organizations that succeed in collaborating to scale causes are willing to share credit. As one informant said: "We are very generous with giving people credit...My view is credit is free, praise is free, thank you is free." This informant went on to describe his view as emanating from "a model of abundance" rather than from "a model of scarcity." As he said, in the abundance model, one assumes that there is "an abundance of money and an abundance of time, an abundance of love and care out there in the world. I'm not worried that if you get something, that somehow diminishes me." He continued, "I think many people in the nonprofit world come from a scarcity model because we are so under resourced."

Theme 1c: Collaboration occurs with strange bedfellows as well as with the expected partners

It has been said that politics makes for strange bedfellows. Policymakers have long realized that to succeed they need to be willing to partner. They must do so with their natural constituencies, and they must be willing to partner with strange bedfellows as well. Nonprofits have been slower to embrace this reality of political life. To the extent that the cause and its sponsoring organization are on a "righteous" crusade, it is sometimes difficult to work with those with less fervor and commitment, let alone those who are sometimes considered "evil." This theme has been explored elsewhere, especially in the literature on the increased interaction between nonprofit organizations and businesses (e.g., Berger et al., 2004). This well-documented phenomenon of the difficulty of collaboration takes on special complexities when the effort is not only to collaborate but to scale. More players, different missions, different values, different cultures, different locales, different measurements, and so on, can increase problems exponentially.

Nonetheless, willingness to collaborate with strange bedfellows is often essential to the diffusion of an idea or behavior beyond its natural constituents. We observed a number of instances of partnerships between unnatural partners—a governmental agency and bars, a gay rights organization and a conservative Christian group, a union and a management organization, organizations competing for the same donor dollars. How did successful scalers find collaborators? One informant put it well: "We've looked for the logical extensions. Who has a dog in the hunt? Who has a reason to help?"

Collaboration with strange bedfellows typically requires special attention to the message so that it can be embraced by the partner. As an example, one promoter of an antidrinking and driving message explained how her organization succeeded in getting bars to collaborate in getting out a responsible drinking message:

> We have been very careful about the message that goes into an establishment whose business is based on beer sales. We don't say, "Don't buy beer," we say, "Designate a driver." We don't say, "Drink, drive, go to jail." We have been sympathetic to the fact that they sell alcoholic beverages; we just want there to be a responsibility message at the point of sale...We found a place of common interests.

Of course, collaboration with unnatural partners is not to the exclusion of more natural allies. With both the strange and expected bedfellows, collaboration is more likely when the request is for something other than money—for example, time, talent, media—and when the time frame is bounded: "By not asking for cash, by not having our hand out all of the time, by tying it to specific campaigns that have a beginning and an end, that's helped in a lot of respects."

Theme 2: Mission

While it is important to be willing to pursue collaborations outside the comfort zone, it is equally important to stay in the center of the organizational mission.

Theme 2a: The cause must fit with the mission of the sponsoring organization

Many organizations are involved in multiple causes, and as such, not all causes can receive priority. Causes that scale fit well with the organization's primary mission. This increases the likelihood that the cause will receive priority and benefit from existing expertise. As one informant remarked, "We have a long history of expertise in the [cause] category... We've been doing it for a long time, and we are very good at it." Failure to scale is typically attributed to lack of priority, which is often caused by a mismatch between the cause and the organization's mission. The fit between an organization's mission and a cause is an important theme in research on partnerships between companies and nonprofits and on corporate social responsibility (e.g., Berger et al., 2004, 2006, 2007, forthcoming).

Theme 3: Branding

Branding is the word and concept of the decade in marketing, and many traditional branding principles apply to causes. However, we found some successful approaches that appeared to contradict traditional branding ideas or at least were counterintuitive, and there were tradeoffs.

Theme 3a: The cause benefits from a separate, stand-alone brand name and identity without an organizational tie

In an increasingly competitive marketplace in which more and more nonprofit organizations vie for fewer and fewer resources, many nonprofits seek to tie their organizational brands closely to every possible cause initiative. They are infatuated with strategies to brand themselves and are frenetically trying to raise the visibility of their organizational brands in any possible way. In contrast to this approach, the causes that scale often are not co-branded with the organization's name. The causes have their own brand names that are generally free of organizational labels. They have independent websites and their own identities. As one informant said: "We made some very conscious decisions around branding the [cause] movement. [The cause] had its own website. It was completely separately branded. In fact, the first year, you would have had a hard time figuring out that we were behind it." One informant referred to branding the cause as "mission branding" as opposed to "organizational branding." Recall theme 1 and the importance of coalitions to scaling. Having a separate, stand-alone brand name and identity opens the door for partnerships with other organizations. Because the initiative to promote the cause is not labeled with one organization's name, partners embrace it more easily and enthusiastically, share ideas more willingly, and are more likely to benefit from it. Partner organizations can create stronger positive brand associations for themselves by promoting the cause if it has a stand-alone brand name and identity.

But there is a downside. The primary organization's brand is not benefitting as much as it would with a co-branded approach in which its own name is highlighted. As a result, the organization may not get as much credit, and fund-raising may be more difficult. As one informant said: "I am very ambivalent about the decision [to have a separate brand name]...Our organization doesn't get the credit it deserves; it kills the development staff...but it is what we needed to do to get the mission accomplished, and we have always thought that the mission is bigger than the organization." Of course organizations want to create name recognition and positive associations for themselves; therefore, informants spoke of needing to find a balance between mission branding and organizational branding. As some pointed out, if the organization is not sustainable, its work on behalf of the mission ends. When it comes to the causes that scaled in our study, however, there is no doubt: mission branding trumps organizational branding.

Theme 3b: The brand is an open source

Traditional branding philosophy involves conveying a consistent brand in a unified manner across the many different brand "touch points." Messages, symbols, colors, taglines, and other manifestations of the brand are uniform. In contrast, scaling causes requires a paradigm shift in brand management. Gone are the days of the brand police, who enforce brand consistency and uniformity. When causes scale, the brand is viewed as an open source in that others are permitted to interpret and customize the brand for themselves. This branding philosophy greatly enhances the dynamics of partnership and the willingness of others to join in. One informant explained what he described as the "secret ingredient" in a highly successful cause initiative:

> We did something there that was deliberate, that was new for us, and that in hindsight was a significant learning for us. What was new was this idea of how do we let people—people can be an advertising agency to an individual to a government agency—how do we let others participate in the program on their own terms—how do we let them have ownership, allowing them to customize...to reflect their needs, their interests, their personalities?...That was the secret ingredient of having so many people participate in such an extensive way.

Another informant described the new type of flexibility that this new approach entailed:

> The lesson to be learned is sometimes we put a campaign out there and say, "Join us, support us, but here's how you have to do that." And a lot of times there are supporters out there who want to join but can't do it on your terms, and you have to learn to let go and provide flexibility so that people can be evangelists for your organization.

This paradigm shift is not an easy one, especially for organizations with a well-established brand. "I wouldn't say that we went into it willingly...Historically as an organization, we've been control freaks. We do it on our terms, and we're very busy policing to make sure that you don't deviate from the brief or what we ask you to do." There are obvious downsides to an open source branding approach. As one informant said: "Sure, there were instances of creative work that we would not have created or chosen, but in the spirit of letting people participate on their own terms, we had to live with that." There are good reasons for brand consistency. However, our informants suggested that the positive benefits of open source branding on partnerships and participation in the scaling efforts outweigh the negative. An often unanticipated upside is that the brand as interpreted by others often has a fresh, innovative, "edgier" tone that appeals to a younger audience. "It's not your mother's [brand]!" one informant exclaimed.

Theme 4: Messages

Marketing and agenda setting both attest to the importance of framing a message. Creating messages that scale presents some special challenges arising both from the individuals involved and from some unique aspects of the scaling task itself.

Theme 4a: Messages are based on consumer insight derived from research and are relatively free of client restraints

Marketers have long appreciated the importance of consumer insight when designing a message, but this approach often runs into bumps when dealing with cause messages. This is true for several reasons, but one we heard about frequently related to the "clients." Scientists, public health specialists, and others who have expertise in a cause often have deeply held convictions about how a cause should or should not be framed. Because of these strong beliefs, consumer research often is not conducted or it has to be ignored because of restrictions the client places on messaging. For example, scientists and social scientists often resist dramatization of the message and forceful statements. As one informant explained, "The client places a lot of restrictions on the messaging...We are not allowed to play the scare card...so it doesn't have a sledgehammer behind it." Another explained: "The client doesn't want to upset people or be forceful [with the message]. When you're trying to create social change, you can't be wimpy. First of all, you have less money than everyone else, and the stakes are higher."

Another problem is due to lack of marketing expertise among some non-profit and government leaders generally. They change messages frequently, sometimes dictated by political concerns, and they often fail to do market research or the research is done poorly. But as we would expect, messages that diffuse effectively are based on customer insight from sound and definitive research designed to understand which groups should be targeted and their perceptions and concerns.

Theme 4b: The message engages the heart

One of the fundamental principles of effective branding is that the brand must have an emotional component as well as a cognitive one. Despite their wonderful material for stories, nonprofits often emphasize facts and statistics, neglecting emotional aspects. As one informant said: "You have to get to people on a gut level. You have to connect with them on an emotional level and tap into why it's important to them and their families, and you do that with emotive and aspirational language rather than with statistics and facts." Another informant elaborated: "It had a hook, and it had humanity. It was one of those campaigns that really had the emotional impact. Lots of campaigns are well crafted, clear, professional, but they don't stick." Engaging the heart oftentimes means telling a meaningful story that connects with people, and scaling causes involves effective storytelling. This sounds simple, but as theme 4a suggests, some cause advocates resist such approaches.

Theme 4c: The message is framed around commonly shared principles rather than around policy positions

As demonstrated in theme 1, coalitions are central to scaling causes, and the manner in which a message is framed can facilitate or hinder coalition building. Major agreements between liberals and conservatives that get an issue on the national agenda often begin with an agreement on principle, and only later are the policy issues hammered out. Likewise, when causes scale, their messages are framed in terms of broad and commonly shared principles that can be embraced by multiple and diverse targets. As one informant said:

> We made a conscious decision to lead with principles, not policy positions...If you go out there at that broader, aspirational level, it resonates with people...[The framing around principles] creates a platform to engage people beyond our membership demographic...[It] provides something that can cut across the spectrum.

In contrast, when causes are framed with policy positions, coalitions do not get off the ground, and even natural allies nit pick. One of the factors that affects the diffusion of an idea is its compatibility with the existing culture and beliefs (Rogers, 1962). Framing around commonly shared principles increases compatibility and enhances the message's ability to diffuse from the innovators and early adopters to others.

Theme 4d: Messages that provide hope that a solution is possible play well

A major premise of the agenda setting literature is the importance of the availability of a solution (Kingdon, 1984). As in politics, when people perceive that a cause presents an intractable problem about which nothing can be done, they find it difficult to invest time, energy, and money in addressing it. This is true for the national agenda in politics, and it is true for scaling causes. This poses a challenge for causes in that messages typically must convey both the gravity of the problem and the possibility of a solution. It is a fine line to walk. A problem must be perceived as serious and worthy of priority, but to energize potential partners, the public, and policymakers, the message must convince them that there is something they can do. As an example from our research, a focus on the tragedy for the victim of drunk driving is less effective than a focus on the perpetrator. Changing the behavior of the perpetrator is possible. As another example, visuals of wells that provide clean water being built in Africa may be more effective than visuals of people suffering the dire consequences of drought. To be effective, the solutions presented in messages must be practical. In analyzing a cause that did not scale, an informant pointed to the ineffectiveness of impractical solutions, "A lot of the things that we say in the message are impractical. You just can't do them." Another benefit of messages framed in positive terms of actions to take to solve a problem is that they are appealing to corporate sponsors, who are reported to be reluctant to take negative messages to their customers. This finding converges with findings of research on partnerships between companies and nonprofits (e.g., Berger et al., 2004).

Theme 4e: Simple messages play well

Solutions to societal problems are often complicated, sophisticated, and multifaceted, and they lend themselves to complicated messages. However, causes that scale tend to have messages that are simple and accessible—something that people understand immediately. Again and again, our informants commented on the simplicity and clarity of effective messages. One must acknowledge that some solutions can be expressed more simply and clearly than others, and as such, some causes are naturally advantaged. This finding converges with the findings of previous research that the complexity of an innovation and the ease of communicating it affect diffusion (Rogers, 1962).

Theme 4f: A compelling and portable visual is crucial

It is a theme as old as marketing itself: one cannot underestimate the importance of a powerful visual. As one informant remarked: "Visuals speak very loudly. You can talk until you are blue in the face, but have a fantastic visual, and it will speak a thousand words...It must be engaging—a wow kind of visual." She went on to express a side benefit of a compelling visual,

"It [the visual] is vivid, and it teaches, but it is totally nonjudgmental." Visuals can teach without being preachy, which is often a difficult task for a textual message. In contrast to words that typically must be customized for different targets, a single, compelling visual often can be used for many targets, even non-consumer audiences such as grantors and scientists.

While the power of a visual is an age old communication theme, a modern twist is that the visual must be "portable," so that people can share it electronically: "The days of driving people to a particular website...those days are long gone...If I go to [cause website], I want to share it on my Facebook and put it on You Tube. All of our content has to be portable...It has to go across networks." Another informant elaborated on the benefits of portability: "People start passing it around, linking to it. Having that begot other things [news media coverage, a television special]...Once you've got something like that, people start coming to you."

Theme 5: Commercial Marketing Communication Approaches

There is resistance to commercial communication approaches within non-profits and cause communities, but the organizations that scale causes successfully overcome this resistance and embrace commercial approaches. As one informant said, "We must think and act like commercial marketers so that we can compete for mindshare."

Theme 5a: A wide variety of communication approaches are integrated

Public relations, celebrity endorsements, paid media advertising, cause marketing, special events, and all types of collateral materials are used. As one informant said: "we aligned our advertising—our air game—with our ground game—our volunteers—and our online presence too." Typically, outside communications help is employed.

Theme 5b: Effective spokespeople are used, many of whom are celebrities

While the downsides to celebrity endorsements are well documented, celebrities with a genuine commitment to the cause can be effective spokespeople who draw media coverage and new supporters. Typically, they have a special and very personal tie to a cause that gives them a claim to a hearing. They include performers, politicians, athletes, or film makers, and they are engaged in a variety of efforts, which includes not only publicity and fund-raising but also volunteering and humanitarian efforts.

Theme 5c: Generating viral/buzz/word-of-mouth marketing is important

When causes scale, nontraditional and social media are used to engage people with the cause in such a way that they become evangelists, which furthers diffusion. Word-of-mouth support is especially important because of its credibility. Marketers know this, and nonmarketing research has found that new media are important in influencing the agendas of the public, policymakers, and even traditional media (McCombs, 2004; Roberts et al., 2002). However, viral marketing is always tricky, and many resources can be squandered in outreach that does not find traction.

Theme 6: Grassroots Movement

To scale, causes need broad based support, which frequently is most effectively engendered through a grassroots movement. An effective grassroots movement calls for effective marketing, branding, and astute politics. As such, it is not surprising that a number of the aforementioned themes tie to facilitate a grassroots movement.

Theme 6a: Grassroots movement are seeded but not ceded

Grassroots movements are often spontaneous and unbridled. However, when causes scale, the grassroots movements are typically seeded and channeled. One way of seeding a grassroots movement is to enlist a preexisting field force. Associations (e.g., professional associations, industry associations) prove to be particularly attractive partners in mobilizing an existing field force. They have a membership base with common interests with whom they communicate regularly. Associations are constantly looking for ways to provide value to their members, and they can portray themselves as providing value by tying their members in with the cause. Participants in cause-related events such as runs or races and a nonprofit's existing volunteer base are other sources of preexisting field forces.

Another way of seeding a grassroots movement is to recruit what one informant referred to as the "keymasters," the individuals who provide access to a community or who attract a community. Often these are people who have been affected by the cause or who have a special tie to it and who have the power to evangelize effectively. Celebrities have long been keymasters for cause-related movements. As one informant said, "Our celebrity ambassadors energize and encourage our grassroots movement." Others pointed to the importance of attracting influential community leaders and bloggers with big followings. These keymasters must be trained to evangelize for the cause so that they can recruit more participants. This process requires effective targeting of keymasters, equipping them to evangelize, and then motivating them to do so. Informants reported that the open source branding philosophy is attractive to keymasters, who typically want to express their own interests and styles as they evangelize. These findings tie to the diffusion of innovation literature, which segments adopters into active and passive categories (Rogers, 1962). It asserts that active adopters must be prompted to evangelize for the innovation, and attempts must be made to convert passive adopters to active ones.

Once seeded, the challenge is to channel the effort of the grassroots movement and tie it to the brand. For example, as a part of its activism for the cause, some preexisting field forces provide advertising creative and other content for the branding efforts, typically through contests similar to those in the commercial world. As one informant explained: "The great thing for us is that it [the contest for consumer generated advertising] is free advertising for our events by the people who care about the events. We didn't have to go out and make videos...People did that for us...We got unlimited B [background] role."

Theme 6b: Corporate partners with retail chains or
operations in many geographical areas are helpful

Corporate partners can be especially valuable if their employees and/or customers are natural constituents for participation in the grassroots movement. The fit of the cause with both the company's employees and customers is an important factor to consider. Considerable support (e.g., training and branded materials) must be provided to enable corporate employees to evangelize effectively.

Theme 6c: Headquarters guide the grassroots efforts, but the local
organizations are given the latitude to customize and implement it

In keeping with the spirit of the open source branding approach, when scaling succeeds, headquarters provide guidance, but the local chapters are engaged, mobilized, and given latitude to customize and implement. A top-down approach that does not involve input from local chapters or freedom to implement the cause program is stifling and ineffective.

Theme 6d: Successful grassroots efforts create brand communities

Much of the ultimate success of a grassroots movement depends upon its ability to create a community among supporters of the cause. As one informant said: "The buzz word for good or ill is 'communities.' People want a community for people interested in things."

Community is also enhanced by providing many broad and varied opportunities for participation. "We had a greater scope of activities for volunteers to do than we had in the past, and we were able to keep them busy. So their enthusiasm grew, and they recruited friends, and we continued to build that." Signing pledges, sponsoring community events of all types, blogging, twittering, entering contests—there are many opportunities for participation at the grassroots level. These activities provide "brand touch points" and outlets for branded materials of all sorts—t-shirts, posters, flyers, coasters, and so on.

It is an age old problem—headquarters versus field. In order to get enthusiasm, buy-in, and so on, some control must be relinquished, but it cannot be completely ceded. Among those in our research who scale causes well, however, the ability to develop robust grassroots movements is important.

Discussion and Conclusion

Our findings offer themes that suggest best practices. Because the best practices are obvious from the themes themselves, we will not reiterate them here. Instead we speculate on some of the implications of our research in light of existing scholarship, particularly that scholarship outside of marketing.

One of the key findings in agenda setting research and in research on corporate societal marketing is the importance of "policy entrepreneurs" (e.g., Kingdon, 1984, Drumwright, 1994, 1996). Policy entrepreneurs are people who have many of the same characteristics as new business entrepreneurs—resourcefulness, creativity, persistence—but rather than investing in a new business venture, they are investing their energies in getting an issue on the agenda. They shepherd an issue throughout its process of getting on the agenda, and they tirelessly advocate for it. Evidence of people who play the role of policy entrepreneur is found in many literatures, and they go by many names—social entrepreneurs, corporate social entrepreneurs, change agents, and enviro-preneurs. In our research, we certainly saw evidence of policy entrepreneurs. For causes to scale and collaborations to proliferate, there is a need for policy entrepreneurs. But given the nature of scaling, we assert that a community of policy entrepreneurs will need to be created. People in this community will need to play key roles in scaling causes—roles that are often slow to be assumed. It will be incumbent upon these people to span the boundaries among the various parties involved—negotiating collaborations, coordinating efforts, sharing best practices, and continually serving as catalysts for further scaling of the cause. More attention should be given to creating mechanisms that build and maintain communities of policy entrepreneurs to increase the chances of successful scaling.

Many worthy causes never make it onto the agenda, and many problems never receive the attention they are due. Importance and worthiness do not guarantee attention either on the political agenda or in the public mind. Agenda setting research discusses the importance of the opening and closing of "policy windows." At times, policy windows open unpredictably when an unexpected event, for example, a crisis, brings an issue into the public consciousness or a new study brings new evidence to light. At other times, policy windows are opened by predictable events such as a new administration or a planning process. As with agenda setting, policy entrepreneurs and other cause advocates need to scan the environment to spot both predictable and unpredictable policy window openings so that they can make the most of them. They also must realize that windows close as well as open. Timing can be crucial to the success of a venture, and often events that lead to good timing are beyond the control of those involved. When the time is right, however, causes must be ready to scale.

Diffusion of innovation research has found that innovations typically diffuse through society by adopter categories—from innovators (estimated at 2.5 percent of the population on average) to early adopters (estimated at 13.5 percent) to the early majority (estimated at 34 percent) to the late majority (estimated at 34 percent) to laggards (estimated at 16 percent) (Rogers, 1962). If causes diffuse like innovations, and there are reasons to believe that they do, attention to adopter categories is prudent. Adoption categories differ on important dimensions. For diffusion that leads to scaling, each adopter category must be identified and the perceptions of its members understood, so that messages and marketing programs can be tailored to a specific group at a specific time. This means that consumer research should support the marketing of causes throughout the scaling process and not just at one phase. Because of limited funds, market research for causes is often not conducted at all, or if it is done, it is conducted only at the beginning of the initiative, which means it focuses disproportionately on innovators and early adopters. For causes to scale, it is particularly critical that the early and late majority categories be understood. This means that research is needed to identify the typical consumer in each category as well as the influence patterns within a category and between categories. Gaining these insights means that more priority and more resources must be given to market research that results in consumer insight throughout the diffusion process.

While the emphasis in scaling causes is often on adopters, diffusion of innovation literature gives considerable attention to rejecters. It asserts that rejecters, especially active rejecters, should be identified, and attempts should be made to neutralize their negative influence. Our informants did not seem to focus on rejecters, yet given the damage that brand terrorists and bad word of mouth can do, they would be well served by turning their research and strategic planning toward identifying and neutralizing rejecters as well as toward identifying and motivating adopters.

Given the importance and centrality of branding in today's world, it is easy for marketers to assume that the brand philosophy and brand strategy should determine aspects of the scaling process, but instead, it is the requirements of the scaling process that should determine the brand strategy and philosophy. For example, in some of our reporting, the need for collaboration and grassroots movements made the separate brand name and identity and the open source branding philosophy both attractive and crucial.

Politics is the art of the possible. This aphorism provides wisdom and guidance to leaders and effective policymakers. It is not a bad guide for those who seek to advance causes and scale them. Indeed, scaling a cause requires political skill. At base, "the art of the possible" means that the great cannot become the enemy of the good. Effective political leaders understand the need for compromise, think outside the box, build almost unthinkable coalitions, marshall grassroots support, and reframe issues in ways that achieve an ultimate goal. That is not to say that all compromises are worth it, but looking for what is possible and not ideal is the everyday reality for political leaders and policymakers. Republicans sometime hate to join with Democrats, and the United States sometimes hates to partner with Russia. Credit sharing is difficult. Reframing universal health care or environmental concerns as economic issues rather than as health or moral issues can stick in the craw of some, but if that gets to an end goal, most political leaders can accept it. Indeed, the best political leaders are masters at reframing issues. Such thinking, however, is often a difficult pill to swallow for many cause advocates; but scaling may require a mindset of the art of the possible.

The phrase also conveys that politics is an art, not a science. To be sure, politics is not all art—Aristotle saw it as a science as does the discipline of political science—but it is not a hard science, and artistic ability is required. Without carrying the metaphor too far, art suggests that cause scalers must think creatively, outside the box, and in some ways contrary to prevailing wisdom. Not only must strange bedfellows be accepted at times and rejected at others, but also judgments must be made about when to control and when to let a thousand flowers bloom. The successful cause scaler will need art and science.

Finally, even the worthiest of ideas, pushed by the most effective leaders, often do not make it onto our national agenda, nor does diffusion occur. Oftentimes there are events, situations, an unwilling public, a limit to what the system can bear, and so on that stymie even the best efforts. Likewise, there is no magical formula to ensure scaling success, and failure does not necessarily mean something was done incorrectly. That said, those who have succeeded at scaling offer insights as to what works and what does not, and upon reflection, their observations make sense in light of theories and scholarship.

Note

1. Although we were unaware of their work when we were conducting our research and drafting our chapter, our findings converge with those of Leslie R. Crutchfield and Heather McLeod Grant in their book, *Forces for Good: The Six Practices of High-Impact Nonprofits*. See their book for an excellent treatment of collaboration in the nonprofit sector.

V

Guiding Funders and Supporters

11

Harnessing Capital Markets to Promote Social Entrepreneurship

David T. Robinson

Increasingly, the world is turning to the private sector to address problems that have historically been dealt with by governments. Bornstein (2008) offers examples that span the globe: social entrepreneurs operate in American schools, supplying instructional content that has been stripped from curriculums. Small socially innovative organizations such as charity:water build wells in the developing world, coupling the development of the well with local instruction to achieve rates of clean water usage over time that far outpaces what the World Bank had been able to achieve before.

Why? Like most economic phenomena, there are two parts to the answer: supply and demand. As the examples in Bornstein (2008) illustrate, the provision of public goods and services by the private sector is in many respects a response to the inefficiency and inadequacy of governmental responses to social ills around the world. In short, social actors are responding to the failures of governments and large-scale NGOs on the supply side.[1]

But equally important, there is a groundswell of consumer consciousness that compels social actors to act in the spirit of benevolence toward the world's marginalized groups. The upsurge in corporate social responsibility, especially among companies that rely on traditionally marginalized groups in their supply chain, is one example. Organizations such as TransFair, which certify fair-trade products in the United States, do so in part because companies that source raw materials using fair trade practices understand that a new class of discerning customers demands that they pay attention to these matters. Thus, the demand side is important as well.

While conditions on the supply-side and the demand-side both favor the development of private sector alternatives to public action, these initiatives face a fundamental challenge. The challenge is that of scale. How can social innovation scale?

My central thesis is that social entrepreneurs must harness financial markets to reach efficient scale. To do this, the financial intermediation sector that serves social innovators must grow.

Typically, when scholars use the term *social entrepreneurship*, they have a specific and narrow set of private-sector actors in mind (Dees, 2001). For the purposes of the present discussion, however, it is more fruitful to group a number of distinct organizational forms together under the rubric of social entrepreneurship. Therefore, I will use *social entrepreneur* or *social innovator* interchangeably to refer to a private-sector economic actor belonging to a broad class of organizational forms that address social change. For reasons that will become clear, a *social entrepreneur* for my purposes will be any social change agent that may rely partly on external funding for their survival and success. This is anathema to those who are keenly aware of the differences in organizational structure, and so on, but the specifics of my argument make it natural to group together entrepreneurs with other actors who strive to change practice to promote social outcomes.

The idea that capital markets can help scale social entrepreneurship is not really a new one.[2] Indeed, business history is replete with examples illustrating the power of capital markets to promote social welfare. One need look no further than to Adam Smith to find descriptions of how impediments to speculative trade served to promote localized famine in rural England (see later). Fast forward some 250 years, and we have not one, but two Nobel Prizes recognizing the power of capital markets for promoting social entrepreneurship: Ned Phelps, the winner of the 2007 Economics Nobel Memorial Prize, stressed the role of entrepreneurial capitalism in ushering forward technological advances that promote human welfare. Meanwhile, Mohammed Yunus won the Nobel Peace Prize in the same year for founding Grameen Bank, the very act of which exemplifies the principles espoused by Phelps himself.

What impediments must be overcome to scale social financial intermediation? I argue there are three. The first is measurement. Simply put, we need more data. We need not only more program evaluation work, but also work collecting and assembling data on administrative practices, more accounting data on social enterprises. The second is governance. With better data, robust governance mechanisms can be put in place that lower the idiosyncratic risk that investors face when they invest in social entrepreneurship. And the third is compensation. The organizational constraints under which most nonprofits work create employee compensation practices. These practices can have adverse incentive effects, especially when social investors work alongside commercial ones.

If these challenges are overcome, the fruits are significant. Questions of efficient scale of an enterprise can be delegated to the market. Indeed, the efficient scale of an organization can be decoupled from the efficient level of aggregate social output in a sector. As a result, market structure can evolve, proliferate, and become an additional force for the promotion of innovative social change.

The remainder of this essay is structured as follows. I begin by defining in detail what it means to harness capital markets to promote social entrepreneurship. Then I address the primary impediments that private sector agents face when they attempt to scale through social entrepreneurship. Following a discussion of the impediments to scaling, I discuss the benefits of scaling through capital markets.

Perhaps we can take encouragement from the fact that social financial intermediaries are already at work promoting social entrepreneurship. I conclude by briefly discussing a few of these key initiatives.

Promoting Social Middle Men

In light of current developments in financial markets, it might seem awkward or ill-timed to suggest that capital markets can and should play a key role in alleviating social ills by reallocating resources toward those who need it most. As Rajan famously argued in 2005, globalization and financial development seem to have increased risk, not risk-sharing.

Nevertheless, my main thesis is that harnessing capital markets is a necessary condition for promoting social entrepreneurship. What does this mean? In principle, it means taking advantage of the vast, anonymous mechanism of the financial market to intermediate the transfer of wealth and facilitate risk-sharing.

As a practical matter, this means promoting the financial middleman. The financial middleman for the social innovator is the economic actor who aggregates the patient capital (Trelstad, 2008) provided by foundations, philanthropists, and socially conscious investors, and in turn acts as a custodian of these funds, investing them in organizations that pursue the social objectives that are congruent with the upstream investors' missions.

As I discuss in greater detail later, each of these economic actors in the social sphere has a direct analog in the commercial sphere. Social financial intermediaries are analogous to VC firms. The vast web of charity comprising foundations, philanthropists, and investors are akin to the limited partners in commercial VC firms. The social entrepreneurs who receive backing are like the portfolio companies in which commercial venture capitalists invest (figure 11.1). While we think of financial intermediaries such as venture capitalists as modern inventions, they are not. They are as old as the problems they help to solve.

Financial Middlemen as Promoters of Social Change

Middlemen have a long history in economics as agents that promote the development of sectors. Chapter 5, Book IV of the Wealth of Nations describes prohibitions against middlemen and profiteering in the time of famine and rightly points to these prohibitions as a primary cause of localized famine in medieval England.

The statute of Edward VI, therefore, by prohibiting as much as possible any middle man from coming in between the grower and the consumer, endeavored to annihilate a trade, of which the free exercise is not only the best palliative of the inconveniences of a dearth, but the best preventive of that calamity; after the trade of the farmer, no trade contributing so much to the growing of corn as that of the corn merchant.

The Edwardian statutes prohibiting middlemen effectively forced farmers to act like local retailers, rather than delegating this (economically distinct) activity to a specialist wholesaler. The crux of Smith's argument is that corn prices would be at least as high if bought from the farmer than if bought from the wholesaler. This is an immediate consequence of the division of labor: forcing the farmer to play retailer forces the farmer to devote capital and labor that could better be used in farming instead toward retailing.

Smith's argument was that prohibitions against speculators, for lack of a better word, actually worked to promote famine, rather than to alleviate it. The distribution of corn to the kitchen table is a distinct economic activity from the production of corn from seed and earth. Because farmers had limited amounts of capital, the capital turned away from farming toward the distribution of corn had to earn a return commensurate with its opportunity cost. This meant less corn, not more corn, and higher, not lower prices.

Outsourcing the Fundraising Function

The same arguments that applied to sixteenth-century English corn farmers apply in spades to twenty-first-century social innovators. Without a

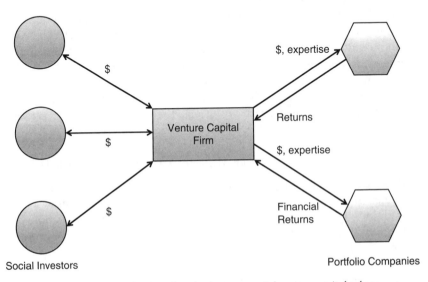

Figure 11.1 Organizational interactions in the commercial venture capital sphere.

fully developed social financial intermediation sector, social entrepreneurs are like the corn farmers who have to move their capital away from farming and devote it to retail endeavors. Without the benefit of social financial intermediation, today's social entrepreneurs take time away from mission to keep their mission alive.

Of course, many social entrepreneurs are strong advocates for their causes. Their passion is persuasive.[3] My argument is not that they lack persuasion. My argument is that their passion is better spent on their mission than on communicating to investors.

As figure 11.2 shows, returns to scale is the key to this argument. In a world with pervasive social financial intermediation, social entrepreneurs will still be required to communicate their passion to outsiders. But their efforts will be more concentrated. They will only communicate their mission to a narrower audience: the social financial intermediary in turn communicates to the broader pool of investors.

Why are social financial intermediaries better able to do this than social entrepreneurs? While they may or may not lack the passion of the social entrepreneur, their role as financiers creates incentives for them to develop reputations among donors. Standard arguments in economics show how the ability to develop and maintain a reputation creates incentives for middlemen to develop expertise in an area.[4] This expertise allows them to develop a comparative advantage over the social entrepreneur, not just by economizing on resources that the social entrepreneur would otherwise devote to the task, but by increasing the efficiency by which the resources are deployed. Because the efficient scale of a reputation in the financial market need not coincide with what is feasible in a small, socially innovative organization, more aggregate social entrepreneurship can be created by introducing a middleman that operates at a different scale than the social innovators it serves.

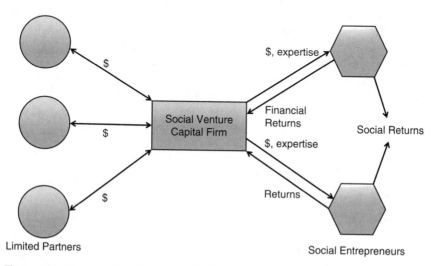

Figure 11.2 Organizational interactions in the social venture capital sphere.

Of course, as this discussion makes clear, it is not as if social entrepreneurs are not active in capital markets. They are. But to draw on another analogy to commercial financial practices, when social entrepreneurs use passion and persuasion to bring in investment capital, they are playing the role of private wealth management experts. I am arguing for the venture capital model to supplant the private wealth management model as the primary mechanism through which social entrepreneurs access financial markets.

While my main focus is on social venture capital, this is not the only type of organization that can carry out social financial intermediation. Indeed, as the Growth Philanthropy Network illustrates, the websites can serve many of the same functions. The website serves as a virtual meeting place where donors, social actors, and many other interested bystanders can gather to share resources and information about social change initiatives. Because the World-Wide Web is so highly scalable, websites provide a powerful aggregation mechanism where numerous small donations from individuals that are interested in various social issues can be put to work. Networks such as GPN also share another feature with social venture capital: their reputation can become an asset that provides assurance to donors that the social ventures represented on the site have passed through a variety of quality or ethical screens.

Impediments and Challenges

To understand what impediments and challenges we face as we urge the social financial intermediation sector to grow, it is worth examining the standard toolkit used by the financial intermediaries of commercial innovation. Venture capitalists rely on prevailing market statistics to determine investment prices. They use sophisticated financial contracts to facilitate careful monitoring of the portfolio companies that receive their investment funds. And their compensation practices allow them to share in the financial upside of the companies in which they invest: this sharpens incentives to monitor investments and to provide assistance and advice.

What pieces, then, need to be in place for social financial innovation to scale? From peering inside the VC's toolkit, we see that there are three:

(1) First, there has to be a robust system of measurement that allows market participants to measure social output and compare efficiency across institutions.
(2) Second, there have to be sound governance practices in place throughout the sector so that widespread trust can be built in the sector.
(3) Third, among the social financial intermediation sector, there have to be robust compensation practices that create incentives to monitor portfolio companies without destroying credible governance and measurement practices.

Each of these impediments is important in its own right, but more importantly, there are interactions between them. For example, better data is a complement to better governance. But taken to the extreme, better compensation practices may cut against governance, and indeed may jeopardize attempts to create meaningful data. Thus, getting the mix right is as important as making headway on any single impediment.

Measuring Social Outcomes

The ultimate goal of any investor is to earn the maximum return for the amount of risk that they choose to bear. This leads quickly to the need to distinguish between well and poorly functioning investments, and in turn, well and poorly functioning organizations.

This involves improving measurement on two fronts. We need both more widespread efforts at program evaluation and more firm- or project-level accounting and control data.

The standard statistical debate in social sciences that program evaluation attempts to address is the question of selection versus treatment. Did a social innovation work because the program was effective, or because the people who chose to participate were somehow different than the nonparticipants in ways that are difficult to observe? Put simply, what if the people helped by the social innovation would have improved anyway, even without the program's help?

Answering this question in the affirmative requires careful research designs, ideally ones that involve random assignment to control and treatment groups. Recent work by Karlan et al. (2006) or Karlan and List (2007) provide recent examples. Such programs are expensive to implement—Trelstad (2008) speaks of costs ranging from $250,000 to $500,000 per evaluation. As a result, there is often skepticism among practitioners surrounding the use of program evaluation. Practitioners build up their knowledge-set case by case through the act of implementing the social enterprise, and thus often view the program evaluation as unnecessary.

The problem with the practitioner perspective is that practitioners only observe the data that confront them. Experience does not offer insights into counterfactual outcomes. Program evaluations are designed to measure exactly this.

Of course, the practitioner's side of the argument is not without merit. Social scientists in academia require draconian standards of proof. To be satisfied that a social effect has occurred in a particular data set, they typically require a 95 percent level of confidence. Perhaps this standard of proof is simply too onerous for the real world. This is akin to "beyond the shadow of a doubt" certainty that is the threshold in criminal proceedings, where a conviction may well deprive the convicted person of their liberty, or worse, even their life. In contrast, civil litigation in the United States only requires a level of professional confidence: the idea that the effect is more likely than not to be responsible for the finding at hand.

The most practical answer may well be to employ lower-cost program evaluations that, because of their lower cost, do not allow conclusions to be drawn at conventional academic levels of statistical confidence, but nonetheless do allow program evaluators to discern likely treatment effects from likely selection effects at conventional "business judgment" standards of confidence. Even if selection and treatment can only be disentangled at conventional levels of business judgment, there is still value in knowing whether results come from selection or treatment. Indeed, if the success of a program comes primarily through selection, then this suggests that a marginal dollar of investment may well be better spent on advertising, rather than on program development.[5]

But more program evaluation is not the only source of additional data we need. Program evaluation is essentially a way of evaluating business models, not businesses. Program evaluation answers questions such as whether people will use more bednets if they are free or if they have to pay for them. We also need data that allow us to evaluate the businesses that implement the business models. These data allow us to answer whether a particular organization is doing an effective job putting bednets into service.

On this second front we need to assemble data that allow us to compare many different types of organizations. Organizations such as Guidestar already do this for the nonprofit sector. But to understand best the most efficient means of achieving a social innovation, we need to know about performance across organizational forms, not just within them. We need data on nonprofits, and then we need to add to that meaningfully comparable data from a range of other forms of social innovation.[6]

Only when we have meaningful performance data from a range of social innovators will we be able to answer the question that is foremost in investors minds: How do I maximize the return I face for a given level of risk? This question is infinitely more complex in the social sphere than in the commercial sphere, but no less important. Measuring returns to social innovation requires measuring the externalities that social change brings about. If the externalities were measurable, it would be possible to internalize them, and they would no longer be externalities. So measuring social return is no small feat. And of course, measuring risk in the social sphere is no easier than measuring returns. Perhaps the prescription of Trelstad (2008) is best: measure social output, worry about social outcomes.

Solving the Governance Problem

Better data, both on the efficacy of business models as well as the efficiency of individual businesses, are the key to addressing what may be the biggest impediment to scaling social innovation: better governance of social entrepreneurs.

This is not to suggest that individual social entrepreneurs are ungovernable or prone to malfeasance. If anything, the problem of governance is simply a communication problem between those who entrust their money to social financial intermediaries and those who receive investments from social financial intermediaries. Governance is simply a mechanism for communicating that puts prespecified rules in place.

The governance problem is exacerbated by the nature of the motives behind those who contribute capital to social financial intermediaries. Too often the act of donating financial capital to a cause is equated to the act of carrying out the cause. When a donor equates giving and doing, they have diminished incentives to monitor how their capital is being deployed. An investor in common equity naturally cares about the point of harvest, in addition to the point of investment. The nature of charitable giving too often obscures the point of harvest from the donor's attention. Thus, a primary function of the social financial intermediary is to use its reputation to increase the salience of harvest.

Getting Compensation Right

Of course, getting corporate governance right inside the socially entrepreneurial organization is complicated by the third critical challenge to scaling social financial intermediation: compensation practices. Current operating practice in the social financial intermediation sector places constraints on compensation. These constraints can have adverse consequences.

Most social intermediaries are organized as charitable organizations. Their 501(c)3 status essentially prevents their employees from earning carried interest on the investments that they make. This is an important point of distinction between social financial intermediaries and their counterparts in the commercial sector.

It is easy to see the logic behind putting constraints on compensation practices in the social financial intermediation sector. Since, by definition, a large component of the returns to social investing will be returns that are difficult to measure and appropriate to investors, tying compensation to the returns to social investment can be problematic. Consider a financial intermediary choosing between two investments. Investment A pays an unmeasured social return of $5Y$ and an appropriable financial return of $X. Investment B pays a social return of $2Y$ and a financial return of $2X. Even though the social intermediary may be dedicated to creating social output Y, excessive performance-based compensation may cause the investor to choose investment B over A, even if A were the socially desirable choice, just because his claim on the marginal $X of financial return may sway his decision-making.

Nevertheless, if the incentives of the social financial intermediary are blunted to the outcomes of the companies in which they invest, this too can lead to bad outcomes. This is because, like commercial venture capitalists, the VCs of the social sphere take an ongoing, continued interest in their social innovators. It is not only important that the social VC thus have the incentives to undertake the appropriate *level* of effort, they must have incentives to undertake the right type of effort for a given effort level. They must not only have incentives to work hard, but to make the right choices.

As long as financial success and social success are positively correlated within the organization, tying the social VCs incentives to the financial success of the company should increase the incentives to undertake the socially optimal action. Indeed, in the earlier example, financial incentives produce distorted outcomes precisely because in the choice between investment A and B, financial and social returns are negatively correlated.[7] Thus, there is an important interaction between the efficient scope of the social innovation organization and the efficient compensation practices of the intermediaries that fund it: compensation practices that work when overseeing one organization will not work for an organization with a different set of financial and social tradeoffs. Getting compensation right requires getting organizational structure right at the same time.

The preceding discussion simply addresses the problems of a single intermediary engaging a single social entrepreneur. Compensation problems inside social financial intermediaries are exacerbated by the fact that social investors often invest alongside commercial ones. Because it is common for commercial investors to share in the economic upside of the businesses in which they invest, the compensation constraints that social intermediaries face create conflicts of interest in the governance of socially entrepreneurial organizations.

The Fruits of Intermediation

While the impediments I have outlined earlier may be seemingly intractable, the gains from scaling social financial intermediation are commensurately large. Disintermediating the funding of social enterprise means that the operating scale of a social movement and the operating scale of a social enterprise need not be interlinked. In short, economies of scale in operations need not be constrained or dictated by economies of scale in fund-raising activities.

Several important implications follow immediately from decoupling the scale of an individual operation and the scale of fund-raising. The first, and most important, is that the aggregate amount of social innovation will grow. If there are decreasing returns to the practice of social innovation, and the efficient scale of fund-raising is larger than the efficient scale of social innovation, then social innovators left to their own devices will necessarily operate at an inefficient operating scale. Breaking this inefficiency through the introduction of increased financial intermediation will, therefore, necessarily increase the output of social innovation.

Once the link between the operating and fundraising scales is broken, there is increased space for organizational innovation in the social innovation sector. Firms that operate on a scale that is dictated or constrained by fund-raising considerations have limited capacity to experiment with organizational design and implementation. Delegating the fund-raising function to an intermediary allows for experimentation that may yield new and better modes of implementing social change.

Increased intermediation will also create competition among organizations, which will further encourage efficiency. This is important because often there is no natural role in the product market for social enterprises to compete against one another, since the products that they supply are offered at reduced or no cost. Introducing competition on the funding side without diverting scarce resources to fund-raising can increase efficiency by more closely tying the output of the social entrepreneur to the social objectives of investors.

All told, this means that we should expect to see a proliferation of market structures in the social innovation sector. In some sectors, growth in one social sector may result in a proliferation of small organizations, all competing against one another for funds in the capital market. In other sectors, growth may favor a dominant player.

Conclusion

Since I began this essay by pointing out that I was not the first to recognize the importance of scaling social entrepreneurship through financial markets, let me then conclude by pointing out that many of the concerns I have addressed are already being addressed; many of my suggestions already underway.

The Acumen Fund and other social VC firms like it provide a case in point. Social venture capitalists such as Acumen make VC-style investments in portfolio companies across the globe that operate hybrid models blending financial sufficiency with social returns. The contracts that they employ bear a striking resemblance to the types of contracts that VCs employ in the commercial sector: they take equity positions or convertible debt positions in socially entrepreneurial startups, employing term sheets that give them board oversight and important business decision-making rights. And even though the compensation problems that I have outlined earlier may impair the social VC's attempts to monitor and guide the company, it is important to note that by using VC-style contracts, social VCs have a positive impact on the incentives that the social entrepreneurs face.

The Acumen Fund has been pivotal in two ongoing initiatives designed to promote better access to data on social entrepreneurship. The first is the Impact Ratings and Investment Standards, or IRIS, initiative. This initiative was spearheaded by The Rockefeller Foundation, Acumen Fund, and BLab. The goal of the IRIS initiative is to promulgate a common accounting standard across organizations that engage in social entrepreneurship. Widespread adoption of IRIS accounting standards mean that it will be increasingly possible to compare the performance of socially innovative organizations. This, in turn, facilitates the greater use of measures such as Social Return on Investment (SROI), currently used by many organizations, or Best Available Charitable Option (BACO), used by Acumen.

The PULSE system is a second industry-wide initiative that stands to improve data availability, and therefore governance outcomes. It is essentially a document repository in which contracts, performance metrics, and outcomes associated with individual investments can be stored. The proliferation of data on funding, and the ability to tie it to social outcomes, holds enormous promise for further academic research in this sector. Modern empirical financial economics got its start when widely available data on stock returns allowed scholars to study the statistical properties of returns—data guided the development of better theory. What if we could take the insights developed over the last fifty years in portfolio management, capital structure, and corporate governance, and apply them to the funding of social enterprise? Widespread adoption of PULSE and IRIS could revolutionize the way academics address social entrepreneurship, which in turn could usher in a new era of practice.

As these initiatives illustrate, practitioners and social scientists are already providing innovative solutions to the problems associated with measuring social enterprise. A more pressing challenge is to develop robust, scalable models of governance provision that allow for transparency and accountability. Changes in accounting rules and standards surrounding multiple bottom line organizations would be a step in the right direction. But the ultimate solution will involve the creation of new market actors whose role is to certify providers of social enterprise. It is hoped that these organizations can learn from the mistakes of their erstwhile cousins in the traditional capital markets, where misaligned incentives created a distorted system of certification that no doubt contributed to the current state of affairs in capital markets. A financial market collapse in the world of social enterprise would be a tragedy indeed.

Notes

1. See Moyo (2009) and Easterly (2006) for more on the problems with large-scale aid as a tool for alleviating supply-side pressures.
2. Indeed, recent work by Bloom (2009) and Bloom and Chatterji (2009) discusses the role that capital provision plays in social entrepreneurship.
3. Indeed, their passion may in some cases be stronger than their managerial or operational skill. But this is all the more reason to introduce sophisticated financial intermediaries. Hellmann and Puri (2002) have argued that one of the key services that commercial venture capitalists provide to small firms is professionalization of the firm's management. If the analogy between social and commercial venture capital holds, then the same argument should push increased social financial intermediation to spur professionalization of social enterprise.
4. See Biglaiser (1993) or Rubinstein and Wolinsky (1987) for classic treatments of this problem.
5. One could as well argue that if a program's efficacy comes through selection, then a marginal dollar of investment is better spent on program development. Allocating the marginal dollar of investment between advertising or program development depends on the elasticity of output of either with respect to investment.
6. The need to compare across organizational forms of social innovation and the ability of social financial intermediaries to channel resources into an array of different types of organizations are precisely why I choose to adopt a broad definition of social entrepreneurship for the purposes of the present arguments.
7. This is essentially the same as the comonotonicity property that Aghion and Bolton (1992) require in their analysis of funding with incomplete contracts.

12

Methodological Issues and Challenges in Conducting Social Impact Evaluations

Cornelia Pechmann and J. Craig Andrews

Conducting meaningful research, or "research that matters," is an important and potentially rewarding activity for many researchers. This type of research has been described as social impact research, social entrepreneurism, social marketing, altruistic marketing, and transformative consumer research (Mick, 2006), among other terms. Research topics that matter are abundant, including smoking, obesity, gambling, alcohol and drug addiction, AIDS, malnutrition, environmental damage, poverty, lack of health coverage, and illiteracy including financial and health illiteracy to name just a few.

In pursuing research that matters, researchers often conduct studies to evaluate the effectiveness of social marketing campaigns, social entrepreneurship programs, or related social initiatives. We will refer to these as social impact evaluations, and they will serve as our focus. They are often done on behalf of government entities, nonprofit groups, or firms. Successfully measuring the effectiveness of social initiatives that affect large segments of a society is an extremely important endeavor (Bloom, 2009) and focusing on behavior change is arguably the ultimate objective (Andreasen, 1994).

However, there can be numerous methodological challenges and problems inherent in such studies that can limit their generalizability and/or their ability to prove causal effects. In many instances, social impact evaluations are subject to research design trade-offs; that is, methodological decisions that increase some aspects of a study's internal or external validity also unfavorably impact other aspects (Cook and Campbell, 1979). While all research involves tradeoffs, they seem to be especially visible and problematic in these evaluations because of the high stakes involved in determining whether a social initiative worked or not, and thus whether it merits further funding.

The purpose of our chapter is to critically evaluate two key aspects of social impact evaluations: design and implementation. More specifically, we first discuss the technical aspects of designing or planning the research. Then, we identify four main design options available to researchers, give examples of each, and discuss the pros and cons of each. These include both expensive, comprehensive, multiyear designs and more limited designs that can be used when there is a shortage of money and/or time.

Under implementation, we examine the human aspects of carrying out social impact research and dealing with the various stakeholders. In particular, we explore some of the challenges in working with different constituencies with widely varying perspectives on the social initiative, in terms of goals and processes. For instance, it is often necessary to balance the conflicting recommendations and mandates of government agencies, funding agencies, advertising agencies, marketing research firms, public relations firms, legislators, government oversight groups, nonprofit groups, consumer advocacy groups, diverse consumer groups, outside evaluators, and/ or academic and practitioner consultants. We then identify several major sources of conflict and discuss potential solutions by drawing on real-world examples from our own research and consulting.

Our background includes work with the Office of National Drug Control Policy on their antimarijuana ad campaign; Health Canada, Massachusetts and Wisconsin on their antismoking ad campaigns; the Risk Communication Advisory Committee of the Food and Drug Administration; the Federal Trade Commission; and the U.S. Census Bureau. In this chapter, we focus on research that we conducted or followed in evaluating the different anti-drug and antismoking campaigns. However, the designs and conflicts we discuss should be broadly applicable to other types of social impact evaluations.

Research Designs for Evaluating Social Impact Programs

The major design dimensions that we consider are whether to conduct experiments or quasi-experiments, and whether to use a lab or field research setting. We do not examine nonexperiments because they cannot assess causal impact (Cook and Campbell, 1979). By experiments, we mean that exposure to the campaign or program is manipulated; the program runs in some communities or during some time periods (the test), but not others (the control). By quasi-experiments, we mean that there is no manipulation of exposure involving test and control groups, or we mean that exposure effects are compared across demographic subgroups that precludes random assignment to subgroup (e.g., participants cannot be randomly assigned to a gender subgroup; they are born into one). This makes it more difficult to assess the causal impact of exposure or why the impact may differ by demographic subgroup, but other approaches can be taken

Table 12.1   The four main types of designs for evaluating social impact programs

Field setting		Lab setting	
Quasi-experiment	*Experiment*	*Quasi-experiment*	*Experiment*
Design 1: Full-scale evaluation	Design 2: Partial evaluation or field test	Design 3: Audience subgroup copy test	Design 4: Message or situational copy test

to allow causal inferences. The most common approach is to try to statistically equate the test and control groups and/or the demographic subgroups using covariates.

We will also consider the research setting dimension. By lab setting, we mean an artificial testing environment, such as a mall research facility or a middle school classroom, where nuisance variables such as distraction can be manipulated or controlled. By field setting, we mean a highly realistic testing environment, such as a mass media advertising broadcast, where such nuisance variables cannot be controlled. Crossing the two dimensions discussed here leads to the four designs in table 12.1.

Design 1: The Field Quasi-Experiment for a Full-Scale Evaluation

We now examine the field quasi-experiment (design 1), which permits a full-scale evaluation of a campaign or program in its final form under realistic conditions. Many government and nonprofit groups and firms prefer or even demand this design. However, it has some weaknesses including no manipulation of exposure and little control over nuisance variables. Steps must be taken to strengthen the design, in order to increase the validity of inferences about causal effects. We will discuss various case examples that differ in the steps taken. We will focus primarily on the design decisions; the original articles contain additional details about samples, measures, and analyses.

> *Case 1.1: National Youth Anti-drug Ad*
> *Campaign full-scale evaluation*

A costly full-scale evaluation of the National Youth Anti-Drug (Antimarijuana) Media Campaign was conducted, using a quasi-field experiment (Hornik et al., 2008). The research questions were whether the campaign, which had already commenced, was effective among adolescents in terms of creating antimarijuana beliefs or reducing intent to use, or at lessening actual marijuana use. No steps had been taken to facilitate the evaluation, which is fairly common. No pre-campaign or baseline data had been collected to provide a control group, and the campaign had aired continually in every market so there were no apparent low-exposure markets or times to create control groups this way.

The researchers surveyed roughly six thousand adolescents annually in their homes; overall, the same adolescents were surveyed four times. It was found that 94 percent of youths reported seeing the ads, and the median frequency was two–three ads per week. In effect, all adolescents had been exposed to the same ad campaign and thus, technically, were in the test condition. However, the researchers used the level of ad recall to identify adolescents with different levels of exposure, and then used the low exposure level as the control and the higher exposure levels as the test. (See figure 12.1 for a stylized illustration of the design.) Since the low and higher exposure groups likely differed in their a priori marijuana use risk propensity, the researchers measured numerous covariates (150) to try to statistically equate the groups using propensity scores to preserve degrees of freedom (Joffe and Rosenbaum, 1999). For instance, differences in risk because of sensation seeking and religiosity were controlled for or factored out in the statistical models.

The study found mixed effects and concluded that overall the campaign was ineffective or even counterproductive. There were some positive effects; as the campaign progressed, antimarijuana beliefs strengthened, but it is unclear whether the campaign caused this or other factors such as general trends, other related-product campaigns (e.g., Truth), or random variation. There were some neutral effects; ad exposure did not predict marijuana beliefs or intent when measured at the same time. There were also negative effects in that higher recall of general antimarijuana ads sometimes predicted more intent to use one year later, and higher recall of specific ads sometimes predicted more pro-marijuana normative beliefs one year later.

However, it is unclear whether these negative effects can be attributed to the campaign. Research shows that ad effects occur within days or weeks of exposure and do not take a year to appear (Koyck, 1959), and this is the case even with pro-drug ads (Pollay et al., 1996) and antidrug ads (Emery et al., 2005). Further, reverse causality may have occurred (Hornik, 2002) in which adolescents who formed intent to use marijuana on account of other risk factors may have paid more attention to marijuana ads, but nonetheless maintained their intent due to those same risk factors. This would create an association between later intent and earlier ad exposure (also between earlier intent and later ad exposure, which was not assessed), but it would be driven by adolescents' own intent rather than the ads, and covariates may not have adequately controlled for this.

With such a potential reverse causality problem, it is unclear whether ad exposure caused intent or intent caused ad exposure. The reverse causality problem arises whenever self-reported ad exposure is used, because the high and low exposure groups are likely to differ fundamentally in terms of use intent; thus, they are noncomparable. In general, consumers with higher intent pay more attention to the ads and recall them better (Pechmann and Stewart, 1990). Therefore, one solution may be an independent measure of ad exposure that is unrelated to viewer's intent (e.g., ad GRPs).[1] This should ensure that ad exposure and prior intent are relatively uncorrelated. Or, one can include a true no-exposure baseline group or a true control

1.1   National Youth Anti-drug Ad Campaign Full-Scale Evaluation (Hornik et al., 2008)

1.2   Truth Anti-smoking Ad Campaign Full-Scale Evaluation (Farrelly et al., 2005)

C + T
C + T
C + C
C + C

and so on, across numerous markets

1.3   Other Full-scale Evaluations with Limited Exposure Variability

a) Pierce et al. (1998)

C + CC
C + TT

b) Emery et al. (2005)

T
C
T
C

and so on, across numerous markets

c) Pechmann et al. (1998)

CCCCCCCCTTTTTTT

2.1   University of Vermont Anti-smoking Ad Campaign Field Test (Flynn et al., 1992)

C + T
C + C
C + T
C + C

2.2   University of Kentucky Anti-marijuana Ad Campaign Field Test (Palmgreen et al., 2001)

CCCCCCCCTTTTCCCCCCCCTTTTCCCCCCCC
CCCCCCCCCCCCCCCCCCCCCTTTTCCCCCCCC

3.   Copy Test of Anti-drug Ads with Different Demographic Subgroups (Foley and Pechmann, 2004)

T—subgroup 1
C—subgroup 1
T—subgroup 2
C—subgroup 2
and so on for twelve demographic subgroups

4.   Copy Test of Anti-smoking Ads with Different Messages (Pechmann et al., 2003)

C
T—message 1
T—message 2
T—message 3

and so on for each of seven message types

Key: T = test, C = control; different rows indicate different markets (geographies)

Figure 12.1   Illustrations of the designs used in various social impact evaluations.

group that is not exposed to the ads in question but is matched to the test group on original intent and demographics.

Overall, the Hornik et al. (2008) antidrug ad campaign evaluation was large and comprehensive. It had several positive features including large, representative samples; a prospective or longitudinal design that tracked the same adolescents over time; and a host of reliable measures and covariates. However, this evaluation also had design limitations that should be avoided whenever possible. Most importantly, each evaluation could include at least one control group that actually receives lower exposure to the campaign or program. The control group should not consist of people who are exposed to the exact same campaign or program but for some reason report getting less exposure; this likely means they are fundamentally different and noncomparable and that their exposure was influenced by prior intent or behavior. Proper low exposure control groups can be found by looking for true exposure variability across markets or times, as discussed later.

Case 1.2: Truth antismoking ad campaign full-scale evaluation
A full-scale evaluation was conducted of the Truth antismoking ad campaign using a quasi-field experiment that employed a completely different design that was far less costly because it relied on secondary or preexisting data (Farrelly et al., 2005). The research question was, "Did the Truth campaign reduce smoking among adolescents?" The campaign had aired in all 210 U.S. media markets, but a careful analysis revealed that there was substantial variability in exposure because some markets (e.g., rural) did not have the smaller network stations (e.g., Fox) or cable stations (e.g., UPN) that were included in the media buys. Therefore, the adolescents in these markets could only see the major network ads and served as a low exposure control group (see figure 12.1). There was about a fivefold difference between the lowest and highest exposure groups; their annual GRPs were about two thousand and ten thousand, respectively, excluding outliers.

Statistical models examined whether exposure to the Truth ads during the first two years of the campaign (2000 and 2001), as measured by cumulative media market GRPs, reduced adolescent smoking. Smoking was assessed using the independent Monitoring the Future survey, which is an annual school-based survey of a representative sample of fifty thousand students across grades 8, 10, and 12. Additional models estimated the smoking trend during the control period of 1997–1999, before the Truth campaign commenced, also using Monitoring the Future. The statistical models included numerous individual covariates (e.g., demographics) as well as media market covariates (e.g., population size, education, income, cigarette prices, tobacco control spending, and market fixed effects).

The study indicates that the Truth campaign was effective; the higher the exposure level, the lower the smoking. It appears that the effect of the campaign continued to increase through ten thousand cumulative GRPs and then began to attenuate. Based on the trend during the control period (1997–1999), the smoking rate during the test period (2001–2002) should have declined from 25.3 to 19.6 percent and it actually declined to 18.0 percent; therefore it was concluded that 22 percent of the decline was due to Truth.

The Farrelly et al. (2005) evaluation was large, comprehensive, and inexpensive; and it included two separate control groups. Baseline control group data for the pre-campaign period was obtained from an ongoing survey that was used to estimate the pre-campaign decline and to show that the decline steepened during the campaign. In addition, the low GRP markets were used as a separate control group to examine what happened when GRPs increased. The high and low GRP markets differed in TV channel availability.

A study limitation is that the markets with low channel TV availability were probably more rural, and characteristics associated with rural markets (e.g., lower education) may have been related to smoking, but covariates were used to factor out these effects. It is preferable for exposure levels to be determined randomly by conducting a full-fledged experiment, but this was not feasible. Another concern is that the smoking rates, as measured by Monitoring the Future, were affected by many variables other than the ads, but this is also true of smoking behavior, and so the aim is to determine if ads matter despite these other factors.

Additionally, it cannot be determined if the students actually saw the ads that were aired in their media markets; GRPs are an imprecise measure of actual exposure. However, trying to assess actual exposure through self-reports can lead to the reverse causality problem discussed earlier; self-reported ad exposure may be highly correlated with intent and so it not possible to ascertain definitively whether ad exposure caused intent or vice versa. Finally, this study did not track the same people over time or prospectively, but doing so can lead to carry-over or demand effects (Cook and Campbell, 1979), and the cross-sectional samples should be comparable due to the sophisticated sampling used (Farrelly et al., 2005).

Case set 1.3: Other full-scale evaluations
with limited exposure variability

Ideally, a full-scale field evaluation will have substantial exposure variability across numerous markets and times including both pre- and post-campaign periods, as in the Farrelly et al. (2005) evaluation. However, this is not always possible. Fortunately, a valid field evaluation can be conducted using data from just a few markets for the pre- and post-campaign periods. An example is Pierce et al.'s evaluation (1998) of the California antismoking campaign that involved just two geographies; it compared the smoking trend in California to the United States based on various surveys. Since the surveys and the geographies were not fully comparable, weights were used to try to equate the samples on gender, age, race, and education level. Within each geography, three time periods were examined: the years prior to California's campaign, the years of California's early campaign when it had high funding, and the years of California's later campaign when it had low funding. This design improved the study's validity because trends in each geography could be compared by period, to see if there were any effects that were unique to California that were not attributable to a general trend over time (figure 12.1). The findings indicate that the early high-funded campaign caused a 50 percent more rapid decline in smoking than had occurred previously, and that this was unique to California, but that campaign efficacy waned when funding was reduced.

A valid field evaluation can also be conducted if there is variability across markets, but no variability across times, for example, no pre-campaign data. See Emery et al. (2005) for an example of this type of evaluation, involving state-funded antismoking ads (figure 12.1). The researchers purchased monthly Nielsen data on antismoking ad GRPs (targeted at adolescents) for seventy-five top media markets for two years when the ads were running. The researchers also purchased Monitoring the Future survey data on adolescent smoking for those same years. Then, the researchers estimated a model to determine if differences in ad exposure across the markets resulted in different smoking rates, after controlling for other market differences, such as cigarette prices and tobacco control policies via covariates. Ad exposure for the four months prior to the survey ranged from zero to roughly two, so exposure levels were low. Nonetheless, the findings indicate that higher ad exposure led to more ad recall, lower smoking rates, and fewer cigarettes smoked.

A valid field evaluation might even be possible if there is variability across times but no variability across markets, although this is the weakest of such designs. Pechmann et al. (1998) used structural time-series models to estimate Canadian smoking trends by age group, and the data spanned the years prior to and during Canada's antismoking ad campaign. With sufficient data points and structural time-series models, one can estimate the trend in behavior prior to a campaign that is independent of ad spending, and then see if the trend changes, that is, if a shock occurs, when the campaign starts (figure 12.1).

The problem with simple comparisons over time (single unit time series) is that anything else correlated with the trend in ad spending is often indistinguishable from the ad effect. For example, ad spending often starts when the problem is at its worst, which means that it will improve regardless. If a structural time-series model can estimate the peak and the subsequent decline that would have occurred without the ads, it can determine if there is a residual ad effect. However, this typically requires very large datasets, with hundreds of monthly or annual observations.

Design 2: The Field Experiment for a Partial Evaluation or Field Test

Next, we will discuss the field experiment (design 2) that permits a partial evaluation or field test of a campaign or program. However, the test takes place under experimental conditions that are carefully monitored, and it occurs in only a few markets or geographies. Government agencies that fund scientific research, such as the National Institutes of Health, often prefer experiments and especially randomized controlled trials. Experiments are considered to be the gold standard for assessing causal effects (Cook and Campbell, 1979), but they are costly because primary or original data must be collected, and sometimes they cannot be carried out due to a lack of a true control market. Virtually all clinical drug trials involve randomized controlled trials, because quasi-experiments are considered inadequate.

However, experiments do have a substantial limitation: it is never entirely clear if the results will generalize to a full-scale campaign or program. For instance, the University of Kentucky antimarijuana ad campaign discussed subsequently produced impressive results (Palmgreen et al., 2001), and so it served as an initial template for the Office of National Drug Control Policy campaign evaluation that produced questionable results (Hornik et al., 2008). A host of decision-makers became involved in the national antimarijuana campaign, and the initial evidence-based template was modified in the hopes of improving it.

Case 2.1: University of Vermont antismoking ad campaign field test
University of Vermont researchers conducted a large field experiment of an antismoking ad campaign that complemented an antismoking school program (Flynn et al., 1992, 1994; Worden et al., 1988). The study was funded by the National Cancer Institute and it was a prospective or cohort study; the same 5,458 students were surveyed annually for five years, starting in grade 4, 5, or 6. The antismoking ads aired for five months the following year, followed by short ad surges for the next three years, providing about seven television and nine radio ad exposures per week. Also, students received an antismoking school program of four hours a year in grades 5–8, and then two hours a year in grades 9–10. The research question was: Did the ads help to deter smoking initiation?

The design was an experiment, in that ad exposure was manipulated. Two test communities received the ads and school program, while the two demographically matched control communities received just the school program (figure 12.1). Two pairs of metropolitan statistical areas were selected based on their having populations between fifty thousand and four hundred thousand, being similar on education, income, and ethnicity, and having independent media markets. Then, schools within these areas were selected that had low levels of parental education and income because these variables are associated with high smoking.

The study found that the ads were effective (Flynn et al., 1992). While smoking prevalence increased as the students aged as expected, the increase was less in the test group (ads and school program), relative to the control group (school program only), resulting in significantly lower smoking prevalence in the last two years. By the final year, 12.8 percent of the test group reported smoking in the past week versus 19.8 in the control group, a 35 percent difference. Results were similar for other measures of smoking behavior and beliefs. Two years later, smoking rates remained lower in the test versus control group (Flynn et al., 1994). The ads reduced smoking but not drinking as expected.

Strengths of this evaluation include the large samples, extensive ad exposure, and the fact that ad exposure was manipulated, which increases the likelihood that the ads at least partially caused the effects. A limitation of this evaluation, and some others like it, is that the intervention or ad manipulation was not entirely clean. In particular, some of the students who were exposed to the ad campaign participated in preliminary research to help design and pretest the ads (Worden et al., 1988), and it is unclear how much these experiences bolstered the ad effects. Also, all students received an extensive school program and so the effects of an ad-only intervention are unknown. We do not know the effects of the school-only intervention because there was no school-only group either. Another limitation is that demographic covariates were measured, but not included in the main models that estimated the ad effects. Finally, standard errors should have been adjusted by school to account for clustering (correlated errors) at the school level, since schools were the primary sampling unit not individual students (Farrelly et al., 2005; Murray and Hannan, 1990).

Case 2.2: University of Kentucky antimarijuana ad campaign field test

University of Kentucky researchers completed a large field experiment of an antimarijuana ad campaign with funding from the National Institute on Drug Abuse (Palmgreen et al., 2001). The study lasted thirty-two months, and involved monthly surveys with one hundred randomly selected adolescents in each of two counties (markets), amounting to about six thousand adolescents overall. The survey assessed marijuana use in the past thirty days, other substance use, and sensation seeking as a personality trait.

The design was an experiment as well, but ad exposure was manipulated differently. One county received the ad campaign for four months in each of two years. The second county received the campaign for four months in just the second year; in essence, it served as a control for the first county in the first year (figure 12.1). The two counties were in the same region and were demographically and culturally similar. At least 70 percent of the targeted adolescents were exposed to three or more ads per week. Surveys were conducted in each county during pre-, post-, and other non-campaign periods to provide control or baseline data; the same surveys were also conducted during the campaigns to provide intervention data.

The ads were shown to be effective in both counties (Palmgreen et al., 2001). When the ads were on the air and for about six months afterward, marijuana use declined significantly; otherwise, marijuana use increased. However, these effects were limited to high sensation seeking adolescents who overall showed a 26.7 percent decline in marijuana use from the ads. Among low sensation seekers, marijuana use was flat; there were no campaign effects and no developmental trends. The positive effects were specific to marijuana use and did not extend to other substances (e.g., alcohol, tobacco, or crack). Strengths of this evaluation include the interrupted time series design with replication, extensive manipulated ad exposure, monthly measurement, and large samples. Yet, some experts view "two city" designs like this as risky, because there is a single treatment and a single control site, and it must be assumed that the sites are equivalent at the start (Hornik, 2002).

Designs 3 and 4: The Lab Quasi-experiment and Experiment for Copy Tests

Now, we will turn to the evaluations conducted in the lab, namely the lab quasi-experiment (design 3) and the lab experiment (design 4), which are typically done to conduct copy tests of campaign or program materials. By lab we mean a controlled exposure setting, such as a mall research facility or a middle school classroom. By lab quasi-experiment, we mean copy tests in a controlled exposure setting among audience subgroups, such as different ages, genders, or ethnicities. These are quasi-experiments because demographic subgroups cannot be manipulated; people were born into them. By lab experiment, we mean copy tests of materials that vary in terms of the message (e.g., theme) or situation (e.g., distraction level). These are true experiments because exposure to these materials or settings can be manipulated and often a control group is included. These are not simple focus groups in which everyone sees the ads and discusses them.

Lab evaluations cost a fraction of full-scale field evaluations (thousands of dollars versus millions), and can be done in a fraction of the time (months versus years). Researchers can conduct lab evaluations with little or no extramural funding, though some agencies will fund them (Pechmann et al., 2003). Also, lab evaluations can simulate interventions that are too controversial or costly to be rolled out, unless their efficacy is demonstrated. For example, a lab simulation was conducted on the effects of antismoking ads in movie theaters because movie theater owners were unwilling to allow the ads in the theater (Pechmann and Shih, 1999). Major movie studios eventually agreed to put antismoking ads on DVDs based on the study results.

The primary concern about lab evaluations is that it is even more uncertain that the results will generalize to a full-scale campaign. Thus, the optimal approach is to start with a lab evaluation and, if the results look promising, continue with a field evaluation. The Office of National Drug Control Policy's antimarijuana ads were copy tested in a lab setting (Foley and Pechmann, 2004) and then evaluated in the field (Hornik et al., 2008).

Case 3: Copy Test of Anti-Drug Ads with Different Demographic Subgroups

The Office of National Drug Control Policy (ONDCP) routinely copy tests its finished or near-finished anti-marijuana TV ads before airing, to ensure the ads are effective and not counterproductive among adolescents (Foley and Pechmann, 2004). An ad will air if it significantly strengthens an anti-drug belief or weakens drug use intent in the copy test, among the overall sample or a demographic subsample such as a specific ethnic subgroup. An ad will not air if it significantly weakens an antidrug belief or strengthens drug use intent in the copy test, among the overall sample or a subsample.

This design is a lab quasi-experiment; another term for quasi-experiment is partially randomized experiment. The comparisons are between test (those exposed to the ad) and control (those not exposed to the ad) and each individual participant is randomly assigned to test or control. Nonetheless, this is a quasi-experiment or a partially randomized experiment because exposure effects are compared among ethnic subgroups or other demographic subgroups that preclude random assignment (e.g., participants cannot be randomly assigned to ethnic subgroup). Therefore, any differences in exposure effects that seem to be moderated by a demographic factor such as ethnicity cannot unequivocally be attributed to that factor. Ethnicity could be confounded with other variables; for instance, one ethnic group may have more knowledge of marijuana than another, affecting their ad comprehension and thus ad impact. If it is critical to know what is causing a differential impact on one demographic subgroup to take corrective action, researchers should try to manipulate a closely related variable (e.g., manipulate the salience of ethnicity) and do full random assignment to all conditions.

For the government's copy tests of antidrug ads, it is not critical to know what is driving ethnicity or other subgroup effects; therefore full random assignment is not needed and partial random assignment or a quasi-experimental design is adequate. However, random assignment to test versus control is needed to assess causal ad effects. Therefore, each adolescent is randomly assigned to be a test or control participant, and this is done for each of twelve demographic subgroups (figure 12.1). The twelve demographic subgroups represent three ethnicity levels (Caucasians, Hispanics, and African Americans), crossed with two grade levels (7–8 and 9–10) and also crossed with gender (male and female). For each copy test, the total sample size is six hundred, including three hundred test and three hundred control participants, with equal numbers of adolescents in each of the demographic subgroups (fifty per subgroup, including twenty-five test and twenty-five control).

Data collection is typically completed in one weekend using about forty shopping malls that have research facilities. Adolescents are approached in the malls, screened based on grade, ethnicity, and gender, offered one dollar to participate (resulting in a 75 percent participation rate), and given an informed assent form; parental consent is also obtained when possible. Next, adolescents are randomly assigned to be test participants, in which case they see the focal antimarijuana TV ad twice, or control participants in which case they do not see this ad. Afterward, all adolescents complete a ten-minute survey on their drug-related beliefs and intent, and the test participants also rate the ad on diagnostic measures. Covariates are also measured, including sensation seeking and exact age.

The effects of seeing the ad (test) versus not seeing it (control) are examined for the overall sample and for the subsamples. Covariates are included in the analyses to help rule out rival explanations for any observed differences between test and control groups or demographic subgroups (e.g., sensation seeking, exact age). Some of the ads may have null effects, or even adverse effects among a subgroup or the total sample, but these ads are not aired until they are revised, retested, and shown to have only desirable effects. The diagnostic measures help to reveal an ad's specific weaknesses. For instance, it may be found that the youngest adolescents miscomprehended certain ad content.

The strengths of this type of evaluation include relatively low cost, speed, manipulation of ad exposure, random assignment to test or control to ensure the groups are comparable except on ad exposure, and the assessment of effects by demographic subgroup. The main concern about this evaluation is whether the results generalize to the real world. For instance, the lab setting ensures that the ads are attended to; but in the real world, there are many distractions and other influences (e.g., word-of-mouth, peers), and the ads may not be attended to and may fail.

After the Office of National Drug Control Policy's copy test system was fully operational, all of the ads that it aired had been shown to reduce marijuana beliefs and/or intent in a copy test. Nevertheless, the Hornik et al. (2008) full-scale field evaluation found that the campaign was ineffective. In part, this may be because the Hornik et al. evaluation commenced before the copy test system was fully operational. Still there are troubling discrepancies in the research findings that call for follow-up studies.

Case 4: Copy Test of Anti-Smoking Ads with Different Messages

Researchers at the University of California, Irvine, obtained state funding to copy test antismoking ads with different messages among adolescents (Pechmann et al., 2003; also Zhao and Pechmann, 2007). There was considerable controversy about which messages to use, because different states had adopted radically different approaches. Research was needed to identify evidence-based approaches, and it would have been costly and time consuming to test the common types in a large field study. Therefore, a lab experiment was conducted, and the seven most prevalent message types were copy tested including long-term health consequences, cosmetic effects, second-hand smoke risks, and tobacco industry manipulation.

The design was a pure lab experiment or a randomized controlled trial involving 1667 adolescents from public schools. The adolescents who assented to participate and had parental consent were released from class, and then each individual was randomly assigned to a different classroom. In each classroom, several ads representing a single message type were shown on a large-screen TV. [Zhao and Pechmann (2007) embedded the ads in a TV show.] Overall, eight different classrooms were set up, in order to randomly assign participants to view one of the seven message types or the control message type (nonsmoking-related public service announcements) (see table 12.1).

After seeing the ads, adolescents completed a short survey on their smoking-related beliefs and intent. It was not feasible to measure the direct impact of the ads on smoking behavior by offering the adolescents cigarettes, for obvious ethical reasons, and one short ad exposure was not expected to affect long-term behavior. Instead, a validated measure of behavioral intent was used to assess how a well-funded ad campaign featuring each message type might impact long-term behavior (Pierce et al., 1995). The analyses compared the smoking beliefs and intent of the adolescents who saw the control ads, versus the adolescents who saw each type of test ad.

The study (Pechmann et al., 2003) found that the messages about the social aspects of smoking (e.g., second-hand smoke) significantly lowered adolescents' smoking intent, relative to the control condition, while the other messages had weaker and nonsignificant effects. The strengths of this evaluation (low cost, control over ad exposure, random assignment) as well as the weaknesses (artificiality) are similar to those discussed earlier.

Methodological Challenges

Choosing a research design to evaluate a social impact intervention almost invariably involves difficult tradeoffs. After-only designs that lack true control groups suffer from possible reverse causality (e.g., higher prior intentions to use drugs leading to greater awareness of antidrug ads). Simple pre-post designs can be problematic with respect to alternative explanations and confounds (e.g., general trends), as well as insufficient time between observations and inadequate resources for the treatment (Pechmann and Reibling, 2000). Cohort or longitudinal designs may be subject to history and maturation effects of participants. If a no-exposure control group is used, one should try to ensure that treatment and control groups (e.g., cities) are comparable a priori and that the treatment does not spill over to the control group. All of these designs can be challenged, yet it should be recognized that no social impact study is flawless.

In some cases, researchers may not be able to utilize a control group in field research. For example, it might not be politically feasible to hold out a portion of the country in a national antidrug campaign; or in an evaluation of a state antitobacco campaign, a matched control state might refuse to participate in the survey measurement. In such instances, insights may still be derived from a study of key relationships affecting intent or behavior, and of possible moderating and mediating effects. In Andrews et al.'s evaluation (2004) of a statewide, adolescent antismoking campaign, ad campaign attitudes, prior trial behavior and social influence (i.e., family and friends who smoked) were all found to significantly affect antismoking beliefs. Ad campaign attitudes also interacted with prior trial behavior to strengthen antismoking beliefs. In addition, the effect of ad campaign attitudes in lessening social influence and prior trial effects on smoking intent persisted even when accounting for antismoking beliefs.

The temptation may arise to rely on focus groups for evaluations, but these should only be used for idea generation and not as a final evaluation. Pressure may also be exerted to test non-comparable stimuli (e.g., ads in near final form rather than final form), use nonstandard or practitioner measures that look good but have no known reliability or validity (e.g., single item scales), ignore power analyses, focus on selective, data-driven (versus hypothesized) results, and the like. However, it is important to try to adhere to generally accepted research principles and not succumb to such pressures.

Dealing with Stakeholders

Researchers who are evaluating social impact studies often face conflicting recommendations and mandates of a wide variety of stakeholders, including government agencies, funding agencies, ad agencies, marketing research firms, public relations firms, legislators, government oversight groups, nonprofit groups, consumer advocacy groups, diverse consumer groups, outside evaluators, and academic and practitioner consultants. A common problem with having too many stakeholders involved in an evaluation is the pressure to want to test everything, whether or not the issues are related to the key policy questions and/or decisions. Helping the stakeholders to differentiate between what is "important" versus "interesting" can lead to a more focused study.

A second stakeholder problem is related to the often controversial nature of social impact research. Well-intentioned advocates may rush to implement the intervention before pre-exposure control or baseline data can be collected. Also, objectively worded and standard measures must be used, rather than biased measures that may lead participants to answer the questions in the desired ways. Finally, research partners have been known at times to make ill-advised suggestions not to pretest treatment stimuli to save on costs because "they know how consumers will react" (i.e., the "sample of one" problem) or because the stimuli have been tested elsewhere (e.g., in a different state than the current one).

Outstanding Practices of Note

We would like to make special note of two design procedures used to copy test ads for social impact research. First, the National Youth Anti-Drug Media Campaign's testing of ads is a thorough procedure that links focus group data with copy test data and finally with the tracking of campaign effects in the field. These data collection efforts are synergistic because the same measures are used and the results are directly compared for additional learning.

The Federal Trade Commission's procedures for testing deceptive advertising are somewhat different, but they are based on generally accepted principles too. Federal Trade Commission researchers normally include test and control ad groups, as well as control questions, and they funnel respondents from open-ended questions to successively narrower questions and ending with closed-ended ones (Andrews and Maronick, 1995). For greater detail on these copy testing methods, readers are encouraged to review the National Youth Anti-Drug Media Campaign and Federal Trade Commission procedures as discussed in Pechmann and Andrews (forthcoming).

Final Recommendations and Conclusions

We now offer some final thoughts and recommendations. First, we feel that it is important that social impact researchers get in on the "ground floor" of the evaluation planning and design process. It is vitally important to engage in planning and design with the right people who understand program evaluation techniques, the importance of a guiding consumer behavior theory, design options, and reliable and valid measures. As such, people are needed that adequately represent the three-legged stool of theory, research, and social issue (Brinberg and McGrath, 1985). Moreover, the use of multiple methods and triangulation certainly aids in offering greater credence to campaign outcomes. As noted by Shimp (1994), there are many different routes to knowledge.

Perhaps the most important consideration in conducting and evaluating social impact research is the selection of a control group to help account for alternative explanations. However, as noted earlier, there are some situations in which a single control group may not be feasible and creative solutions might be considered (e.g., comparing areas with different ad exposure levels; see also Hornik, 2002). In addition, given the many stakeholders involved in most social impact research decisions, we feel that it is critical to truly understand the many different disciplines that are involved. For example, some may focus on maximizing the amount of information provided in the campaign, rather than the effects on consumers who may have limited processing capabilities (Mazis, 1980). Finally, although there is no such thing as a perfect social impact study, researchers should try not to compromise on generally accepted, research principles.

Note

1. A GRP (gross rating point) is a measure of exposure opportunity, and it is calculated from the media buy reach x frequency. For example, an annual GRP of two thousand might mean that 100 percent of the target consumers received 20 weekly exposure opportunities or about .5 a week; while an annual GRP of ten thousand might mean that 100 percent of the target consumers received 100 weekly exposure opportunities or about 2 a week.

Bibliography

Aaker, D. (1991). *Managing brand equity: Capitalizing on the value of a brand name.* New York: The Free Press.

———. (1996). *Building strong brands.* New York: The Free Press.

Aghion, P. and Bolton, P. (1992). An incomplete contracts approach to financial contracting. *Review of Economic Studies*, 59, 473–494.

Ahlert, D., Ahlert, M., Duong Dinh, H.V., Fleisch, H., Heußler, T., Kilee, L., and Meuter, J. (2008). *Social franchising: A way of systemic replication to increase social impact.* Berlin: Bundesverband Deutscher Stiftungen.

Ahuja G. (2000). The duality of collaboration: Inducements and opportunities in the formation of interfirm linkages. *Strategic Management Journal*, 21, 317–343.

AIDSroko Twitter site. www.twitter.com/aidsroko, September 12, 2009.

Alvord, A.H., Brown, L.D., and Letts, C.W. (2004). Social entrepreneurship and societal transformation. *Journal of Applied Behavioral Science*, 40, 260–282.

Andreasen, A.R. (1994). Social marketing: Its definition and domain. *Journal of Public Policy and Marketing*, 13, 108–114.

Andrews, J.C. and Maronick, Thomas J. (1995). Advertising research issues from FTC versus Stouffer Foods Corporation. *Journal of Public Policy and Marketing*, 14, 301–327.

Andrews, J.C., Richard G.N., Burton S., Moberg D.P., and Christiansen A. (2004). Understanding adolescent intentions to smoke: An examination of relationships among social influence, prior trial behavior, and antitobacco campaign advertising. *Journal of Marketing*, 68, 110–123.

Annim, S.K. (2009). Targeting the poor versus financial sustainability and external funding: Evidence of microfinance institutions in Ghana, *SSRN,* May 21, http://ssrn.com/abstract=1408063.

Ansari, S., Fiss, P.C., and Zajac, E.J. (2010), Made to fit: How practices vary as they diffuse. Academy of Management Review, 35: 67–92.

Arango, T. and Brian, S. (2009). Messages with a mission, embedded in TV shows. *New York Times*, April 1, http://www.nytimes.com/2009/ 04/02/arts/ television/02gates.html.

Armendariz de Aghion, B. and Morduch, J. (2000). Microfinance beyond group lending. *Economics of Transition*, 8, 401–420.

Arole, M. and Arole, R. (1994). *Jamkhed: A comprehensive rural health project.* Bombay, India: Archana Art Printers.

Aspen Institute, The. (2005, 2007). *Beyond grey pinstripes.* Retrieved from http://www.beyondgreypinstripes.org.

Atuahene-Gima, K. and Evangelista, F. (2000). Cross-functional influence in new product development: An exploratory study of marketing and R and D perspectives. *Organization Science*, 46, 1269–1284.

Austin, J. (2000). *The collaboration challenge: How nonprofits and businesses succeed through strategic alliances.* San Francisco, CA: Jossey-Bass Publishers.

Austin, J., Stevenson, H., and Wei-Skillern, J. (2006). Social and commercial entrepreneurship: Same, different, or both? *Entrepreneurship: Theory and Practice*,
30(1), 1–22.

Bamford, J., Ernst, D., and Fubini, E.G. (2004). Launching a world class joint venture.
Harvard Business Review, 82(2), 90–100.

Banerjee, A., Dulo, E., Glennerster, R., and Kinnan, C. (2009). *The miracle of microfinance? Evidence from a randomized evaluation*. MIT Department of Economics
and Abdul Latif Jameel Poverty Action Lav. Working Paper.

Bartlett, C. and Ghoshal, S. (1990). Matrix management: Not a structure, a frame of
mind. *Harvard Business Review*, 68(4), 138–145.

Basu, P. (2006). *Improving access to finance for India's rural poor*. Washington, D.C.:
The World Bank.

BBC. (2007). Solar loans light up rural India. April 29, http://news.bbc.co.uk/2/hi/
science/nature/6600213.stm.

Berger, I.E., Cunningham, P.H., and Drumwright, M.E. (2004). Social alliances:
Company/nonprofit collaboration. *California Management Review*, 47, 58–90.

———. (2006). Identity, identification, and relationships through social alliances.
Journal of the Academy of Marketing Science, 68, 128–137.

———. (2007). Mainstreaming corporate social responsibility: Developing markets for
virtue. *California Management Review*, 49, 132–157.

———. (2010). The integrative benefits of social alliances: Balancing, building, and
bridging. In Smith, N.C. et al. (eds.), *Global challenges in responsible business*.
Cambridge: Cambridge University Press, 49–77.

Bhandari, A., Dratler, S., Raube, K., and Thulasiraj, R.D. (2008). Specialty care systems: A pioneering vision for global health. *Health Affairs*, 27(4), 964–976.

Biener, L., Ji, M., Gilpin, E.A., and Albers, A.B. (2004). The impact of emotional tone,
message, and broadcast parameters in youth anti-smoking advertisements. *Journal
of Health Communication*, 9, 259–274.

Biglaiser, G. (1993). Middlemen as experts. *Rand Journal of Economics*, 24,
212–223.

Biscoux, T. (2008). Uniting nations, uniting business. *Baized*, July/August, 16–21.

Bishop, Matthew and Green, Matthew. (2008). *Philanthrocapitalism: How the Rich
Can Save the World and Why We Should Let Them*. New York: Bloomsbury.

Blau, P.M. (1970). A formal theory of differentiation in organizations. *American
Sociological Review*, 35(2), 201–218.

Block, L.G., Morwitz, V.G., Putsis, W.P., and Sen, S.K. (2002). Assessing the impact
of anti-drug advertising on adolescent drug consumption: Results from a behavioral
economic model? *American Journal of Public Health*, 92, 1346–1351.

Bloom, P.N. (2009). Overcoming consumption constraints through social entrepreneurism. *Journal of Public Policy and Marketing*, 28, 128–134.

Bloom, P.N. and Chatterji, A.K. (2009). Scaling social entrepreneurial impact.
California Management Review, 51, 114–133.

Bloom, P.N. and Dees, J.G. (2008). Cultivate your ecosystem. *Stanford Social Innovation
Review*, 6, 46–53.

Bogg, T. and Roberts, B.W. (2004). Conscientiousness and health-related behaviors:
A meta-analysis of the leading behavioral contributors to mortality. *Psychological
Bulletin*, 130(6), 887–919.

Boxenbaum, E. and Battilana, J. (2005). Importation as innovation: Transposing managerial practices across fields. *Strategic Organization*, 3, 355–383.

Bornstein, D. (2004). *How to change the world: Social entrepreneurs and the power of
new ideas*. New York: Oxford University Press.

Bradach, J.L. (1997). Using the plural form in the management of restaurant chains.
Administrative Science Quarterly, 42, 276–303.

――――. (2003). Going to scale: The challenge of replicating social programs. *Stanford Social Innovation Review*, 1, 19–25.

Brett, J.A. (2006). We sacrifice and eat less: The structural complexities of microfinance participation. *Human Organization*, 65(1), 8–19.

The Bridgespan Group. (2005). *Growth of youth-serving organizations.*

Brinberg, D. and McGrath, J.E. (1985). *Validity and the research process*. Newbury Park, CA: Sage Publications.

Budde, R. (1989). Education by charter. *Phi Delta Kappan*, March, 518–520.

Bull, F.C., Holt, C.L., Kreuter, M.W., Clark, E.M., and Scharff, D. (2001). Understanding the effects of printed health education materials: Which features lead to which outcomes? *Journal of Health Communication*, 6, 265–279.

Bulloch, G. (2009). *Development collaboration: None of our business?* Accenture.

Buzzell, R.D. (2004). The PIMS program of strategy research: A retrospective appraisal. *Journal of Business Research*, 57, 478–483.

California Department of Education. (2009). *Ed-Data Education Data Partnership*. Retrieved from: http://www.ed-data.k12.ca.us/welcome.asp.

Campbell, A., Whitehead, J., and Finkelstein, S. (2009). Why good leaders make bad decisions. *Harvard Business Review*, 87(2), 60–66.

Campbell, K., Taft-Pearman, M., and Lee, M. (2008). *Getting replication right: The decisions that matter most*. The Bridgespan Group.

Carson E.G., Madhu A., and Varian, E.G. (2003). Information processing moderators of the effectiveness of trust-based governance in interfirm R and D collaboration. *Organization Science*, 14(1), 45–56.

CASE. (2006). *Scaling Social Impact Research Project: Practitioner Survey Executive Summary*. Duke University: Center for the Advancement of Social Entrepreneurship.

Cerven, J. and Ghazanfar, S. (1999). Third world microfinance: Challenges of growth and possibilities for adaptation. *Journal of Social, Political, and Economic Studies*, 24, 444–462.

CGAP. (2004). *Effectiveness initiative: Microfinance donor peer reviews.*

――――. (2007). *Banco Compartamos: Interest rates, profits, and an initial public offering.*

――――. (2007). *Beyond Good Intentions: Measuring the Social Performance of Microfinance Institutions*. CGAP Focus Note #41.

――――. (2008). *Who is Funding Microfinance: Results of the First Global Survey of Funders' Microfinance Portfolio.*

Chang, V. and Meyerson, D. (2008). *The "tipping point" and Green Dot Public Schools*. Case Study: SI-109. Stanford, CA: Stanford University Graduate School of Business.

Chenhall, R.H. (2003). Management control systems design within its organizational context: Findings from contingency-based research and directions for the future. *Accounting, Organizations & Society*, 28(2), 127–168.

Child, J. and Yan, Y. (2003). Predicting the performance of international joint ventures: An investigation in China. *Journal of Management Studies*, 40(2), 283–320.

CHIP. (2005). Research brief on "The causes of the high rate of drop-out amongst micro-finance borrowers" Civil Society Human And Institutional Development Programme (CHIP).

Christen, R.P. and Drake, D. (2001). Commercialization: The new reality of microfinance. In Drake, D. and Rhyne, E. (eds.), *The commercialization of microfinance: Balancing business and development*. Bloomfield: Kumarian Press.

Churchill, C. (2000). Bulletin Highlights and Tables—*Reaching the Poor: The Microbanking Bulletin*, 5, http://www.calmeadow.com/mbb2_index.html.

Churchill, G. (1979). A paradigm for developing better measures of marketing constructs. *Journal of Marketing Research*, 16, 64–73.

Clarkeson, J. (1990). Jazz vs. symphony. Reprinted in Stern, C.W. and Deimler, M.S. (eds.), *Boston Consulting Group on strategy: 2nd edition, 2006.* San Francisco: Jossey-Bass, 330–333.

Coburn, C.E. (2003). Rethinking Scale: Moving beyond numbers to deep and lasting change. *Educational Researcher,* 32 (6), 3–12.

Colby, S., Carttar, P., and Stone, N. (2003). Zeroing in on impact. *Stanford Social Innovation Review,* 2, 24–33.

Colby, S., Smith, K., and Shelton, J. (2005). *Expanding the supply of high-quality public schools.* The Bridgespan Group.

Colgate's "Toothman." http://www.colgate.com/app/Kids-World/US/Game_Toothman. vsp; accessed on September 12, 2009.

Collins, J. (2005). *Good to great and the social sectors.* New York: HarperCollins.

Common Interest Groups: Swine Flu. facebook; http://www.facebook.com/search/?init= srpandsfxp=andq=swine+fluando=69andc1=4; accessed on September 12, 2009.

Cook, T.D. and Campbell, D.T. (1979). *Quasi-experimentation: Design and analysis issues for field settings.* Boston, MA: Houghton Mifflin.

Copestake, J. (2003). Unfinished business: the need for more effective microfinance exit monitoring. *Journal of Microfinance,* 4(2), 1–30.

———. (2004). A challenge to the orthodoxy concerning microfinance and poverty reduction. *Journal of Microfinance,* 5(2), 7–42.

Copestake, J.G. (2007). Social performance management in microfinance: from mission drift to mainstream. *World Development,* 35(10), 1721–1738.

Crutchfield, L.R. and Grant, H.M. (2008). *Forces for good: The six practices of high-impact nonprofits.* San Francisco: Jossey-Bass.

Cuban, L. (2006). Educational entrepreneurs redux. *The Future of Educational Entrepreneurship.* Cambridge: Harvard Education Press.

Cull, R., Demirguc-Kunt, A., and Morduch, J. (2009). Microfinance meets the market. *Journal of Economic Perspectives,* Winter, 23(1), 167–198.

Daley-Harris, S. (2006). *State of the microcredit summit campaign report.* Washington, D.C.: Microcredit Summit Campaign.

Das, O.K. and Teng, B.S. (1999). Trust, control and risk in strategic alliances: An integrated framework. *Organization Studies,* 22(2), 251–283.

Datar, S.M., Epstein, M.J., and Yuthas, K. (2008). In microfinance, client must come first. *Stanford Social Innovation Review,* 6, 38–45.

Dees, J.G. (1998a). The meaning of "social entrepreneurship." Stanford University: *Draft Report for the Kauffman Center for Entrepreneurial Leadership.*

———. (1998b). Enterprising non-profits. *Harvard Business Review,* 76, 55–67.

———. (2001). The meaning of social entrepreneurship. Working paper, Center for the Advancement of Social Entrepreneurship, Duke University.

Dees, J.G. and Elias, J. (1996). *City year enterprise.* Boston: Harvard Business School Publishing Case 396196.

Dees, J.G., Anderson, B.B., and Wei-Skillern, J. (2002). Pathways to social impact: Strategies for scaling out successful social innovations. *CASE Working Paper Series No. 3.*

———. (2004). Scaling social impact: strategies for spreading social innovations. *Stanford Social Innovation Review,* 1, 24–32.

Deighton, J., Romer, D., and McQueen, J. (1989). Using drama to persuade. *Journal of Consumer Research,* 16, 335–343.

Demirgüç-Kunt, A., Beck, T., and Honohan, P. (2008). Finance for all: policies and pitfalls in expanding access. *World Bank Policy Research Report.*

Desa, G. and Kotha, S. (2006). Ownership mission and environment: An exploratory analysis into the evolution of a technology social venture. In Mair, J. et al. (eds.), *Social Entrepreneurship.* New York: Palgrave MacMillan, 155–179.

Deutsche Bank. (2007). *Microfinance: An emerging investment opportunity.* Deutsche Bank Research, December 19.

Dexter, L.A. (1970). *Elite and Specialized Interviewing.* Evanston, IL: Northwestern University Press.

DFID. (2005). Banking the underserved: New opportunities for commercial banks: Exploring the business case. *Policy Division Working Paper,* Commissioned by Financial Sector Team, Policy Division, Department of International Development, London, April.

Diamantopoulos, A. and Winklhofer, H. (2001). Index construction with formative indicators: an alternative to scale development. *Journal of Marketing Research,* 38, 269–277.

DiMaggio, P.J. and Powell, W.W. (1983). The iron cage revisited: Institutional isomorphism and collective rationality in organizational fields. *American Sociological Review,* 48, 147–160.

Djelic, M. (1998). *Exporting the American model: The postwar transformation of European business.* Oxford, UK: Oxford University Press.

Doh, J.P., LiPuma, J.A., and Newbert, S.L. (2007). Institutional quality and the environment for entrepreneurship in emerging markets. Presented at *Academy of Management Conference,* Philadelphia, Pennsylvania, August 3–8.

Draper Richards Foundation. (2009). See http://www.draperrichards.org/process/proposal.html.

Drumwright, M.E. (1994). Socially responsible organizational buying: Environmental concern as a noneconomic buying criterion. *Journal of Marketing,* 58, 1–19.

———. (1996). Company advertising with a social dimension: The role of noneconomic criteria. *Journal of Marketing,* 60, 71–88.

Duflo, E., Helms, B., Latortue A., and Seidek, H. (2004). *Global results: Analysis and lessons: Aid Effectiveness Initiative.* Paris: CGAP.

Eagley, A. and Chaiken, S. (1993). *The psychology of attitudes.* Orlando, FL: Harcourt Brace Jovanovich College Publishers.

Easterly, W. (2006). *The white man's burden: Why the west's efforts to aid the rest have done so much ill and so little good.* New York: Oxford University Press.

Economist.com. (2009). Froth at the bottom of the pyramid; Is microfinance going the same way as subprime mortgages?, August 25.

Education Sector. (2009). Growing pains: Scaling up the nation's best charter schools. *Education Sector Reports,* Washington, D.C.

Edwards, M. and Hulme, D. (1992). *Making a difference: NGOs and development in a changing world.* London: Earthscan.

Eisenhardt, K.M. (1989). Building theories from case study research. *Academy of Management Review,* 14, 488–511.

Elder, J.P., Ayala, G.X., Parra-Medina, D., and Talavera, G.A. (2009). Health communication in the Latino community: Issues and approaches. *Annual Review of Public Health,* 30, 227–251.

Elkington, J.B. and Hartigan, P. (2008). *The power of unreasonable people: How social entrepreneurs create markets that change the world.* Boston, MA: Harvard Business School Press.

Emery, S.L., Wakefield, M.A., Terry-McElrath, Y., Saffer, H., Szczypka, G., O'Malley, P.M., Johnston, L.D., Chaloupka, F.J., and Flay, B.R. (2005). Televised state-sponsored antitobacco advertising and youth smoking beliefs and behavior in the United States, 1999–2000. *Archives of Pediatric Adolescent Medicine,* 159(7), 639–645.

Enright, K.P. (2006). Inspiration and ideas from philanthropy's latest frontier. *Investing In Leadership,* 2. Retrieved from Grantmakers for Effective Organizations Website: http://www.geofunders.org/leadershipdevelopment.aspx.

Epstein, M.J. and Yuthas, K. (2009). Mission impossible: Diffusion and drift in the microfinance industry. Working Paper, Rice University.

Etzioni, A. (1961). *A comparative analysis of complex organizations*. New York: Free Press.

Farrelly, M.C., Davis, K.C., Haviland, M.L., Messeri,P., and Healton, C.G. (2005). Evidence of a dose-response relationship between "Truth" antismoking ads and youth smoking prevalence. *American Journal Public Health*, 95 (3), 425–431.

Feder, G., Lau, L., Lin, J., and Luo, X. (1990). The relationship between credit and productivity in Chinese agriculture: A microeconomic model of disequilibrium. *American Journal of Agricultural Economics,* 72, 1151–1157.

Feinberg, M. (2008). Commentary. *Forbes*, January 23: http://www.forbes. com/2008/01/22/solutions-education-feinberg-oped-cx_mfei_0123feinberg.html.

Floyd, S.W. and Lane, P.J. (2000). Strategizing throughout the organization: Managing role conflict in strategic renewal. *Academy of Management Review*, 25(1), 154–177.

Flynn, B.S., Worden, J.K., Secker-Walker, R.H., Badger, G.J., Geller, B.M., and Costanza, M.C. (1992). Prevention of cigarette smoking through mass media intervention and school programs. *American Journal of Public Health*, 82, 827–834.

Flynn, B.S., Worden, J.K., Secker-Walker, R.H., Pirie, P.L., Badger, G.J., Carpenter, J.H., and Geller, B.M. (1994). Mass media and school interventions for cigarette smoking prevention: Effects two years after completion. *American Journal of Public Health*, 84, 1148–1150.

Foley, D. and Pechmann, C. (2004). The national youth anti-drug media campaign copy test system. *Social Marketing Quarterly Special Issue*, 10, 34–42.

Ford, N., Williams, A., Renshaw, M., and Nkum, J. (2005). Communication strategy for implementing community IMCI. *Journal of Health Communication*, 10, 379–401.

Forster, S. and Reillie, X. (2008). Foreign capital investment in microfinance: balancing social and financial returns. *CGAP Focus Note 44*.

Foster, W. and Fine, G. (2007). How nonprofits get really big. *Stanford Social Innovation Review*, 5(2), 46–55.

Foster, W.L., Kim, P., and Christiansen, B. (2009). Ten nonprofit funding models. *Stanford Social Innovation Review*, Spring, 32–39.

Foundation Center, The. (2008). *Survey of foundations with over $1M in assets or over $100K in grantmaking in 2005–2006*. Available from Foundation Center database.

Frumkin, P. (2007). *The five meanings of scale*. Social Edge Online Discussion Forum: A Program of the Skoll Foundation.

Fuglesang, M. (2009). Presentation at workshop on "Solar Entrepreneurs" organised by Alejandro Litovsky at the Tällberg Forum, Sweden.

Gerbing, D. and Anderson, J. (1988). An updated paradigm for scale development incorporating unidimensionality and its assessment. *Journal of Marketing Research*, 25, 186–192.

Gladwell, M. (2000). *The tipping point: How little things can make a big difference*. Boston: Little, Brown, and Company.

Gokhale, K. (2009). A global surge in tiny loans spurs credit bubble in a slum. *Wall Street Journal.com*.

Goldberg, N. (2005). *Measuring the impact of microfinance: taking stock of what we know*. Grameen Foundation, USA.

Goldstein, S., Usdin, S., Scheppers, E., and Japhet, G. (2005). Communicating HIV and AIDS, what works? A report on the impact evaluation of soul city's fourth series. *Journal of Health Communication*, 10, 465–483.

Gonzalez, A. (2008). Microfinance, incentives to repay, and overindebtedness: Evidence from a household survey in Bolivia. Dissertation, The Ohio State University.

Gonzales, A. and Rosenberg, R. (2006). The state of microfinance—Outreach, profitability, and poverty. Findings from a database of 2600 microfinance institutions. Presentation at World Bank Conference on Access to Finance, May 30, 2006.

Govindarajan, V. and Fisher, J. (1990). Strategy, control systems, and resource sharing: Effects on business-unit performance. *Academy of Management Journal*, 33(2), 259–285.

Gram Vikas. (2002). Every household counts: Ensuring community participation in Orissa. Available from: info@gramvikas.org.

———. (2008). Annual report 2007–2008. Available from: info@gramvikas.org.

———. (2009). Annual Report 2008–2009. Available from: info@gramvikas.org.

Grant, H.M. and Crutchfield, L.R. (2007). Creating high-impact nonprofits. *Stanford Social Innovation Review*, 5, 32–41.

Greene, K. and Brinn, L.S. (2003). Messages influencing college women's tanning bed use: Statistical versus narrative evidence format and a self-assessment to increase format and a self-assessment to increase perceived susceptibility. *Journal of Health Communication*, 8, 443–461.

Gregory, A.G. and Howard, D. (2009). The nonprofit starvation cycle. *Stanford Social Innovation Review*, 7, 48–53.

Griffin, A. (1997). PDMA research on new product development practices: Updating trends and benchmarking best practices. *Journal of Product Innovation Management*, 14, 429–458.

Griffin, A. and Page, A.L. (1996). PDMA success measurement project: Recommended measures for product development success and failure. *Journal of Product Innovation Management*, 13, 478–496.

Grossman, A. and Wei-Skillern, J. (2003). The Nature Conservancy, Harvard Business School.

Gulati R. (1998). Social structure and alliance formation patterns: A longitudinal analysis. *Administrative Science Quarterly*, 40, 619–652.

Guth, W.D. and Ginsberg, A. (1990). Guest editors' introduction: Corporate entrepreneurship. *Strategic Management Journal*, 11, 5–15.

Haines, H. (1984). Black radicalization and the funding of civil rights, 1957–1970. *Social Problems,* 32(1), 31–43.

Hansen, M.H. (1994). Trustworthiness: Can it be a source of competitive advantage? *Strategic Management Journal*, 15, 175–203.

Harvey, J. and Rainey, L. (2006). *High-quality charter schools at scale in big cities: Results of a symposium.* National Charter School Research Project, Seattle, WA.

Hashemi, S.M., Schuler, S.R., and Riley, A.P. (1996). Rural credit programs and women's empowerment in Bangladesh, *World Development*, 24(4), 635–653.

Hellmann, T. and Puri, M. (2002). Venture capital and the professionalization of start-up firms: empirical evidence. *Journal of Finance*, 57 (1), 169–197.

Hill, R.P. (2001). Service provision through public-private partnerships: An ethnography of service delivery to homeless teenagers. *Journal of Service Research*, 4, 278–299.

———. (2010). A naturological approach to marketing exchange: Implications for the bottom of the pyramid. *Journal of Business Research*, 63, 602–607..

Hinyard, L.J. and Kreuter, M.W. (2007). Using narrative communication as a tool for health behavior change: A conceptual, theoretical, and empirical overview. *Health Education and Behavior*, 34, 777–792.

Hishigsuren, G. (2007). Evaluating mission drift in microfinance: Lessons for programs with social mission. *Evaluation Review*, 31, 203–260.

———. (2008). *Scaling up and mission drift: Can microfinance institutions maintain a poverty alleviation mission while scaling up?* Working paper presented at the Economic Self-Reliance Conference, November.

Hoffman, A.J. (2009). Shades of green. *Stanford Social Innovation Review*, 7, 40–49.

Hoffman, J. (2009). When the cellphone teaches sex education. *New York Times*, http://www.nytimes.com/2009/05/03/fashion/03sexed.html?_r=1andsq=birds%20and%20bees%20textandst=nytandscp=1andpagewanted=all; May 1.

Hornik, R.C. (2002). Epilogue: Evaluation design for public health communication programs. In Hornik, R.C. (ed.), *Public Health Communication: Evidence for Behavior Change*. Mahwah, NJ: Lawrence Erlbaum Associates, 385–405.

Hornik, R., Jacobsohn, L., Orwin, R., Piesse, A., and Kalton, G. (2008). Effects of the national youth anti-drug media campaign. *American Journal of Public Health*, 98(12), 2229–2236.

Hsu, M. (2007). The international funding of microfinance institutions: An overview. *ADA Microfinance Expertise research report*, November 23.

Hubbard, B. (2006). A grantmaker's framework for understanding nonprofit leadership development. *Investing In Leadership*, 1. Retrieved from Grantmakers for Effective Organizations Web site: http://www.geofunders.org/leadershipdevelopment.aspx.

Huggett, J. and Kramer, K. (2008). *Boystown: Using RAPID to clarify decision-making roles between headquarters and sites*. The Bridgespan Group.

Huggett, J. and Moran, C. (2008). Who decides? Mapping power and decision making in nonprofits. *Nonprofit Quarterly*, 14.

Huggett, J. and Saxton, A. (2006). *Focusing on impact*. The Bridgespan Group.

Huggett, J., Smith-Milway, K., and Kramer, K. (2009). *Increasing effectivness in global NGO networks*. The Bridgespan Group.

Hwang, H. and Powell, W.W. (2009). The rationalization of charity: The influences of professionalism in the nonprofit sector. *Administrative Science Quarterly*, 54, 268–298.

Iansiti, M. and Levien, R. (2004). Strategy as ecology. *Harvard Business Review*, 82(3), 68–81.

IndiaStat. (2004). *Report on prevalence of blindness and estimated number of blind persons in India*.

Inkpen A.C. and Beamish P.W. (1997). Knowledge, bargaining power, and the instability of international joint ventures. *Academy of Management Review*, 22(1), 177–202.

Jaeger, A.M. and Baliga, B.R. (1985). Control systems and strategic adaptation: Lessons from the Japanese experience. *Strategic Management Journal*, 6(2), 115–134.

Jenkins, J.C. and Eckert, C. (1986). Channeling black insurgency: Elite patronage and the development of the civil rights movement. *American Sociological Review*, 51, 812–830.

Jenkins, J.C. and Halcli, A.L. (1999). Grassrooting the system? The development and impact of social movement philanthropy, 1953–1990. In Lagemann, E.C. (ed.), *Philanthropic foundations: New scholarship, new possibilities*. Bloomington: Indiana University Press, 229–256.

Jensen, R.J. and Szulanski, G. (2007). Template use and the effectiveness of knowledge transfer. *Management Science*, 53(11), 1716–1730.

Jensen, R.J., Szulanski, G., and Casaburi, M.V. (2003). *Templates and the effectiveness of knowledge transfer*. Academy of Management.

Joffe, M.M. and Rosenbaum, P.R. (1999). Propensity scores. *American Journal of Epidemiology*, 150(4), 327–33.

Johnson, S. (2001). *Emergence: The connected lives of ants, brains, cities and software*. New York: Touchstone, 11–12.

Jones, J.L. and Leary, M.R. (1994). Effects of appearance-based admonitions against sun exposure on tanning intentions in young adults. *Health Psychology*, 13(1), 86–90.

Jordan, C.M., Lee, P.A., Olkon, R., and Pirie, P.L. (2007). Messages from moms: Barriers to and facilitators of behavior change in a lead poisoning preventive education project. *Journal of Health Communication*, 12, 771–786.

Kamath, R., Mukherji, A., and Ramanathan, S. (2008). Ramanagaram financial diaries: Loan repayments and cash patterns of the urban slums. IIMB Working Paper, No. 268.

Kanter, R.M. (1999). From spare change to real change: The social sector as beta site for innovation. *Harvard Business Review*, 77(3), 122–132.

Karamchandani, A., Kubzansky, M., and Frandano, P. (2009). *Emerging markets, emerging models: Market based solutions to the challenges of global poverty.* Cambridge, MA: Monitor Group.

Karlan, D. and List, J.A. (2007). Does price matter in charitable giving? Evidence from a large-scale natural field experiment. *American Economic Review, American Economic Association*, 97 (5), 1774–1793.

Karlan, D. and Valdivia, M. (2006). Teaching entrepreneurship: Impact of business training on microfinance institutions and clients. Yale University Economic Growth Center, Working Paper.

Karlan, D. and Zinman, J. (2009). Expanding microenterprise credit access: Using randomized supply decisions to estimate the impacts in Manila. Yale University, Dartmouth College, and Innovations in Poverty Action Working Paper.

Karlan, D., Ashraf, N., and Yin, W. (2006). Tying Odysseus to the mast: evidence from a commitment savings product in the Philippines. *The Quarterly Journal of Economics*, 121 (2), 635–672.

Karnani, A. (2007). Microfinance misses its mark. *Stanford Social Innovation Review*, 5, 34- 40.

Keane, J. (2009). Interview of John Keane by Alejandro Litovsky, Dar es Salaam, Tanzania, February 28.

Kees, J., Burton, S., Andrews, J.C., and Kozup, J. (2006). Tests of graphic visuals and cigarette package warning combinations: Implications for the framework convention on tobacco control. *Journal of Public Policy and Marketing*, 25(2), 212–223.

Keirns, P. (2007). *Water supply and sanitation services for the rural poor: The Gram Vikas experience.* Warwickshire, UK: Practical Action Publishing.

Keller, P.A. and Lehmann, D.R. (2008). Designing effective health communications: A meta-analysis. *Journal of Public Policy and Marketing*, 27(2), 117–130.

Keller, K.L. (1993). Conceptualizing, measuring and managing customer-based brand equity. *Journal of Marketing*, 57, 1–22.

———. (2003). *Strategic brand management: Building, measuring, and managing brand equity.* Upper Saddle River, NJ: Prentice Hall.

Kelly, K. (1998). *New rules for the new economy: 10 ways the network economy is changing everything.* New York: Viking Penguin.

Khandker, S. (1998). *Fighting poverty with microcredit: Experience in Bangladesh.* Oxford: Oxford University Press.

Khanna T., Gulati R., and Nohria N. (1998). The dynamics of learning alliances: Competition, cooperation, and relative scope. *Strategic Management Journal*, 19, 193–210.

Khanna T., Palepu K.G., and Sinha J. (2005). Strategies that fit emerging markets. *Harvard Business Review*, 83(6), 63–76.

King, B.G., Clemens, E.S., and Fry, M. (Forthcoming). Coherence or differentiation? The emergence of identity in Arizona's charter schools. *Unpublished manuscript*.

Kingdon, J.W. (1984). *Agendas, alternatives, and public policies.* Boston: Little Brown and Company.

Kirchhoff, B.A. (1994). *Entrepreneurship and dynamic capitalism: The economics of business firm formation and growth.* Westport, CT: Praeger.

Kirsch, L.J. (1996). The management of complex tasks in organizations: Controlling the systems development process. *Organization Science*, 7(1), 1–21.

Korten, D.C. (1980). Community organization and rural development: A learning process approach. *Public Administration Review*, 40(5), 480.

Kostova, T. and Roth, K. (2002). Adoption of an organizational practice by subsidiaries of multinational corporations: Institutional and relational effects. *Academy of Management Journal*, 45, 215–233.

Kotler, Philip. (1975). *Marketing for Nonprofit Organizations*. Englewood Cliffs, NJ: Prentice-Hall.

Koyck, L.M. (1959). *Distributed lags and investment analysis*. Amsterdam, The Netherlands: North Holland Publishers.

Kramer, K. (2008). Becoming a highly effective organization. Retrieved from http://bridgespan.org/LearningCenter/ResourceDetail.aspx?id=2624&parentID=236&taxid=320.

Kreuter, M.W. and McClure, S.M. (2004). The role of culture in health communication. *Annual Review of Public Health*, 25, 439–455.

La France Associates. (2006). *Scaling capacities: Supports for growing impact*. LLC, July.

Lake, R.J. (2007). *Identifying and replicating the "DNA" of successful charter schools: lessons from the private sector*. Research brief from the National Charter School Research Project, Seattle, WA.

Lane P., Salk J.E., and Lyles M.A. (2001). Absorptive capacity, learning and performance in international joint ventures. *Strategic Management Journal*, 22, 1139–1161.

Larkey, L.K. and Gonzalez, J. (2007). Storytelling for promoting colorectal cancer prevention and early detection among Latinos. *Patient Education and Counseling*, 67, 272–278.

Leadebeater, C. (1997). *The rise of the social entrepreneur*. London: Demos.

Lebas, M. and Weigenstein, J. (1986). Management control: The roles of rules, markets and culture. *Journal of Management Studies*, 23(3), 259–272.

Ledgerwood, J. (1999). *Microfinance handbook: An institutional and financial perspective*. Washington, DC: The World Bank.

Letts, C.W., Williams, R., and Grossman, A. (1997). Virtuous capital: What foundations can learn from venture capitalists. *Harvard Business Review*, 75 (2), 36–44.

Lincoln, Y.S. and Guba, E.G. (1985). *Naturalistic inquiry*. London: Sage Publications.

Lindenberg, M. and Bryant, C. (2001). *Going global: Transforming relief and development NGOs*. Bloomfield, CT: Kumarian Press.

Low, M. and MacMillan, I. (1988). Entrepreneurship: Past research and future challenges. *Journal of Management*, 14, 139–161.

Lubienski, C. (2003). Charter school innovation in theory and practice: Autonomy, R&D, and curricular conformity. In Bulkley, K.E. and Wohlstetter, P. (eds.), *Taking account of charter schools: What's happened and what's next?* New York: Teachers College Press.

Lunch Crunch. (2009). *Playnormous Health Game and Teacher Guide*. http://www.playnorm ous.com/game_lunchcrunch.cfm; September 12.

Maddy, M. (2001). Dream deferred: The story of a high-tech entrepreneur in a low-tech world. *Harvard Business Review*, 79(5), 57–69.

Madiath, J. and Jayapadma, R.V. (2004). Facing up to the challenges in water and sanitation: How complex? How urgent? Available from: info@gramvikas.org.

Mair, J. and Marti, I. (2006). Social entrepreneurship research: A source of explanation, prediction, and delight. *Journal of World Business*, 41(1), 36–44.

Malkin, E. (2008). Microfinance's success sets off a debate in Mexico. *New York Times*, March 4.

March, J.G. and Simon, H.A. (1958). Cognitive limits on rationality. In *Organizations*. New York: McGraw-Hill.

Marcus, M.B. (2008). Grey's study shows viewers remember TV health messages; *USA Today*, http://www.usatoday.com/news/health/2008-09-16-tb-health-message_N.htm; September 17.

Marr, A. (2004). A challenge to the orthodoxy concerning microfinance and poverty reduction. *Journal of Microfinance*, 5(2), 7–42.

Matin, I., Hulme, D., and Rutherford, S. (1999). *Financial services for the poor and poorest: Deepening understanding to improve provision*. Finance and development research program Working paper Series, no. 9, IDPM, University of Manchester, October.

Mazis, M.B. (1980). An overview of product labeling and health risks. In Morris, L., Mazis, M., and Barofsky, I. (eds.), *Labeling and health risks*, Banbury Report 6, Cold Spring Harbor Laboratory, Cold Spring Harbor, NY, 1–9.

McCall M.J. (2009). Personal conversation with Pamela Hartigan, Geneva, October 9.

McCarthy, J.D. and Zald, M.N. (1977). Resource mobilization and social movements: A partial theory. *American Journal of Sociology*, 82, 1212–1241.

McCombs, M. (2004). *Setting the agenda: The mass media and public opinion*. Cambridge: Polity.

McDonald, C.J. (1998). The evolution of Intel's "Copy Exactly!" technology transfer method. Intel Technology Journal, Q4: 1–6.

McIntosh C. and Wydick, B. (2005). Competition and microfinance. *Journal of Development Economics*, December, 78(2), 271–298.

McLaughlin, M.W. and Mitra, D. (2001). Theory-based change and change-based theory: Going deeper, going broader. *Journal of Educational Change*, 2, 301–323.

McLeod G.H. and Crutchfield, L.R. (2007). Creating high-impact non profits. *Stanford Social Innovation Review*, 32–41.

Meyerson, D. and Chang, V. (2008). The tipping point and green dot public schools. Stanford Graduate School of Business Case SI-109, Stanford, CA.

Meyerson, D., Quinn, R., and Tompkins-Stange, M. (2009). Elites as agents of institutional change: The case of philanthropic foundations in the California charter school movement. Unpublished Manuscript, Stanford University, Stanford, CA.

Mick, D.G. (2006). Meaning and mattering through transformative consumer research. Presidential address to the Association for Consumer Research. In Pechmann, P. and Price, L.P. (eds.), *Advances in Consumer Research*, v. 33. Provo, UT: Association for Consumer Research, 1–4.

Microcredit Summit Campaign. (2009). State of the Microcredit Summit Campaign Report 2009, Washington, D.C.

Miles, M.B. and Huberman, A.M. (1994). *Qualitative data analysis*, 2nd ed. Newbury Park, CA: Sage Publications, Inc.

Miller, C. (2005). The looking-glass world of nonprofit money: Managing in for-profits' shadow universe. *The Nonprofit Quarterly*, 12.

Morduch, J. (2000). The microfinance schism. *World Development*, 28(4), 617–629.

Mossfeldt, C. (2009). Personal conversation with Alejandro Litovsky, Dar es Salaam, Tanzania.

Moyo, D. (2009). *Dead aid: Why aid is not working and how there is a better way for Africa*. New York: Farrar, Straus and Giroux.

Mulgan, G. (2008). *The art of public strategy*. Oxford: Oxford University Press.

Murphy, G., Trailer, J., and Hill, R. (1996). Measuring performance in entrepreneurship research. *Journal of Business Research*, 36, 15–23.

Murray, D.M. and Hannan, P.J. (1990). Planning for the appropriate analysis in school-based drug-use prevention studies. *Journal of Consulting and Clinical Psychology*, 58 (4), 458–468.

Natchiar, G., Thulsiraj, R.D., and Sundaram, R.M. (2008). Cataract surgery at Aravind eye hospitals: 1988–2008. *Community Eye Health Journal*, 21(67), 40–42.

National Center for Education Statistics. (2009). Public elementary/secondary school universe survey, 1997–98 to 2006–07, *Common Core of Data*. Retrieved from http://nces.ed.gov/.

National Charter School Research Project. (2007). *Quantity counts: The growth of charter school management organizations*. Seattle, WA.

Noar, S.M., Benac, C.N., and Harris, M.S. (2007). Does tailoring matter? Meta-analytic review of tailored print health behavior change interventions. *Psychological Bulletin*, 133(4), 673–693. Nonaka, I. (1994). A dynamic theory of organizational knowledge creation. *Organization Science*, 5(1), 14–37.

Obama, B. (2009). Remarks on community solutions agenda. Speech, The White House, Washington, D.C.

O'Keefe, D.J. and Jensen, J.D. (2007). The relative persuasiveness of gain-framed loss-framed messages for encouraging disease prevention behaviors: A meta-analytic review. *Journal of Health Communication*, 12, 623–644.

Olivares-Polanco, F. (2005). Commercializing microfinance and deepening outreach?: Empirical evidence from Latin America. *Journal of Microfinance*, 7, 47–69.

Olsen, M.E. (1978). *The process of social organization*. New York: Holt Rinehart & Winston. Olson, L. (1994). Growing pains, *Education Week*, 29.

Oster, S.M. (1996). Nonprofit organizations and their local affiliates: A study in organizational forms. *Journal of Economic Behavior & Organization*, 30(1), 83–95.

Ouchi, W.G. (1979). A conceptual framework for the design of organizational control mechanisms. *Management Science*, 25(9), 833–848.

———. (1980). Markets, bureaucracies, and clans. *Administrative Science Quarterly*, 25(1), 129–141.

Overholser, G.M. (2010). *Nonprofit growth capital: Defining, measuring and managing growth capital in nonprofit enterprises*. Part One: Building is not buying. Retrieved from http://www.nonprofitfinancefund.org/docs/Building%20is%20Not%20Buying.pdf.

Pagura, M.E. (2004). Client exit in microfinance: A conceptual framework with empirical results from Mali. CSAE Conference, St. Catherine's College, Oxford.

Palmgreen, P., Donohew, L., Lorch, E.P., Hoyle, R. H., and Stephenson, M.T. (2001). Television campaigns and adolescent marijuana use: Tests of sensation seeking targeting. *American Journal of Public Health*, 91(2), 292–296.

Pascale, R. (1985). The paradox of "corporate culture": Reconciling ourselves to socialization. *California Management Review*, 27(2), 26–41.

Pawlak, K. and Matul, M. (2004). Client desertion—a microfinance plague: How to diagnose it successfully? MFC Spotlight Note #11.

Pechmann, C. and Andrews, J.C. (Forthcoming). Copy test methods to pretest advertisements. In Belch, M. and Belch, G. (eds.). *Wiley international encyclopedia of marketing: Chapter 4: Integrated marketing communication*. Chichester, UK: Wiley.

Pechmann, C. and Reibling, E.T. (2000). Antismoking advertising campaigns targeting youth: Case studies from USA and Canada. *Tobacco Control*, 9 (Supplement II), ii18-ii31.

Pechmann, C. and Shih, C.F. (1999). Smoking scenes in movies and antismoking advertisements before movies: Effects on youth. *Journal of Marketing*, 63(3), 1–13.

Pechmann, C. and Stewart, D.W. (1990). The effects of comparative advertising on attention, memory, and purchase intentions. *Journal of Consumer Research*, 17(2), 180–191.

Pechmann, C., Dixon, P., and Layne, N. (1998). An assessment of U.S. And Canadian smoking reduction objectives for the year 2000. *American Journal of Public Health*, 88(9), 1362–1367.

Pechmann, C., Zhao, G., Goldberg, M.E., and Reibling, E.T. (2003). What to convey in antismoking advertisements for adolescents? The use of protection motivation theory to identify effective message themes. *Journal of Marketing*, 67(2), 1–18.

Peredo, A.M. and McLean, M. (2006). Social entrepreneurship: A critical review of the concept. *Journal of World Business*, 41(1), 56–65.

Perl, D. and Phillips, M.M. (2001). Grameen bank, which pioneered loans for the poor, has hit a repayment snag. *Wall Street Journal*, November 27.

Perry, H.W., Jr. (1991). *Deciding to decide: Agenda setting in the U.S. Supreme Court.* Cambridge, MA: Harvard University Press.

Perry, P. (2009). *Rebuilding a country.* July 13, pp. 40–42.

Petty, R.E. and Cacioppo, J.T. (1996). Addressing disturbing and disturbed consumer behavior: Is it necessary to change the way we conduct behavioral science? *Journal of Marketing Research*, 23, 1–8.

Phelps, E. (2006). Macroeconomics for a modern economy. *American Economic Review*, 97, 543–561.

Phills, J.A., Deiglmeier, K., and Miller, D.T. (2008). Rediscovering social innovation. *Stanford Social Innovation Review*, 6, 34–43.

Pierce, J.P., Farkas, A.J., Evans, N., and Gilpin, E.A. (1995). An improved surveillance measure for adolescent smoking. *Tobacco Control*, 4 (Supplement 1), S47-S56.

Pierce, J.P., Gilpin, E.A., Emery, S.L., White, M.M, Rosbrook, B., and Berry, C.C. (1998). Has the California tobacco control program reduced smoking. *Journal of the American Medical Association*, 280(10), 893–99.

Pitt, M.M. and Khandker, S. (1995). Household and intrahousehold impacts of the Grameen Bank and similar targeted credit programs in Bangladesh. Manuscript. Providence, R.I.: Brown Univ., Dept. Econ.

Pitt, M.M., Khandker, S., Chowdhury, O.H., and Millimet, D. (2003). Credit programs for the poor and the health status of children in rural Bangladesh. *International Economic Review*, 44(1), 87–118.

Podsakoff, P. and Organ, D. (1986). Self-reports in organizational research: Problems and prospects. *Journal of Management*, 12, 531–544.

Podsakoff, P.M., MacKenzie, S.B., Lee, J.-Y., and Podsakoff, N.P. (2003). Common method biases in behavioral research: A critical review of the literature and recommended remedies. *Journal of Applied Psychology*, 88, 879–903.

Polanyi, M. (1966). *The tacit dimension.* London: Routledge & Kegan.

Pollay, R.W., Siddarth, S., Siegal, M., Haddix, A., Merritt, R.K., Giovino, G.A., and Eriksen, M.P. (1996). The last straw? Cigarette advertising and realized market shares among youths and adults, 1979–1993. *Journal of Marketing*, 60(2), 1–16.

Powell, W.W., Gammal, D.L., and Simard, C. (2005). Close encounters: The circulation and reception of managerial practices in the San Francisco bay area nonprofit community. In Czarniawska, B. and Sevón, G. (eds.), *Global ideas: How ideas, objects and practices travel in the global economy.* Malmö, Sweden: Liber and Copenhagen Business School Press, 233–258.

Prahalad, C.K. and Hammond, A. (2002). Serving the world's poor, profitably. *Harvard Business Review*, 80(9), 48–57.

Racine, D. (2003). Dissolving dualities: The case for commonsense replication. *Nonprofit and Voluntary Sector Quarterly*, 30(2), 307–314.

Rajan, R. (2005). Has Financial Development Made the World Riskier? Working Paper, University of Chicago.

Reille, X., Glisovic-Mezieres, J., Berthouzoz, Y., and Milverton, D. (2009). MIV performance and prospects: Highlights from the CGAP 2009 MIV benchmark survey.

Reynolds, P. (2000). National study of U.S. business start-ups: Background and methodology. In Katz, J. (ed.), *Advances in entrepreneurship, firm emergence and growth: Vol. 4.* Stamford, CT: JAI, 153–228.

Rijal, K. (2007). Interview with Alejandro Litovsky, Santander, Spain.

Roberts, J. (2003). Stanford Graduate School of Business Alumni Lecture, October 17.

Roberts, M., Wanta, W., and Dzwo, T.H. (2003). Agenda setting and issue salience on-line. *Communication Research*, 24(9), 256–265.

Rogers, E.M. (1962). *Diffusion of innovations*. New York: The Free Press.

Rothaermel, F.T. and Boeker, W. (2008). Old technology meets new technology: Complementarities, similarities, and alliance formation. *Strategic Management Journal*, 29: 47–77.

Rubinstein, A. and Wolinsky, A. (1987). Middlemen. *Quarterly Journal of Economics*, 102, 581–594.

Santos, F.M. (2009). A positive theory of social entrepreneurship. INSEAD Working Paper 23/EFE/ISIC.

Schervish, P.G., Havens, J.J., and O'Herlihy, M.A. (2006). Charitable giving: How much, by whom, to what, and why? In Powell, W.W. and Steinberg, R. (eds.), *The nonprofit sector: A research handbook*. New Haven, CT: Yale University Press, 542–567.

Schumacher, E.F. (1973). *Small is beautiful: A study of economics as if people mattered*. New York: Harper and Row.

Schumpeter, J.A. (1934). *The theory of economic development*. Cambridge, MA: Harvard University Press.

Schwarzer, R. and Renner, B. (2000). Social-cognitive predictors of health behavior: Action self-efficacy and coping self-efficacy. *Health Psychology*, 19(5), 487–495.

Skocpol, T. (2003). *Diminished democracy: From membership to management in American civic life*. Norman: University of Oklahoma Press.

Secret Life of The American Teenager-Official TV Show. abc Family Channel; http://abcfamily.go.com/abcfamily/path/section_Shows+Secret-Life-Of-The-American-Teenager/page_Detail; accessed on September 12, 2009.

Sen, A. (1981). *Poverty and famines: An essay on entitlement and deprivation*. Oxford: Clarendon Press.

Shane, S. and Venkataraman, S. (2000). The promise of entrepreneurship as a field of research. *Academy of Management Review*, 25(1), 217–226.

Shanker, A.F. (1988). Convention plots new course—A charter for change. *New York Times*, July 10, Section 4, 7.

Sharir, M. and Lerner, M. (2005). Gauging the success of social ventures initiated by individual social entrepreneurs. *Journal of World Business*, 41, 6–20.

Sherman, D.A. (2006). Social entrepreneurship: Pattern-changing entrepreneurs and the scaling of social impact. Working Paper, Case Western Reserve University.

———. (2007). Entrepreneurial social sector organizations: Factors that facilitate growth and performance. Working Paper, Case Western Reserve University.

Shimp, T.A. (1994). Academic appalachia and the discipline of consumer research. Presidential Address to the Association for Consumer Research. In Allen, C.T. and John, D.R. (eds.), *Advances in Consumer Research*, Vol. 21, 1–7.

Short J.C., Moss T.W., and Lumpkin, G.T. (2009). Research in social entrepreneurship: past contributions and future opportunities. *Strategic Entrepreneurship Journal*, 3(2), 161–194.

Simanowitz, A. (2000). Client exit surveys: A tool for understanding client drop-out. *Journal of Microfinance*, 2(1), 112–137.

Sireau, N. and Leggett, J. (2009). Interview by Alejandro Litovsky, available at: http://www.volans.com/volans-solutions/pathways/conversations-on-scale/.

Skocpol, T. (2003). *Diminished democracy: From membership to management in American civic life*. Norman: University of Oklahoma Press.

Smith, A. (1776). *An enquiry into the nature and causes of the wealth of nations*. London: Strahan and Cadell.

Smith, K. and Petersen, J.L. (2006). What is educational entrepreneurship? In Hess, F.M. (ed.), *Educational entrepreneurship: Realities, challenges, possibilities*. Cambridge, MA: Harvard Education Press, 21–44.

Sneeze. (2009). Miniclip free games; http://www.miniclip.com/games/stop-swine-flu/en/; September 12.

Snyder, L.B., Hamilton, M.A., Mitchell, E.W., Kiwanuka-Tondo, J., Fleming-Milici, F., and Proctor, D. (2004). A meta-analysis of the effect of mediated health communication campaigns on behavior change in the United States. *Journal of Health Communication*, 9, 71–96.

Soule, S. and King, B. (2008). Competition and resource partitioning in three social movement industries. *American Journal of Sociology*, 113(6), 1568–1610.

Srinivasan, N. (2009). *Multiple borrowing or multiple lending—who is to blame for debt fatigue?* CGAP.

Stacey, R.D. (1993). *Strategic management and organizational dynamics*. London: Pitman.

Stephen A. and Coote, L. (2007). Interfirm behavior and goal alignment in relational exchange. *Journal of Business Research*, 60(4), 285–295.

Stid, D. and Bradach, J. (2008). *Strongly led, under managed*. The Bridgespan Group.

Strauss, A.L. (1990). *Qualitative Analysis for Social Scientists*. Cambridge: Cambridge University Press.

Stiglitz J.E. (1997). *Economics*, 2nd edition. New York: W.W. Norton Company

Stuart T.E. (2000). Interorganizational alliances and the performance of firms: A study of growth and innovation rates in a high technology industry. *Strategic Management Journal*, 21, 791–811.

Sunlabob Renewable Energy. (2008). Solar recharging stations: selling hours of solar lighting in the evenings, http://www.sunlabob.com/documents/08–05-Solar_Lamp_Paper.pdf, last accessed July 14, 2009.

SustainAbility. (2007). *Growing opportunity: Entrepreneurial solutions to impossible problems*. London: SustainAbility for the Skoll Foundation.

———. (2008). *The social intrapreneur: A field guide for corporate changemakers*. London: SustainAbility for the Skoll Foundation.

Szulanski, G. and Jensen, R.J. (2006). Presumptive adaptation and the effectiveness of knowledge transfer. *Strategic Management Journal*, 27, 937–957.

Tangari, A.H., Burton, S., Andrews, J.C., and Netemeyer, R.G. (2007). How do antitobacco campaign advertising and smoking status affect beliefs and intentions? Some similarities and differences between adults and adolescents. *Journal of Public Policy and Marketing*, 26(1), 60–74.

Tannenbaum, A. (1968). *Control in organizations*. New York: McGraw-Hill.

Taylor, M.A., Dees, J.G., and Emerson, J. (2002). The question of scale: Finding an appropriate strategy for building on your success. In Dees, J.G., Emerson, J., and Economy, P. (eds.), *Strategic tools for social entrepreneurs: Enhancing the performance of your enterprising nonprofit*. New York: John Wiley and Sons, Inc., 235–266.

Townsend, D.M. and Hart, T.A. (2008). Perceived institutional ambiguity and the choice of organizational form in social entrepreneurial ventures. *Entrepreneurship: Theory and Practice*, 32(4), 685–700.

Trelstad, B. (2008). Simple measures for social enterprise. *Innovations*, 3, 105–118.

Tushman, M.L. and Nadler, D.A. (1978). Information processing as an integrating concept in organizational design. *Academy of Management Review*, 3(3), 613–624.

UnLtd Ventures Social Enterprise Replication Series. (2008). Social enterprise replication overview: Planning and key considerations for social enterprises planning growth through replication.

US DHHS Office on Women's Health Twitter site. www.twitter.com /womenshealth; September 12, 2009.

Uvin, P. (1995). Fighting hunger at the grassroots: Paths for scaling up. *World Development*, 23(6), 927–939.

Uvin, P. and Miller, D. (1996). Paths to scaling-up: Alternative strategies for local nongovernmental organizations. *Human Organization*, 55(3), 344.

Uvin, P., Jain, P., and Brown, L.D. (2000). Think large and act small: Toward a new paradigm for NGO scaling up. *World Development*, 28(8), 1409–1419.

Volans. (2009). *The Phoenix economy: 50 pioneers in the business of social innovation*. London: Volans Ventures for the Skoll Foundation.

Waddock, S.A. and Post, J.E. (1991). Social entrepreneurs and catalytic change. *Public Administration Review*, 51(5), 393–401.

Wakefield, M., Flay, B., Nichter, M., and Giovino, G. (2003). Effects of anti-smoking advertising on youth smoking: A review. *Journal of Health Communication*, 8, 229–247.

Wallace, S.L. (1999). Social entrepreneurship: The role of social purpose enterprises in facilitating community economic development. *Journal of Developmental Entrepreneurship*, 4, 153–174.

Webster, M. and Walker, P. (2009). *One for all and all for one*. Feinstein International Center, Tufts University.

Weerawardena, J.and Sullivan-Mort, G. (2006). Investigating social entrepreneurship: A multidimensional model. *Journal of World Business*, 41(1), 21–35.

Wei-Skillern, J. and Anderson, B.B. (2003). Nonprofit geographic expansion: Branches, affiliates, or both? CASE Working Paper Series, No. 4, Duke University's Fuqua School of Business, Durham, NC.

Wei-Skillern, J. and Marciano, S. (2008). The networked nonprofit. *Stanford Social Innovation Review*, 6(2), 38–43.

Wells, A.S., Grutzik, C., Carnochan, S., Slayton, J., and Vasudeva, A. (1999). Underlying policy assumptions of charter school reform: The multiple meanings of a movement. *The Teachers College Record*, 100, 513–535.

Wells, A.S., Lopez, A., Scott, J., and Holme, J.J. (1999). Charter schools as postmodern paradox: Rethinking social stratification in an age of deregulated school choice. *Harvard Educational Review*, 69, 172–204.

Wells, R., Feinberg, M., Alexander, J., and Ward, A. (2009). Factors affecting member perceptions of coalition impact. *Nonprofit Management & Leadership*, 19 (3), 327–348.

Williams, C. (2007). Transfer in context: Replication and adaptation in knowledge transfer relationships. *Strategic Management Journal*, 28, 867–889.

Winter, S. G. and Szulanski, G. (2001). Replication as strategy. *Organization Science*, 12, 730–743.

Wolfred, T. (2008). Building leadership organizations: Succession planning for nonprofits. *Executive Transition Monograph Series*, 6.

Worden, J.K., Flynn, B.S., Geller, B.M., Chen, M., Shelton, L.G., Secker-Walker, R.H., Solomon, D.S., Solomon, L.J., Couchey, S., and Costanza, M.C. (1988). Development of a smoking prevention mass media program using diagnostic and formative research. *Preventive Medicine*, 17 (5), 531–58.

Yin, R.K. (2009). *Case study research: Design and methods*, 4th ed. Thousand Oaks, CA: Sage Publications.

"Your Disease Risk." Washington University School of Medicine Siteman Cancer Center; http://www.yourdiseaserisk.wustl.edu; September 12, 2009.

Yunus, M. (2008). *Creating a world without poverty*. New York: Public Affairs.

Zald, M.N. (2004). Making change: Why does the social sector need social movements? *Stanford Social Innovation Review*, 2(1), 25–34.

Zald, M.N. and McCarthy, J.D. (1980). Social movement industries: Cooperation and conflict amongst social movement organizations. In Kreisberg, L. (ed.), *Research in social movements, conflict, and change* (3). Greenwich, Conn.: JAI Press, 1–20.

Zaman, H. (2004). The scaling-up of microfinance in Bangladesh: Determinants, impact, and lessons. World Bank Policy Research Working Paper, no. 3398.

Zhao, G. and Pechmann, C. (2007). The impact of regulatory focus on adolescents' response to antismoking advertising campaigns. *Journal of Marketing Research*, 44 (4), 671–687.

Index